# The Meritocracy Myth

# The Meritocracy Myth

Stephen J. McNamee and Robert K. Miller Jr.

ROWMAN & LITTLEFIELD PUBLISHERS, INC.
Lanham • Boulder • New York • Toronto • Oxford

ROWMAN & LITTLEFIELD PUBLISHERS, INC.

Published in the United States of America
by Rowman & Littlefield Publishers, Inc.
A wholly owned subsidiary of The Rowman & Littlefield Publishing Group, Inc.
4501 Forbes Boulevard, Suite 200, Lanham, MD 20706
www.rowmanlittlefield.com

PO Box 317, Oxford OX2 9RU, UK

British Library Cataloguing in Publication Information Available

**Library of Congress Cataloging-in-Publication Data**

McNamee, Stephen J., 1950–
    The meritocracy myth / Stephen J. McNamee and Robert K. Miller.
        p.   cm.
    Includes bibliographical references and index.
    ISBN 0-7425-1055-7 (cloth : alk. paper) — ISBN 0-7425-1056-5 (pbk. : alk.
paper)
    1.  Social mobility—United States. 2.  Equality—United States. 3.  Social capital
(Sociology)—United States. I.  Miller, Robert K., 1948–

HN90 .S65 M35 2004
                                                                    2003616371

Printed in the United States of America

∞™ The paper used in this publication meets the minimum requirements of
American National Standard for Information Sciences—Permanence of Paper
for Printed Library Materials, ANSI/NISO Z39.48-1992.

# Contents

Acknowledgments     vii

1   The American Dream: Origins and Prospects     1

2   On Being Made of the Right Stuff: The Case for Merit     21

3   The Silver Spoon: Inheritance and the Staggered Start     49

4   It's Not What You Know But . . . : Social and Cultural Capital     71

5   Making the Grade: Education and Mobility     95

6   Being in the Right Place at the Right Time: The Luck Factor     117

7   I Did It My Way: Self-Employment and Mobility     137

8   An Unlevel Playing Field: Racism and Sexism     155

9   Discrimination by Any Other Name: Other Isms     181

10   Running in Place: The Long Wage Recession     197

Index     211

About the Authors     219

# Acknowledgments

Several people made the completion of this project possible. We would like to thank the editors at Rowman & Littlefield including Dean Birkenkamp, Susan McEachern, and Alan McClare for shepherding the book along. We would also like to thank Rowman & Littlefield's editorial staff including Alison Sullenberger and April Leo for their assistance and many helpful suggestions.

We would also like to acknowledge the intellectual debt we owe to our mentors. For Stephen McNamee, these include John Murray, Norbert Wiley, Reeve Vanneman, and William Form and, for Robert Miller, they include William Yancey, Leo Rigsby, Richard Juliani, and Bruce Mayhew. In addition, we extend special appreciation to Jeffrey Rosenfeld and Susan McEachern who provided many useful comments and suggestions on the manuscript. We are grateful for their insights and inspiration, although we assume full responsibility for the content of this book.

We are grateful for the institutional support provided by the University of North Carolina at Wilmington. To our colleagues in the Department of Sociology and Criminal Justice at the University of North Carolina at Wilmington, we extend our gratitude for their encouragement. We would especially like to recognize the support of our Department Chair, Cecil Willis, and our Dean, Jo Ann Seiple.

We also thank our wives, Christine McNamee and Mary Susan Miller, for their love, understanding, and patience. Finally, we thank our children, Gregory McNamee, Catherine McNamee, and Emory Miller for accepting our legacy of love as the greatest bequest we can provide.

# 1

# The American Dream: Origins and Prospects

*The reason they call it the American Dream is because you have to be asleep to believe it.*

—George Carlin, *Brain Droppings* 1997, 83

In the image of the American Dream, America is the land of opportunity. If you work hard enough and are talented enough, you can overcome any obstacle and achieve success. No matter where you start out in life, the sky is the limit. You can go as far as your talents and abilities can take you.

Although most Americans enthusiastically endorse this image in abstract terms (Huber and Form 1973; Kluegel and Smith 1986; Ladd and Bowman 1998), their lived experiences often tell them that factors other than individual merit play a role in getting ahead: "It takes money to make money" (inheritance); "It's not what you know but who you know" (connections); "What matters is being in the right place at the right time" (luck); "There is not an even playing field" (discrimination); and "He or she married into money" (marriage).

Americans have great ambivalence about economic inequality. Indeed, Americans often simultaneously hold contradictory principles about how income and wealth should be distributed. While most Americans, for instance, proudly proclaim the virtues of "getting out of the system what you put into it" (meritocracy), they also steadfastly defend the right of individuals to dispose of their property when they die "as they personally see fit" (inheritance). These beliefs, however, pose a fundamental contradiction between freedom of choice at the individual level and equality of opportunity at the societal level. Simply put, to the extent that income and wealth are distributed on the basis of inheritance, they are not distributed on the basis of merit.

1

The principle of meritocracy is closely tied to the idea of the "American Dream." The latter term was first popularized by historian James Truslow Adams in his 1931 best-selling book, *The Epic of America*. Adams defined it as "that dream of a land in which life should be better and richer and fuller for every man, with opportunity for each according to his ability or achievement" (1931, 404). In a general way, people understand the idea of the American Dream as the fulfillment of the promise of meritocracy. The American Dream is fundamentally rooted in the historical experience of the United States as a new nation of immigrants. Unlike European societies historically dominated by hereditary aristocracies, the ideal in America was that its citizens were "free" to achieve on their own merits. The American Dream was the hope of fulfillment of individual freedom and the chance to succeed in the "New World."

In *Facing Up to the American Dream* (1995), Jennifer Hochschild identifies four tenets of the American Dream: (1) Who?—everyone regardless of origin or station, (2) What?—reasonable anticipation or the hopefulness of success, (3) How?—through actions under one's individual control, and (4) Why?—True success is associated with virtue in various ways; that is, "virtue leads to success, success makes a person virtuous, success indicates virtue, or apparent success is not real success unless one is also virtuous" (Hochschild 1995, 23).

These meritocratic tenets are deeply ingrained in the American consciousness. Survey research repeatedly confirms that most Americans enthusiastically subscribe to them. But the endorsement of meritocracy is not evenly distributed among Americans. Reflecting the reality of their life circumstances, nonwhites and those with less income are more likely to identify "family background," "who you know," and "discrimination" as relevant factors in where people end up in the system. Nevertheless, the overall pattern is clear: Most Americans not only believe that meritocracy is the way the system *should* work; they also believe that meritocracy is the way the system *does* work.

Together, the tenets of the American Dream comprise an ideology of inequality. Ideologies provide a socially acceptable explanation for the kind and extent of inequality within society (Jost and Major 2001; Brown 2002). Ideologies also include guidelines for behavior within a system of inequality. These guidelines include social cues for showing or receiving deference from others, depending on one's relative position in the social pecking order of society. Deferential forms of address (e.g., "sir" in the military, "your honor" in the courtroom), gestures (e.g., saluting, bowing, curtsying), and other behaviors (e.g., standing when the judge enters the courtroom) signal and reinforce social hierarchies.

Ideologies are ultimately based on persuasion as a form of social power. Persuasion entails not just making claims but getting others to go along as well. It is not enough for some to simply have more than others. For a system of inequality to be stable, those who have more must convince those who have less that the distribution of who gets what is fair, just, proper, or the natural order of things. The greater the level of inequality, the more compelling and persuasive these explanations must appear to be.

The type of explanation or ideology varies depending on the type of inequality. In feudal societies, for instance, the aristocracy used "birthright" and the idea of "the divine right of kings" to justify power and privilege over commoners and peasants. In slave societies, slave owners used either the idea of "spoils of victory," or "innate superiority" to justify their ownership of other human beings. In traditional Indian caste societies, inequality was legitimized on the basis of the idea of "reincarnation"; that is, one's place in this life was based on one's performance in past lives.

In industrial societies such as the United States, inequality is justified by an ideology of meritocracy. America is seen as the land of opportunity where people get out of the system what they put into it. Ostensibly, the most talented, hardest working, and most virtuous get ahead. The lazy, shiftless, and indolent fall behind. You may not be held responsible for where you start out in life, but you are responsible for where you end up. If you are truly meritorious, you will overcome any obstacle and succeed.

An important aspect of ideologies of inequality is that they do not have to be objectively "true" to persuade those who have less to accept less. Racism, for instance, is predicated on the false assumption of racial superiority. Racism involves a double falsehood—that there are biologically distinct subcategories within the human population (a view that modern biology soundly rejects) and that these "races" are hierarchically ranked. Americans, including people of color, were long persuaded to accept these myths about themselves. It has taken centuries of struggle, a civil rights movement, and a black power movement to begin to counter these beliefs. Likewise, women long accepted a definition of themselves as inferior to men, and many accepted the prevailing definition of the "proper" place for women in society as "barefoot, pregnant, and in the kitchen." Consciousness raising associated with the women's movement challenged these definitions, and they are now largely rejected.

Racism and sexism rest ultimately on biological assumptions of superiority and inferiority that can be demonstrated empirically to be false. From the point of view of those in power, however, an *ideal* ideology is one that *cannot* be proven true or false, such as "reincarnation" or the "divine right of kings." As long as people *believe* an ideology to be "true," then it is "true" for them in its consequences. People do not act on the world as it is but as they perceive and make sense of it. For ideologies of inequality to "legitimize" particular social arrangements, it is not necessary that the ideology be objectively true or even falsifiable; what matters is that people accept and act on it.

The acceptance of meritocracy in America is predicated not on what "is" but on the *belief* that the system of inequality is "fair" and it "works." According to the ideology of meritocracy, inequality is seen to be "fair" because everyone presumably has an equal (or at least an adequate) chance to succeed, and success is determined by *individual* merit. The system ostensibly "works" because it is seen as providing an individual incentive to achieve that is good for society as a whole; that is, those who are most talented, the hardest working, and the most virtuous *get* and *should get* the most rewards.

## INDIVIDUALISM AND THE ORIGINS OF THE AMERICAN DREAM

The American Dream has as its core an emphasis on the individual. According to the ideology of the American Dream, we are "masters of our own fate." We "go our own way" and "do our own thing." For Americans, "it all comes down to the individual." The American emphasis on individualism is not a historical accident but is firmly rooted in the religious, political, economic, and cultural experience of America as a nation of immigrants.

One source of American individualism is the religious backgrounds of the European colonists in America, who were mostly members of various Protestant religious sects. These sects were part of the many splinter groups that formed in the aftermath of the Protestant Reformation, which began in Europe in the sixteenth century. The conquering English population, as part of the spoils of victory, established the rules of the game. Those who followed had to adopt those rules or risk isolation or exclusion. In this way, the cultural ideals of the conquering white Anglo-Saxon Protestants (WASPs) became the dominant cultural force in America.

Among the early WASP settlers were a group of religious dissidents who landed in 1620 on the rocky shores of Massachusetts at a place they called "Plymouth," named after the town in England from which their flagship, the *Mayflower*, sailed. These religious dissidents had split from the Church of England, which had earlier split from Catholicism. They came to those shores to flee religious persecution at the hands of the official Anglican hierarchy. These "separatists" practiced an extreme form of religious piety, referred to as "Puritan." These Puritans of Plymouth became the vanguard of American cultural values and the wellspring for what became the American upper class.

The constellation of cultural values that became known as the "Protestant ethic" found its greatest expression among the various Puritan sects that formed the dominant religious backgrounds of the early American colonists. The principles of the Protestant ethic were analyzed by the German sociologist Max Weber in his classic work, *The Protestant Ethic and the Spirit of Capitalism* (1905). The core of Weber's argument is that the twin ethics of diligence and asceticism were associated with the early development of capitalism. Diligence stimulated productivity, and asceticism encouraged savings. Capitalism—particularly early capitalism—needed both a highly motivated labor force and investment "capital." Because people worked hard, they became productive, while the self-denial of asceticism encouraged saving by discouraging self-indulgence.

As part of the break with Catholicism, Protestantism emphasized an individual rather than communal relationship with God. Puritans in particular eschewed Catholicism's communalism and the elaborate ritual system associated with it. Instead, the emphasis was on a direct relationship with God through individual prayer and reading of the Bible. The Protestant Reformation also shifted the traditional Catholic view of work as "punishment" for "original sin" to the idea of work as a sacred calling, a mission from God to subdue nature and gain control over it. People should become instruments of God's will on earth and were called upon to transform the world and remake it in God's image, what Weber called "world mastery."

The greatest expression of this ethic was in the Puritan sect of Calvinism. The Calvinists believed in predestination, which meant that people did not earn salvation but were "elected" to it by God. This belief created among the followers what Weber called "salvation anxiety," which led individuals to attempt to ascertain whether they were among the elect. Individuals came to believe that worldly success could be taken as a sign of God's grace. So, driven by "salvation anxiety," people worked very hard to become successful so that they could "prove" to themselves and others that they were among the elect.

These Puritan values of individual "industry, frugality, and prudence" were reflected in early American moralistic novels (Wiess 1969) and were integrated into the core of an emerging national culture. The best known of these was a popular series of 107 "rags to riches" novels by Horatio Alger (1832–1899). Alger was the son of a Unitarian minister and a Harvard graduate who for a short time also served in the ministry. Puritan themes were reinforced as well in a series of widely used early American primary school "readers," written by William McGuffey, who was also a minister turned writer.

While the hard work/no play twin ethic may have been useful for stimulating the early development of capital, it was not as useful for sustaining the continued expansion of capital. The problem is that the twin ethic contains within it an internal economic contradiction. With everyone working hard to succeed, it does not take long to produce more than enough goods to meet minimum standards of living. The asceticism part of the ethic, while good for savings, depresses the demand for goods. The work hard/no play combination eventually results in an imbalance between supply and demand. For supply and demand to be reasonably balanced, something has to give. People either need to produce less or consume more.

Americans clearly decided to consume more. This was most evident especially in the period of prosperity following World War I, commonly known as "the roaring twenties." The inhibitions, frugality, and austerity associated with the ascetic "no-play" part of the Puritan ethic waned. Consumption was redefined, not as an evil of self-indulgence but as just reward for hard work. The "work hard" part of the ethic was retained but transformed. People no longer worked hard simply for the glory of God but increasingly for self-enhancement. In this way, the *Protestant* ethic has lost most of its religious underpinnings and survives now in American culture simply as the "work ethic," the moral underpinnings of which have severely eroded (Wuthnow 1996). Secularized vestiges of the Puritan tradition persist in the American values of self-reliance, independence, and responsibility.

Politically, the American emphasis on individualism was born in revolution. Shedding the grip of the aristocratic monarchy, the American colonists would embark on the bold experiment of democracy. In 1776, the Declaration of Independence proclaimed the sovereignty of a new nation and the inalienable right of its citizens to "life, liberty, and the pursuit of happiness." These were God-given rights that the state could not abridge. The spirit of *individual* freedom contained in this document became the "blueprint" for how the political system of the new nation would operate. The details of the new political blueprint were later expanded with the Articles of Confederation, adopted in 1781, and finalized with the ratification of the U.S. Constitution in 1788. In the spirit of the previous documents, the Constitution outlined a contract between the citizen and the state, emphasizing (especially in the Bill of Rights) the limits of state power over individual freedoms.

The early European settlers who reached the shores of the New World were not a cross section of the populations they left behind. Those who left were no doubt different than those who remained. Some were fleeing persecution and, in some cases, prosecution. The New World offered an opportunity for freedom and a chance to start over. For others, the lure was one of adventure and economic opportunity. Others saw themselves in service to the crown, expanding the British Empire. Still others came to America as indentured servants or were brought as slaves.

The colonists under British rule gradually became more and more resentful of the political and economic constraints imposed by the Crown. More than a century after the first permanent settlements, the colonists organized a revolt. With the success of the American Revolution, a new government was established. The revolutionaries who laid out the plan for the new government had risked everything to gain political and economic freedom, and they were determined not to re-create the same tyranny they had fought so bitterly to defeat. The new government would have no king, no monarchy, and no unilateral system of control. In the aftermath of battles with the Crown, the framers of the new government were leery of centralized systems of political control. A constitutional system of "checks and balances" was formed to diffuse power and to hold those who wielded power accountable.

A compromise plan—the federal system—was worked out to balance the need for national unity with the desire for localized control. Democracy, American style, was born. "Freedom" was a key ingredient in this formulation, although it had different meanings for different individuals—religious freedom for some, freedom to acquire wealth for some, freedom from tyranny for others.

Alexis de Tocqueville wrote the much-celebrated book, *Democracy in America*, in 1835. In it, he praised America for the early success of its radical experiment of democracy. Key to that success, according to Tocqueville, was the American emphasis on individualism and equality. By individualism, Tocqueville meant "a mature and calm feeling, which disposes each member of the community to sever himself from the mass of his fellow creatures" (1967, 118). He was careful to distinguish individualism from egotism: "Egotism is a vice as old as the world, which does not belong to one form of society more than another; individualism is of democratic origin, and it threatens to spread in the same ration as the equality of conditions" (1967, 118–19). By "equality" Tocqueville meant the absence of aristocracy, which he also links to individualism:

> Aristocracy has made a chain of all the members of the community, from the peasant to the king: democracy breaks that chain, and severs every link to it. As social conditions become more equal, the number of persons increases who, although they are neither rich enough nor powerful enough to exercise any great influence over their fellow creatures, have nevertheless acquired or retained sufficient education and fortune to satisfy their own wants. They owe nothing to any man, they expect nothing from any man; they acquire the habit of always considering themselves as standing alone, and they are apt to imagine that their whole destiny is in their own hands. (1967, 120)

In short, Tocqueville maintained that in America individuals are free to achieve, not by virtue of hereditary title but by their own merit, creating, as Thomas Jefferson put it, an "aristocracy of talent." Thus the emerging ideal of the American Dream incorporated two meanings of freedom—both political freedom from tyranny and economic freedom to achieve on one's own merits.

Freedom from political tyranny, however, is not the same as "free market," although the two are often mistakenly viewed as inextricable. Free markets mean that prices, profits, and wages are determined by the "free" flow of market forces. In free market societies, businesses are for sale, open for profit, and open for investment, but free markets do not guarantee democracy, civil liberties, or political freedom.

In what is one of the great coincidences of American history, America's economic blueprint for a free market economy was laid out in the same year—1776—as its political blueprint for a democratic government. In that pivotal year, the Scottish economist Adam Smith published *The Wealth of*

*Nations*, which became adopted in the United States as the informal "bible" of American "free market" capitalism. It emphasized rational *self*-interest, *individual* competition, *private* ownership, and *laissez-faire* principles. At the time of the publication of Smith's book, roughly three-fourths of the new nation's labor force was self-employed, comprising mostly small farmers, merchants, and artisans. A large number of mostly small producers encouraged market competition. Government regulation of business was minimal. The economic blueprint seemed to fit.

In feudal economies, everyone essentially works for the aristocracy. Peasants did not own land and had little opportunity to move up in the system. With the decline of feudalism and the rise of market economies, "free markets" emerged. Individuals could own their *own* land and be their *own* bosses and have a chance to move up on the basis of their *own* efforts. In America, the absence of a feudal past and the abundance of land enhanced these opportunities, thus grounding these notions in the formative stages of the development of America's national values.

It is important to point out, however, that the democratic-free market blueprint in America has never applied equally to everyone. From the very beginning, indentured servants, slaves, Native Americans, women, and others were systematically excluded from both the protections of the Constitution and the opportunities of "free market" capitalism. Despite these exclusions, the dominant cultural image of "individual rights" and the "free market" prevailed.

The "can do" individualism associated with the American Dream was further reinforced by the experience of the American Western frontier. Historian Frederick Jackson Turner, in his classic book, *The Frontier in American History* argued that the frontier was central to the development of American individualism:

> From the condition of frontier life came intellectual traits of profound importance. . . . The result is that to the frontier the American intellect owes its striking characteristics. That coarseness and strength combined with acuteness and inquisitiveness; that practical inventive turn of mind, quick to find expedients; that masterful grasp of material things, lacking in the artistic, but powerful to effect great ends; that restless, nervous energy; that dominant individualism, working for good and for evil and withal that buoyancy and exuberance which comes with freedom—these are the traits of the frontier. (1947, 37)

Turner further linked the rugged individualism of the pioneer with the ideals of democracy: "[Q]uite as deeply fixed in the pioneer's mind as the ideal of individuals was the ideal of democracy. He had a passionate hatred for aristocracy, monopoly and special privilege; he believed in simplicity, economy and the rule of the people" (1947, 37).

Contemporary historians have sharply criticized Turner's largely nostalgic and romantic view of the frontier. They correctly point out that Turner paid little attention to Indians or slaves, that he had little to say about governmental aid to expansion, much less its selective character, and that his portrayal of the frontier was concentrated on the humid middle West to the neglect of the arid West (Limerick 1995). But it is precisely this idealized image of the American frontier that has filtered into the American consciousness—reinforced by countless books, TV westerns, and Hollywood feature films. The frontier is portrayed as a rough and dangerous place but one with abundant opportunity. Those who were able and willing could tame the wilderness, overcome any obstacle, and realize the American Dream.

## DOWNSIZING THE AMERICAN DREAM

The American Dream implies not just a general hopefulness for the future and a formula for success but also a sense of what the fulfillment of the Dream would mean. Although specifics vary, several outcomes are generally associated with the fulfillment of the American Dream, including home ownership, improving life chances for children (especially defined now as sending children to college), having a chance to get rich, and achieving a secure and comfortable retirement. The prospects for fulfillment of the American Dream have been dimmed in recent years, and American workers are responding by becoming more pessimistic about the future (Starks 2003).

In a U.S. Census study appropriately entitled *Tracking the American Dream,* F. John Devaney (1994) examined housing trends in the fifty-year period between 1940 and 1990. In terms of fulfillment of the dream, the results are mixed. Between 1890 and 1940, rates of home ownership remained at slightly less than one-half of the American population. In the post–World War II period, stimulated by postwar prosperity and veterans loans as part of the GI Bill, rates of ownership increased dramatically, from 44% in 1940 to 62% in 1960. Subsidized by government highway funds that linked surrounding communities with central cities, this was also the period of rapid expansion of American suburbs. For many, the ranch house in the suburbs with the two-car garage and meticulously maintained lawn symbolized the fulfillment of the Dream. Commuters in these "bedroom" communities, who worked in the urban areas and had access to its cultural amenities, felt shielded from the "problems" of central cities. For them, it was the best of both worlds. Economic success, resulting in "white flight" to the suburbs in the postwar period, however, exacerbated the problems of central cities and, in many cases, increased rates of segregation and racial tension. The tax base of urban areas eroded along with public services including schools, police and fire protection, and urban sanitation. The fulfillment of the Dream for some was, for others, a nightmare of inner-city crime, drugs, unemployment, poverty, and despair.

Since 1960, home ownership rates have increased more slowly, from 61.9% in 1960 to 63.9% in 1985 to 66.8% in 1999 (U.S. Census Bureau 2000b, Table 1213). While the overall trend is one of modest increase in home ownership over the past fifty years, the *cost* of home ownership has increased. Since as early as 1960, Americans have been paying a higher proportion of their incomes for housing. For example, in 1975, the median cost of existing housing was about 3 times the median family income; by 1999, it had increased to 3.26 times the median family income. Similarly, in 1980 the median cost of new housing was 3.65 times the median family income; by 1999 it had increased to 3.9 times the median family income (calculated by the authors from Tables 1199 and 1201, U.S. Census Bureau 2000b and U.S. Census Bureau 2000a, Table H-6). Also, a substantially higher proportion of "home ownership" involves mortgages rather than outright ownership. In other words, mortgaged "homeowners" don't really "own" their homes until they pay off their mortgages. In 1890, 72% of American homeowners actually "owned" their own homes; by 1990, the corresponding figure was only 35% (Devaney 1994). In short, in this century more Americans live in "owner-occupied housing," but a higher portion of them have gone into debt to do so.

Another aspect of the American Dream is the idea that each new generation would have better opportunities than the previous one. Reports from survey data show inconsistent trends in this regard (Ladd and Bowman 1998, 58–78). Results vary depending on how and when the question was posed, but in general, recent data suggest that most Americans feel that the next generation will be worse off than the current one. If asked about their own children's futures, however, Americans are more optimistic. A clearer picture emerges in terms of providing a college education for children. An increasing proportion of Americans is achieving this aspect of the American dream. In 1900, only 4% of American eighteen to twenty-one year olds were college students. By 2001, 62% of the American eighteen to twenty-one year olds were college students. In 1940, 4.6% of the population twenty-five years and older had completed four years or more of college. By 2001, that figure had increased to 26.1%. Although more Americans are entering college than ever before, the costs of college education have been increasing at a rate far greater than either increases in family income or the general cost of living.

Despite low rates of inflation, the cost of a college education continues to soar. For the 2003–2004 academic year, the average annual costs for tuition, fees, room, and board was $10,636 at a public four-year college and $26,884 at a private four-year college. Adjusted for inflation, these costs in constant 2003 dollars are more than double what they were in 1980–1981 for private colleges ($11,876) and almost double for public colleges ($5,416) (The College Board 2003, 9). What is more, the cost of higher education grew at a faster rate than did median income and disposable per capita income during the late 1980s and early 1990s (U.S. Department of Education 2002b). Parents of the average American college student are increasingly unable to afford these growing costs. As a result, more students themselves are working, taking longer to graduate, and taking on heavy debt loads to finance their own education. Between 1992–1993 and 1999–2000, undergraduate borrowing increased significantly. The percentage of full-time undergraduates who relied on federal student loans to help pay for their college education increased from 30 to 43% overall. After adjusting for inflation, the average amount of a federal student loan also increased, from about $3,900 to $4,800. While no increase in the percentage of students borrowing was detected for undergraduates in the lowest income quartile—roughly half borrowed during the period—the likelihood of borrowing increased for both middle-income undergraduates (from 32 to 45%) and high-income undergraduates (from 15 to 31%) (U.S. Department of Education 2002b, 2).

With so many Americans receiving college degrees, however, the overall return on the investment has declined. To put it simply, the labor force is being flooded with new college graduates. There are fewer "college level" jobs being produced by the economy than there are new college graduates. The result has been an increase in both underemployment (e.g., college graduates waiting tables) and credential inflation (employers requiring higher levels of education for positions without a corresponding increase in the demands of the positions themselves). Under these conditions, many students perceive that getting a college education would not help them so much as the lack of a college education would hurt them. In what appears to be spiraling credential inflation, increasing numbers of students are responding to the education "arms race" by pursuing graduate and professional degrees—not so much because they have an intrinsic interest in education but to get a jump on the competition. Between 1970 and 1999, graduate and professional school enrollments both increased by 75% (U.S. Department of Education 2002a).

Having at least a chance to get rich holds great appeal for most Americans. The appeal is keenly felt, as evidenced by the excitement generated by jackpot lotteries that soar into the millions and by the popularity of such TV game shows as *Who Wants to Be a Millionaire?* The Internet has become the equivalent of a modern "gold rush" as entrepreneurs anxiously seek to stake their "dot-com" electronic claims. Survey data show that a substantial majority of Americans (78% in 1998) believe that it is possible to "start out poor in America, work hard, and become rich" (Ladd and Bowman 1998, 57). But, as we will show, the mere *possibility* of getting rich is not the same as the *likelihood* of getting rich.

Self-employment, which we will examine in greater detail in chapter 7, is relevant here because most meteoric rises in personal wealth come not from wages and salaries but through entrepreneurial activity—starting and owning businesses. With the decline of the family farms and businesses and the ascendance of corporations in the twentieth century, however, rates of self-employment plummeted. New business starts are notoriously risky. For most Americans, these factors have decreased rather than increased the likelihood of "rags to riches" scenarios.

A secure and comfortable retirement is in many ways the closing chapter of the American Dream. In modern America, a comfortable retirement is achieved through a combination of savings, investments, pensions, and Social Security. In earlier times, people rarely "retired." Those who lived on farms, for instance, relied on adult children to provide for them if they were no longer able to work. Through much of the earlier history of the United States, life expectancy was short, savings limited, pensions rare, and Social Security nonexistent. With the rise of industrial America and union-negotiated contracts, pensions became more common. In 1933 as part of Franklin D. Roosevelt's New Deal initiatives, the federally sponsored Social Security system was established. Until the mid-1970s, poverty rates for those over sixty-five were substantially higher than for other age groups. Many retirees were faced with small and fixed incomes and the erosion of purchasing power as prices increased. The longer they lived, the poorer they became. In the mid-1970s, however, Social Security benefits were adjusted to the Consumer Price Index, and Social Security benefits became the largest government social services program. This, combined with post–World War II economic prosperity, greatly improved the economic condition of elderly Americans, who now have a rate of poverty below the national average.

Nevertheless, the future of secure retirements is in serious jeopardy. The Social Security fund is in trouble. Unless taxes are raised or benefits reduced, the Social Security system will become insolvent. Projections are that at current rates the fund will become exhausted by 2041 (Board of Trustees, Federal Old-Age and Survivors Insurance and Disability Insurance Trust Funds 2002, 3). Although the Social Security fund currently has a surplus, the surplus will be drained as the large cohort of postwar baby boomers becomes eligible for benefits. There are other ominous developments. Savings rates for Americans are declining, the proportion of Americans receiving employer-sponsored pensions is also declining (Collins et al. 1999), and the pensions themselves are not as secure as previously assumed. The population as a whole is "graying" as life expectancy continues to increase and birthrates continue to decline. The costs of health care continue to increase at a rate much higher than the general increase in costs of living. This is significant because the greatest proportion of health care expenditures is for the elderly.

In some ways, then, the Dream has been downsized in recent years. Whatever the likelihood might be of attaining the American Dream in the future, however, one thing is certain—it will be more attainable for those closer to the top of the system than toward the bottom.

## PLAN OF THE BOOK

In chapter 2, "On Being Made of the Right Stuff," we identify key factors usually associated with the meritocratic formula for success—innate talent, hard work, proper attitude, and moral virtue. We then examine the relationship between these individual traits and where people end up in the system. We point out that each of these individual traits, especially having the right attitude and moral character, is difficult to measure; that it is difficult to assess the independent contribution of each to getting ahead; and that the entire line of argument is largely tautological—that is, those who get ahead or who are successful are labeled as having the right stuff after the fact.

If getting ahead were simply a matter of "being made of the right stuff," we would have a relatively short and simple story to tell. However, there is much more to it than this, and we devote the remainder of this book to telling that story. We begin by suggesting that if intelligence were actually the primary determinant of getting ahead, then one might expect that the distributions of income and wealth would closely mirror the bell-shaped distribution of intelligence. But they don't even come close.

In fact, the most important determinant of where people end up in the economic pecking order of society is where they started in the first place. Inheritance and the "staggered start" are nonmerit factors discussed in chapter 3, "The Silver Spoon." Instead of a race to get ahead that begins anew with each generation, the "race," if it could be called that, is more aptly described as a relay race in which children inherit different starting points from parents. The advantages of being born wealthy are cumulative and substantial. Inheritance, broadly defined as one's initial starting point in life based on parental position, includes a high standard of living during childhood, having friends and relatives in high places, cultural advantages, infusion of parental capital while parents are still alive and insulation against failure, better health and greater life expectancy, and the inheritance of bulk estates when parents die. Growing up in a privileged family means greater opportunities to acquire and develop individual competence as well as having that competence recognized and rewarded. Further, much intergenerational transfer of wealth and privilege occurs between the living. Offspring of the wealthy do not have to wait until the death of their parents to receive the benefits of familial wealth. The size and timing of such inter vivos transfers significantly affect standards of living and quality of life and provide the means to their augmentation through further achievement. Finally, at death the wealthy tend to leave the bulk of their estates to their immediate families—spouses, children, and, increasingly, grandchildren.

The chapter ends with a discussion of America's ownership class—the roughly 1% of the American population that owns nearly 40% of all the available net worth. We argue that this class is set apart from other Americans not only by the sheer amount of wealth held but by an exclusive, distinctive, and self-perpetuating way of life that reduces opportunities for merit-based mobility into it.

In chapter 4, "It's Not What You Know But . . . ," we discuss two important nonmerit factors that, while part of the American folklore of social placement, are nevertheless typically underestimated in their effects—"who you know" (social capital) and "fitting in" (cultural capital). S*ocial capital* refers to individual and family "connections" in the larger community, at school, and at work that mediate access to opportunity. *Cultural capital* refers to a set of cultural resources—bodies of often esoteric and specialized information and knowledge including style, bearing, manner, and self-presentation skills—that are needed to travel and be fully accepted in high-powered social circles. Like social capital, cultural capital mediates access to opportunity. In essence, cultural capital is a set of cultural credentials that certify eligibility for social and economic opportunity. To "look and know the part" is to possess cultural capital.

As with the ownership of wealth, the possession of social and cultural resources is not necessarily evidence of "individual merit." Wealth can be converted into social and cultural capital, providing distinct nonmerit advantages to the children of the rich and powerful. The social and cultural capital of George W. Bush, president and son of a president and the most politically powerful person in the world, is provided as an example.

Finally, we discuss the related phenomenon of social climbing. Social climbing refers to conscious efforts by individuals to attain membership in a group (usually higher in status) by emulating the cultural capital of that group. Strategies employed by social climbers include the conscious construction and use of social networks, conspicuous and invidious consumption, and the purposeful acquisition of prestigious cultural capital. Instead of gaining social acceptance that they desire, their efforts may backfire, and social climbers are often viewed as snobs within their own groups and as impostors or poseurs by those in the group to which they aspire to belong.

In chapter 5, "Making the Grade," we examine the complex relationship between education and the American Dream by evaluating competing arguments concerning the relationship between education and social mobility. We begin by presenting the conventional view that education serves as a mechanism that identifies and selects intelligent, talented, and motivated individuals, regardless of class background, and provides educational training in direct proportion to individual merit. The amounts and kinds of education achieved are taken as indicators of merit and are used as criteria of eligibility for occupations and the material rewards attached to them.

A radically different view of the role that education plays denies that education operates to promote equality of opportunity or that it serves as an avenue of social mobility. In this alternate view, education is tracked by social class and reproduces the class system. In short, schools both reflect and re-create existing inequalities in society. Schools reward children of the privileged by enhancing and certifying their social and cultural capital with valuable diplomas and degrees that provide access to occupational and economic opportunity. On the other hand, schools punish children of low socioeconomic status for their lack of such capital, consigning them to teachers, curricula, tracks, and the self-fulfilling prophecies of low expectations that these produce. The results are that less-privileged children are awarded credentials of lesser value, and inequality is largely reproduced across generations. Inequality reproduced across generations is substantial but far from complete. Some parents, regardless of class position, are more successful in promoting the futures of their children, and some children, regardless of class position, are more capable than others. As a result some rich kids fail and some poor kids succeed. These exceptions help to sustain at least the outward appearance of meritocracy and the American Dream.

There can be little doubt that being bright, working hard, and getting more education help people get ahead. But the competition for success is structured by an educational system that does not provide equality of opportunity, and quite independent of individual ability, the demands of a complex and changing corporate economy condition opportunities and the likelihood of success within it.

In chapter 6, "Being in the Right Place at the Right Time," we discuss factors in addition to individual characteristics and beyond the immediate control of individuals that significantly affect occupational attainment and life chances. We first examine the relationship between the *supply* of people available to fill jobs and the *demand* for the kind of jobs that need to be filled. The demand for workers is based on the number and kinds of jobs that the economy generates, and these differ from place to place and change over time. In the preoccupation with the supply side—worker skills, experience, and other individual characteristics—defenders of the American Dream often ignore the demand side. The American Dream assumes unlimited and equal demand for everyone who has merit. However, the numbers and types of jobs available not only affect levels of opportunity, competition, and social mobility, but the very meaning of merit itself. That a job that maximizes any particular person's set of skills becomes available for that person when he or she is ready for it is at least to some degree a matter of luck. While individuals do have some control over how skilled they are, they do not have control over what kinds of jobs are available, how many jobs are available, or how many others are seeking those jobs.

We show that changes in American industrial and occupational structures over time have occurred independently of the capacities of discrete individuals —how smart or talented they are, how hard they work, or how motivated they are to get ahead. In short, it matters—beyond individual merit—what shape the economy is in when individuals enter it. It also matters how many people are chasing how many jobs. When one is born—a factor beyond individual control and unrelated to individual merit—nevertheless bears on the conditions of employment at the time of labor force entry and for future life chances. Place also matters: both job opportunities and compensation for work vary depending on where one works. Finally, for the same kinds of work performed equally well, the characteristics of the employing organization also matter, with large, private sector, capital-intensive firms paying the best. In short, the simple fact is that there is far more talent, intelligence, hard work, and ability in the population than there are people who are lucky enough to find themselves in a position to exploit it.

Beyond income from jobs, we also show that being at the right place at the right time also matters for acquiring great wealth. Striking it rich—be it through inheritance, entrepreneurial ventures, investments, or even hitting the lottery—necessarily involves at least some degree of just plain dumb luck.

Americans embrace the ideal of the "self-made person" who starts with little or nothing and grows a successful business. In chapter 7, "I Did It My Way," we discuss the myth of entrepreneurship and its central place in the American Dream. Put simply, it is claimed that America's vast opportunities provide any and all reasonably bright, hardworking (meritorious) individuals an excellent chance to establish their own successful businesses and become their own boss. Our evaluation of this claim leads us to examine the rise of the giant corporations, the concomitant decline in self-employment, the numerous barriers to self-employment, and their implications for entrepreneurial activity.

We find that despite the mystique of self-employment, the reality is often less than glamorous because most discussions of self-employment focus only on its *voluntary* entrepreneurial form. Recognizing that such discussions are incomplete, we also examine *nonvoluntary* forms of self-employment. Generally unacknowledged by proponents of the American Dream, various forms of involuntary self-employment have always existed side by side with the voluntary entrepreneurial form. For example, an unknown number of the self-employed are displaced labor and are disproportionately women, minority, and older workers who do odd jobs "off the books" and "under the table." Likewise, many of today's "consultants" and "freelancers" are in reality laid off and struggling white-collar workers, hardly the exalted entrepreneurs of the American Dream. Others, including franchisees, professionals who work in group practices, and subcontractors who have only one client, lack the autonomy associated with the traditional petty bourgeoisie. Still others operate in the "irregular" or "underground" economy engaging in various forms of illegal economic activity.

The ascendance of large corporations in the American economy has contributed significantly to the decline in self-employment. The collective assets and associated economies of scale of the corporate giants tend to undercut competition from small companies and discourage new entrants. Americans cling to the historical legacy and language of free enterprise and the entrepreneurial spirit even though it no longer accurately describes the circumstances of the vast majority of the labor force that now works for somebody else. Although the odds are long, some individual entrepreneurs do succeed, sometimes phenomenally. We briefly look at one important case, Bill Gates, the wealthiest American and cofounder of Microsoft Corporation, and show that—like most success stories—his is not one of individual merit alone but a combination of merit and nonmerit factors.

In chapter 8, "An Unlevel Playing Field," we discuss two of the most obvious nonmerit barriers to getting ahead in America—race and gender discrimination—and their implications for the American Dream. Simply put, discrimination is the antithesis of merit. Where there is discrimination, there is no meritocracy because discriminatory allocations of opportunity and rewards discount or ignore merit and instead replace it with nonmerit criteria. Discrimination allows some (who are not necessarily meritorious) to get ahead at others' expense. What is more, discrimination creates a terrible irony—the very discrimination that invalidates the American Dream for many Americans creates conditions that seem to validate it for others, enabling them to embrace it so fervently. By excluding entire categories of people from equal access to opportunity, discrimination has reduced competition and increased the chances of others to get ahead who mistakenly conclude that their success is based exclusively on their own individual "merit."

We briefly review America's long history of discrimination against minorities and women—a history of unequal starting points and playing fields that have been anything but level. We argue that although discrimination is on the decline, the effects of various forms of discrimination from the past endure into the present. We also argue that modern forms of discrimination, although less blatant, continue to deny their victims full access to the American Dream. Although minorities and women have both suffered from discrimination, the class advantages of women have enabled them to take advantage of new opportunities as they have become available. Simply put, larger proportions of racial and ethnic minorities start at or near the end of the line. Thus even when new opportunities do become available, "catching up" means having more distance to make up. Finally, those who face multiple jeopardy—those subjected to discrimination along the axes of class, race, and gender—have the most to overcome.

Chapter 9, "Discrimination by Any Other Name," completes our discussion of discrimination. Although discrimination against minorities and women is its most visible and damaging form, at least in terms of costs and numbers affected, other forms of discrimination also interfere with the pursuit of the American Dream. We present brief treatments of several additional forms of discrimination, including heterosexism, ageism, discrimination against the disabled, religious bigotry, regionalism, and "lookism" (preference for the attractive). It could be argued that each of these is a relatively minor form of discrimination. After all, compared to discrimination against minorities and women, each clearly claims fewer victims. Nevertheless, it would be difficult to convince the victims of these forms of discrimination that their effects are any less real. What is more, these forms of discrimination often become components of cumulative disadvantage, which we refer to as "multiple jeopardy." We conclude that discrimination trumps merit; the more forms of discrimination that are operative, the stronger the trump.

In the concluding chapter, "Running in Place," we outline the implications of deindustrialization, the long wage recession, and increasing economic inequality over the past twenty years for the sustainability of the American Dream. We examine strategies that individual Americans have developed to cope with the problems created by these changes. In an attempt to keep up and make ends meet, many working Americans have increasingly resorted to multiple wage earners, working longer hours and moonlighting, and increasing levels of debt. Ultimately, such individualistic solutions become unsustainable. Each has upper limits that are quickly being realized—there are only two spouses who can work, any one person can only work so many hours a week, and a spiral of borrowing and spending more than one earns ultimately ends in bankruptcy.

Such individual coping strategies will not change the fundamental way that resources are distributed in society. They will not make the system more equal, more meritocratic, or more fair. Changes of this magnitude would require reductions in socially structured inequality, especially inequalities of wealth and power. We suggest how such change could be effected. To be consistent with the American Dream, our society would need to become one that truly creates equal opportunities to develop merit, recognize genuine merit, and equitably reward it. Since a level playing field is a premise of the American Dream, an obvious strategy is to continue efforts to eliminate all forms of discrimination. Because discrimination remains a major source of nonmerit inequality, stronger antidiscrimination laws could be developed and more effectively enforced. Affirmative action programs in education and employment must be revitalized, and new forms of class-based affirmative action could be instituted that directly target wealth inequality. In class-based affirmative action critical services like education, housing, health care, care for the elderly, and the like could be decommodified and provided to the less fortunate regardless of the ability to pay. In the spirit of the philosophy that for whom much is given much is expected, economic policies could be developed that encourage noblesse oblige and philanthropy among the privileged in ways that genuinely lift the prospects of the underprivileged. Another way to both decrease the nonmerit advantages of inheritance and increase opportunities for those who start out life at the end of the line would be to impose a more heavily progressive system of taxation on the wealthy. Measures such as these would help to create a more equal playing field and a more authentically meritocratic society.

Many of these structural proposals, however, are politically infeasible because they appear to violate the underlying individualism of the American Dream or because they threaten the interests of the powerful and privileged. In the meantime, the meritocracy myth is sustained even in the face of pervasive discrimination, vast and growing inequalities of wealth and income, and frequently unfair and unjust social institutions. We thus conclude that, although true equality of opportunity is probably not possible, the *myth* of meritocracy in America is itself harmful because its legitimation of inequalities of power and privilege rests on claims that are demonstrably false.

## REFERENCES

Adams, James Truslow. 1931, *The Epic of America*. New York: Blue Ribbon Books.

Bellah, Robert, et al. 1985. *Habits of the Heart: Individualism and Commitment in American Life*. Berkeley: University of California Press.

Board of Trustees, Federal Old-Age and Survivors Insurance and Disability Insurance Trust Funds. 2002. *The 2002 Annual Report of the Board of Trustees of the Federal Old-Age and Survivors Insurance and Disability Insurance Trust Funds*. Washington, D.C.: U.S. Government Printing Office.

Brown, Richard H. 2002. "Ideology after the Millennium: Problems of Legitimation in American Society." Pp. 185–232 in *Bringing Capitalism Back for Critique by Social Theory*, edited by Jennifer M. Lehmann. New York: JAI.

Carlin, George. 1997. *Brain Droppings*. New York: Hyperion.

The College Board. 2003. *Trends in College Pricing: 2003*. Princeton, N.J.: CEEB.

Collins, Chuck, Betsy Leondar-Wright, and Holly Sklar. 1999. *Shifting Fortunes: The Perils of the Growing American Wealth Gap*. Boston: United For A Fair Economy.

Davis, James A., and Tom W. Smith. 1989. *General Social Surveys, 1972–1989*. Chicago: National Opinion Research Center.

Devaney, F. John. 1994. *Tracking the American Dream: 50 Years of Housing History from the Census Bureau: 1940–1990*. Washington, D.C.: U.S. Census Bureau.

Hochschild, Jennifer. 1995. *Facing Up to the American Dream: Race, Class and the Soul of the Nation*. Princeton, N.J.: Princeton University Press.

Huber, Joan, and William Form. 1973. *Income and Ideology: An Analysis of the American Political Formula*. New York: Free Press.

Jost, John T., and Brenda Major, eds. 2001. *The Psychology of Legitimacy: Emerging Perspectives on Ideology, Justice, and Intergroup Relations*. Cambridge, U.K.: Cambridge University Press.

Kluegel, James R., and Eliot R. Smith. 1986. *Beliefs about Inequality: Americans' Views of What Is and What Ought to Be*. New York: de Gruyter.

Ladd, Everett Carll, and Karlyn H. Bowman. 1998. *Attitudes toward Economic Inequality*. Washington, D.C.: EI Press.

Limerick, Patricia Nelson. 1995. "Turnerians All: The Dream of a Helpful History in an Intelligible World." *American Historical Review* 100, no. 3: 697–717.

Starks, Brian. 2003. "The New Economy and the American Dream: Examining the Effect of Work Conditions on Beliefs about Economic Opportunity." *The Sociological Quarterly* 44, no. 2: 205–25.

Tocqueville, Alexis de. [1835] 1967. *Democracy in America*. New York: Schocken Books.

Turner, Frederick Jackson. [1920] 1947. *The Frontier in American History*. New York: Henry Holt.

U.S. Census Bureau. 2000a. *Current Population Survey, Historical Income Tables*. Washington, D.C.: U.S. Government Printing Office.

———. 2000b. *Statistical Abstract of the United States*. Washington, D.C.: U.S. Government Printing Office.

U.S. Department of Education. 2002a. *The Condition of Education 2002*. Washington, D.C.: National Center for Educational Statistics.

———. 2002b. "What Students Pay for College: Changes in Net Price of College Attendance between 1992–1993 and 1999–2000." Washington, D.C.: U.S. Government Printing Office.

Weber, Max. [1904–1905] 2002. *The Protestant Ethic and the Spirit of Capitalism*. Translated by Stephen Kahlberg. Los Angeles: Roxbury Publishing.

Wiess, Richard. 1969. *The American Myth of Success: From Horatio Alger to Norman Vincent Peale*. New York: Basic Books.

Wuthnow, Robert. 1996. *Poor Richard's Principle: Recovering the American Dream through the Moral Dimensions of Work, Business, and Money*. Princeton, N.J.: Princeton University Press.

# 2

## On Being Made of the Right Stuff: The Case for Merit

*The rich feel full of merit.*

—Mason Cooley, U.S. aphorist (b. 1927)

In 1959, seven astronauts were chosen for NASA's Mercury space program. These seven men were selected from an initial pool of thousands of military pilots.[1] They were considered the best and the brightest, the strongest and the bravest. In short, they were made of the "right stuff."[2] Getting ahead in America is widely seen in these terms. The popular perception in America is that those who are made of the right stuff are the cream of the crop that rises to the top.

Although there are variations on the theme of meritocracy, we have identified four key ingredients in the American formula for being made of the right stuff: being talented, having the right attitude, working hard, and having high moral character. We will review each of these in terms of its impact on getting ahead.

### INNATE TALENTS AND ABILITIES

In 1994, Richard Herrnstein and Charles Murray published *The Bell Curve: Intelligence and Class Structure in American Life*. The central thesis of this book is that intelligence is largely genetically inherited and that it largely determines socioeconomic success. Herrnstein and Murray contend that the distribution of intelligence in the general population takes the form of a symmetrical "bell curve," or what statisticians refer to as a "normal distribution." In normal distributions, the most common score is the average, with most cases bunched closely around it. Variation around the middle is symmetrical in either direction (below and above the average), with most cases close to the average and the number of cases dropping off rapidly the farther away from the average, becoming rare at either end of the distribution. The shape of this curve resembles a bell; hence the name. Many occurrences in nature are "normally" distributed in this manner. The argument made by Herrnstein and Murray is that intelligence is another indication of this more general tendency in nature. But from the start, human IQ is distributed normally only by definition. The standard distribution of IQ scores is, by definition, "normal." We don't really know how intelligence is distributed in "nature"—it is only distributed this way because the tests are constructed to produce normal distributions.

Herrnstein and Murray further argue, with little compelling evidence, that barriers to upward mobility on the basis of natural talent have largely been eliminated and that a new "cognitive elite" is emerging in America. They contend that as colleges and universities have opened opportunities to a broader economic spectrum of students, educational attainment is increasingly based on academic performance and less on the inheritance of wealth and privilege. Moreover, with new technological demands, there is an increasing premium in society on intellectual prowess. In short, *The Bell Curve* contends that intellectual capability is increasingly replacing socioeconomic background as the new axis of economic inequality in society.

At face value, this argument does not fit the facts. If intelligence is shaped like a bell curve, and if it is what is mostly behind economic outcomes, then why are income and wealth distributions not also bell curve shaped? Indeed, income and especially wealth are very highly skewed, with small percentages of the population getting most of what there is to get (see chapter 3.). Is billionaire Bill Gates really billions of times smarter than you are? More generally, does income vary directly with intelligence?

This question is, of course, unfair, since Herrnstein and Murray did not claim that intelligence causes wealth for any one person. They were interested in overall patterns of results. Another reason that the curves of intelligence and wealth are not the same is that factors other than intelligence affect economic outcomes. Herrnstein and Murray acknowledge that other factors such as family background affect income but, according to their calculations, family background is only one-third as important as IQ in predicting income. One could also argue that the differences between intelligence and economic outcomes are not directly proportional because even a small difference in intelligence might be multiplied many times over in producing social and economic consequences. Finally, Herrnstein and Murray looked at income but not wealth in accounting for economic consequences. This is important because wealth is not only much more skewed in its distribution than income, it is also much more subject to family background differences.

Nevertheless, the burden is great on those who claim that such dissimilarly shaped curves (intelligence and economic outcomes) can be strongly related in cause and effect terms.

Not surprisingly, the publication of *The Bell Curve* was met with a barrage of criticism. Among the many critical responses, for instance, was *Inequality by Design: Cracking the Bell Curve Myth* (1996). This book was written by a team of six sociologists at the University of California at Berkeley and provides a systematic, chapter-by-chapter and point-by-point refutation of the arguments and conclusions contained in *The Bell Curve*. As the authors of *Inequality by Design* state, "the devil is in the details" (Fischer et al. 1996, 229). The methodological details go far beyond what we can adequately address here. The upshot of the many criticisms of *The Bell Curve*, however, is that in terms of social and economic outcomes, Herrnstein and Murray greatly overestimated the influence of intelligence (nature) and greatly underestimated the influence of environmental factors (nurture).

Specifically, the critics contend that there are serious questions surrounding Herrnstein and Murray's measurement of intelligence itself. First, is intelligence a single capacity, or does it have multiple dimensions? Herrnstein and Murray argue that there is a general intelligence factor (sometimes called the "g" factor) that is highly related to separate dimensions of intelligence. Other experts, however, dispute the idea that the complexities of human intelligence are reducible to a single number. Whatever single number is produced is at best only an estimate of whatever general intelligence means. Second, to what extent is intelligence heritable? In their review of the psychometric literature on IQ tests, Herrnstein and Murray suggest that between 40 and 80% of the scores on IQ tests are heritable, so they simply split the difference and accept an estimate of 60%. Other research, however, estimates that the inheritability of intelligence is much lower and is unlikely to exceed 40% (Feldman, Otto, and Christiansen 2000). This means that most of the variation in IQ tests scores is due to environmental factors and how environmental factors interact with intellectual ability. Also, other research has found that the particular measure of "intelligence" that Herrnstein and Murray used in their study—the Armed Forces Qualifications Test—is a better marker for family background than inherent intellectual capacity (Currie and Thomas 1999).

The critics also note that even though Herrnstein and Murray initially point out that IQ scores are at least 40% subject to environmental influences, they nevertheless proceed to discuss the results of "IQ" effects as if these measured intelligence alone. There are other puzzles of IQ test scores that Herrnstein and Murray's analysis does not explain. Average scores on IQ tests have been rising consistently and sharply in recent generations. Since the 1940s, average IQ scores have risen more than twenty points in the United States and much of the industrialized world, more rapidly than could be explained by genetic change. In short, genetically based traits simply don't "evolve" that fast. This average increase in IQ scores is called the "Flynn Effect," named after James Flynn, the researcher who first noticed and documented the trend. As educational attainment of a population increases, for instance, so do scores on IQ tests, which suggests that schooling (an environmental factor) makes people "smarter." Herrnstein and Murray acknowledge that school makes people smarter at a rate of about three-fourths of a point of IQ per year of education, although other estimates are more than three times as high (Winship and Korenman 1997). Herrnstein and Murray do not directly include education as an independent variable in their prediction of social outcomes, since they argue that smarter individuals get more schooling, and education is also highly correlated with social class background. There is a substantial literature, however, that suggests that education has strong and independent effects on labor force outcomes such as income and occupational attainment (see chapter 5). Herrnstein and Murray also do not control for gender, which is known to have independent effects on earning power, the accumulation of wealth, and the probability of poverty. These effects are not due to women being less intelligent than men but rather to women being at higher risk for poverty and more likely to experience wage discrimination in the workplace (see chapter 8).

The critics also took issue with Herrnstein and Murray's measurement of "socioeconomic background." Herrnstein and Murray estimate socioeconomic background with a single variable, the Blau-Duncan socioeconomic index. This index is a combined measure of parental income, education, and occupational status. Fischer et al. (1996) show that this combined score masks the independent effects of the component variables. Allowing each of these dimensions of socioeconomic status (SES) to be entered into the analysis separately increased the effects of each factor. In a subsequent analysis, Murray (1998) responded to the critics in this regard by redoing the original analyses of *The Bell Curve*, comparing siblings as a control for environmental effects. The reasoning is that children who grow up in the same households have the same environment, which gets around measurement problems associated with other estimates of environmental effects. In this subsequent analysis, Murray (1998) claims that the effects of IQ versus social background remain the same. However, Murray does not control for number of siblings, birth order, or gender, which are factors known to influence the amount of resources that parents invest in the children's futures. In a more detailed treatment of sibling comparisons using more inclusive and robust measures of family background, Korenman and Winship (2000) show that family background is at least as important and may be more important than IQ scores in determining economic success.

Among the more controversial parts of *The Bell Curve* is the chapter on IQ differences among racial minorities. Herrnstein and Murray point out that blacks tend to score about one standard deviation less than whites (about sixteen points) on IQ tests. The implication is that this difference is real; that is, not the effect of cultural bias of tests results and, therefore, substantially responsible for gaps in white/black socioeconomic attainment. Many scholars (Oliver and Shapiro 1995), however, dispute this conclusion. Indeed, the validity of "race" itself is disputed (cf. Harris 1990, 106–14). "Race" implies discrete subcategories within the human population. However, most biologists point out that genetic differences that produce superficial physical differences such as skin color are matters of degree and not of kind and vary considerably within groups, and are not related to other important genetic markers. The very term "race" is a social construct and not a biological distinction. Beyond the "continuum-category" issues surrounding "race," the dispute is not that IQ scores tend to be lower among those who self-identify as "black" but what the causes of those differences might be. Are those differences attributable to differences in innate intellectual capacity or the cumulative effects of the experience of being black in a white-dominated society? One factor, for instance, that can suppress intellectual development is the first environmental influence in a person's life: the environment of the womb. Lack of prenatal care, poor nutrition, and other environmental conditions experienced disproportionately by minorities and the poor can depress the potential for intellectual development. And from womb to tomb, those closer to the bottom of the economic ladder are more disadvantaged by environmental conditions. Finally, at all social levels, the costs of being black are substantial. Institutionalized discrimination creates structural impediments to mobility (see chapter 8).

Under the assumption that genetic endowments are fixed at birth and that these endowments are largely responsible for social outcomes, the policy implication of Herrnstein and Murray's conclusions is that money spent on social programs designed to improve the environmental opportunities of the poor and underprivileged is wasted. Indeed, Herrnstein and Murray suggest that money spent on such programs should be diverted to programs for the academically gifted. Again, their critics dispute this assertion based on the assumptions built into it. First, following this logic can create a self-fulfilling prophecy. Thus the poor are seen to be poor because they are not smart. Because they are not smart, they end up living in deprived environments. Changing the environment will do nothing to help the economic circumstances of the dull people who live there, and this becomes justification for nonintervention.

Overall, the evidence for the effects of "raw intelligence" is inconclusive. Beyond the difficulties of defining and measuring "intelligence," separating out the effects of innate intelligence on life outcomes from environmental factors that might affect success is difficult. As soon as infants are born, they are subject to environmental influences in addition to whatever genetic endowments they may possess. What matters is not raw intellectual capacity or environment alone but both in conjunction with one another. That there are differences in intellectual capacity among people is not in dispute. How much these differences make a difference is at the heart of the matter. The best evidence available suggests that intellectual capacity is only very modestly associated with getting ahead. Newer evidence estimates, for instance, that—at best—intelligence accounts for less than 10% of the variance in income (Cawley et al. 1999; Fisher et al. 1996). Because wealth is even more subject to environmental influences than income, it is likely that the effects of intelligence on the amount of wealth someone has are even smaller. Intelligence matters, but not nearly to the extent that most people presume.

Besides raw intellectual capacity, other presumably innate talents and abilities are also popularly perceived as part of the merit formula. These include—but are not limited to—athletic and artistic abilities. These traits are often associated with meteoric social mobility. The view that such talent can propel someone from rags to riches is not entirely without foundation. When people think of who is really rich in America, often the people who come to mind first are professional athletes and artists (actors, singers, writers, etc.), who command huge salaries for their services. Although star entertainers and athletes such as Tom Hanks, Oprah Winfrey, Tiger Woods, and Jennifer Aniston earn huge annual incomes for their services ($55 million, $180 million, $78 million, and $35 million respectively) (*Forbes* 2003a), the really big money in America comes not from working for a living but from owning income-producing property. Among the 100 highest paid celebrities in America who are athletes or entertainers (as opposed to owners, directors, and producers), only one—Oprah Winfrey—is among the wealthiest 400 Americans, making the cut at number 224 (*Forbes* 2003b). It is instructive that Ms. Winfrey also owns her own production company, HARPO. The other two nonperforming "entertainers" included in the list of the wealthiest 400 Americans, George Lucas (number 56) and Steven Spielberg (number 71), also own their own production companies (*Forbes* 2003b).

Although typically among the wealthiest of all Americans, athletes and actors, however, are celebrities who are well known to the general public. Some, such as Oprah Winfrey, come from modest social origins. The phenomenal success of these celebrities tends to reinforce the public perception that in America, you can go as far as your talents and abilities can take you.

Despite these images, the reality is that many are called but few are chosen. In athletics, for instance, sociology of sport expert Stanley Eitzen notes that:

> The dream of financial success through a professional sports career is just that, however, a dream for all but an infinitesimal number. A career in professional sport is nearly impossible to attain because of the fierce competition for so few openings. For example, in 1992, there were approximately 1.9 million American boys playing high school football, basketball, and baseball. That same year about 68,000 men were playing those sports in college and 2,490 participated at

the major professional level. In short, one in twenty seven high school players in these sports will play at the college level and *only one in 736 high-school players will play at the major professional level (.014%)*. (1999, 136)

Of those, only a few have long careers, with the average career lasting just five years. One could argue that these "elites" are truly talented and have extraordinary physical qualities not available to the average person (size, speed, agility, hand–eye coordination, etc.). "Raw" talent alone, however, is not enough. The talent has to be cultivated through recruitment and opportunities for training. Potential talent can go unnoticed, particularly in the absence of opportunities to develop and exhibit it. Training may be expensive and not easily available to people of modest means, particularly in such sports as golf, tennis, swimming, and figure skating.

Sociologist William Chambliss (1989), who studied the world of champion Olympic swimmers, suggests that the concept of inherent talent in and of itself is essentially useless since inherent talent as cause cannot be separated from its effects. That is, talent cannot be used to distinguish success and failure because one does not "know" it is there until success occurs. Chambliss argues that the thresholds for natural ability needed for athletic success (minimum physical strength, coordination, heart/lung capacity, and the like) are remarkably low. Many of the key factors to success in the swimming world are unrelated to raw talent—living in warm climates, having wealthy and supportive parents, and the availability of expert coaching. Where milliseconds often separate "winners" and "losers," Chambliss points that what distinguishes champions from mere contenders is not inherent physical superiority but more mundane considerations such as technique and training.

Historically, the conspicuous lack of people of color in these individual middle- and upper-middle-class sports is telling. Team sports such as baseball, basketball, and football have generally been more accessible (at least more recently), and this is reflected in the racial and socioeconomic makeup of the athletes in these professional sports. Overall, there is a strong relationship between type of sport and the race and class of origin of the professionals within it, which strongly suggests that differential recruitment and opportunity are at work rather than athletic prowess alone. In this regard, it is also noteworthy that athletics as a means of upward social mobility—regardless of talent level—is more available to males than females since there are more paid professional opportunities in men's sports. Even in sports in which both men and women compete, until quite recently prize money has been much greater for men.

The notion of raw "artistic" talent as a means of upward social mobility is even more suspect. Although "talented" Hollywood actors make millions, it is not clear that the potential pool of "talent" is small. It is unknown how many potential Dustin Hoffmans are out there, but chances are great that there are more of them than potential Michael Jordans. While there may be millions in the general population who could become movie stars (if "discovered," with the "right" breaks, the "right" acting coaches, the "right" roles, the "right" looks, etc.), there is probably a much smaller potential pool of individuals who can dunk a basketball from the foul line. This is indicated, for instance, by the high number of "crossovers" from sports to acting (or broadcasting) but not the other way around. Besides acting, the full extent of the potential pool of "innate" talent in the other performing arts (music, painting, sculpture, writing) is also equally unknown. As with other extraordinary "gifts," these too have to be nurtured even to be noticed much less developed to an elite level.

The presumed link between raw talent and celebrity athletes and artists reinforces the meritocracy myth. The presumption is that if *some* celebrities with these talents came from humble origins, then *anyone* who had those potential talents could do the same. However, it does not follow that if *only* those with talent rise to the level of celebrity athlete or artist, all those with talent will *become* celebrity athletes or artists. Indeed, as we suggested, the actual probabilities of social ascent through athletics or the arts are very small. And, as Norbert Wiley (1967) has pointed out, the illusion of potential success in these glamour areas ends up being a "mobility trap" for many youthful aspirants, who invest time and effort in the long-shot pursuit of fame and fortune at the expense of more realistic avenues of social mobility.

The National Basketball Association draft illustrates this principle. In 2003, there were fifty-eight players drafted into the NBA. Of these slots, twenty-one went to foreign players, leaving thirty-six filled by Americans. In 2003, there were approximately 15,000 college players in various National Collegiate Athletic Association men's teams playing in the United States. The statistical probability that any one of these players could realize their "hoop dreams" of being drafted to play in the NBA were about 1 in 417, or less than three-tenths of 1%. This means that many outstanding players with superb skills honed and cultivated by many hours of practice on the courts will get passed over in the draft.

The central issue here is not whether being smart or clever or shrewd or talented helps at least some people get ahead. It clearly does. The issue is how *much* it matters and how much difference makes a difference. This is a complex issue, and it is difficult to know precisely what mix of innate endowments and environmental influences has an effect on life outcomes. But even in the meritocratic formula for success, it is clear that capacity alone accounts for nothing. Any inherent capacities must be put to use, and this requires having the right attitude.

## HAVING THE RIGHT ATTITUDE

Beyond cognitive skills such as intelligence, various attitudes and behavioral traits are often presumed to be associated with economic success. In more familiar terms, these attitudes and traits are summarized by the phrase "having the right attitude." "Having the right attitude" is associated with qualities such as being ambitious, energetic, motivated, and trustworthy. It may also involve more subtle traits such as good judgment, sense of personal responsibility, willingness to defer gratification, persistence in the face of adversity, getting along with others, assertiveness, and the like. Conversely, lack of "proper attitudes" as evidenced by laziness, shiftlessness, indolence, lack of self-discipline, unreliability, disruptiveness, and so on, is associated with the failure to achieve.

It would seem that these represent two sides of the same coin. However, which side is emphasized makes a big difference in estimating the effects of attitudes and values on life outcomes. Most of the research linking attitudes with mobility has focused not so much on how the "right" values help one get ahead but on how the "wrong" values keep one from getting ahead. This implies that, in effect, one could have the "right" values but not get ahead anyway. Having the "wrong" values, however, would prevent one from getting ahead and may even be responsible for falling further behind.

One of the early attempts to link attitudes to the prospects for attainment is the "culture of poverty" theory. This theory was developed initially in the 1960s by anthropologist Oscar Lewis (1959, 1966), who conducted ethnographic studies of Mexican families living in poverty. This general perspective was later applied mainly to African Americans in the United States (Banfield 1970). For proponents of culture of poverty theory, the cause of poverty in these settings is not rooted in inherent individual biological deficiencies but in the "culture" of the poor. The "subculture" of poverty in the groups Lewis studied were said to be fatalistic, hedonistic, and impulsive. There was a high incidence of early initiation into sexual activity, consensual unions, and familial disruption. Lewis interpreted this subculture of poverty as pathological and self-perpetuating. Poor people hang around with other poor people as these values are reinforced in interaction within the group. Children are socialized into anti-work, anti-school, anti-family, anti-authority values passed on from one generation to the next in what becomes a "vicious cycle of poverty."

One of the central issues in the culture of poverty debate is whether poverty creates deviant values or whether deviant values create poverty. For Lewis, it is both. Lack of opportunity creates conditions that favor the development of these values, which—while adaptive to a life of poverty—are maladaptive to prospects for upward mobility. Lewis argued that the poor become so ingrained with a lifestyle of poverty that they reject opportunities to move ahead even when opportunities to do so become available. To this extent, poverty is a freely chosen lifestyle. However, the "blame" is not on individuals but on the group to which individuals belong, and the group itself is seen as resistant to change.

Culture of poverty theory has been sharply criticized on several grounds. It rests on the twin assumptions that the poor have values different than the nonpoor and that these values are responsible for the condition of poverty itself. Critics (Coward, Feagin, and Williams 1974; Della Fave 1974; Gould 1999; Rodman 1963; Valentine 1968) have attacked both of these key assumptions. According to critics of the theory, the poor do not have values significantly different from the nonpoor. Rather, the poor—like everyone else—adjust their perceptions of reality to accommodate the reality of the situation, resulting in what Rodman refers to as "the lower class value stretch." It is one thing, for instance, to say that the poor have a "present time orientation" because they are hedonistic thrill seekers who live for the moment. However, it is another thing altogether to say that—regardless of one's personal value system—one is forced to focus on the present if one is not sure where one's next meal might come from. The middle and upper classes have the luxury to be able to plan ahead and defer gratification (going to college instead of accepting a low-paid service job) precisely because their present is secure. Similarly, the poor may have modest ambitions, not because they are unmotivated, but because they make a realistic assessment of limited life chances. In this formulation, exhibited behaviors and perceptions associated with a "culture of poverty" reflect the *effects* of poverty—not the causes.

The idea of a situational view of poverty is consistent with the psychologist Abraham Maslow's well-known "hierarchy of needs" theory. According to Maslow (1970), humans have a hierarchical order of needs that begins at the fundamental levels of food, clothing, and shelter and advances to "higher order" needs for independence and "self-actualization." Maslow points out that one cannot attend to higher order needs if the lower order needs are not satisfied. In other words, poverty keeps people stuck at lower order needs, regardless of their desire for higher order fulfillment.

Although it appeared that the critics had discredited the "culture of poverty" theory, the concept seems to have resurfaced under the new label of an "underclass," which has the wrong values. Two prominent books popularized the term: *The Declining Significance of Race* (1980) by a sociologist, William Wilson, and *The Underclass* (1982) by a journalist, Ken Auletta. In an analysis of the evolution of the change in terminology from "culture of poverty" to "underclass," Michael Morris (1989) notes that both liberals and conservatives have adopted the new term. The term lends itself to either a cultural or structural argument regarding the causes of poverty. For Wilson, an urban underclass was created by structural changes in declining economic opportunities in cities following the post–World War II era. Following the white flight movement in the 1950s and civil rights movement of the 1960s, blacks became more internally stratified. There was simultaneously an increase both in the number of middle-class blacks and the number of impoverished blacks. Like other members of the middle class, educated middle-class blacks fled the problems of the cities. Despite the progress of the 1960s, poor blacks with little education and declining economic opportunities became trapped in the inner cities.

At a time when urban manufacturing centers were rapidly closing or being displaced, inner-city ghettos became increasingly associated with high risks for crime, drug abuse, and out of wedlock births. Conservatives (Murray 1984; Gilder 1981) argued that growing welfare programs designed to alleviate poverty actually encouraged an underclass of economically dependent welfare recipients who lacked incentives to work or get married. In both applications, the concept of "the underclass" is more closely tied to the minority poor—especially the urban minority poor. Research, however, has shown that black urban poor in the United States are committed to mainstream work and family values (Wilson 1996; Barnes 2002). In the face of limited opportunities, however, inner-city blacks may resort to expending capacities and talents in the irregular economy—hustling, pimping, drug dealing, and the like. In a systematic review of the culture of poverty debate related to inner-city blacks, sociologist Mark Gould concludes that:

> Inner-city blacks are not stuck in a "culture of poverty." Instead, the value commitments that most maintain are congruent with mainstream values, while the cognitive expectations they have formulated in response to their opportunity structures are accurate and functional. If these opportunity structures were to change, creating mainstream opportunities for inner-city blacks, most are committed, because of their orthodox values, to adopting those changes. (1999, 195–96)

Gould further suggests that since Americans believe that in the post–civil rights era equality of opportunity has been achieved, "the failure of blacks to succeed (in employment or education) is 'evidence' that there is something wrong with blacks," and cites other research showing that employers perceive workers from the inner city as "unskilled, uneducated illiterate, dishonest and lacking an understanding of work, without personal charm and with no family life or role models" (Gould, 1999, 189). These stereotypes, in turn, become a basis for employment discrimination. That is, employers discriminate against blacks not because they are black but because of a false perception that blacks are high employment risks. Gould refers to this as a "new racism," justified on presumed "rational" economic criteria.

Beyond the culture of poverty debate, there has been surprisingly little systematic research into the effects of noncognitive attitudes and behavioral traits on who gets ahead in America. The results of what research has been done have been mixed at best (see Farkas 2003 for a systematic review). The lack of research findings in this area is at least partly due to the difficulty in clearly separating out effects of all the possible "causes" of who gets ahead (and conversely who falls behind). With respect to attitudes and values, the question becomes *which* attitudes and *which* values? Moreover, do these attitudes and values produce *independent* effects on life outcomes, or are they merely related to other possible causal factors? And finally, how are attitudes related to behavior? Humans have a habit of saying one thing (expressed attitudes) but doing something else (exhibited behavior). Also, is the direction of influence clear? That is, do attitudes influence behavior, or does behavior influence attitudes?

Some research (Inoue 1999; Sewell, Haller, and Ohlendorf 1970) has shown that, for high school students, educational aspirations (intent to go to college) and occupational aspirations (occupational plans) of high school students have some effect on their subsequent levels of educational and occupational attainment. Aspirations, however, are only part of what predicts these outcomes—family background, academic aptitude, academic performance, and encouragement from significant others also matter. What is more, the "attitudes" examined in these studies are limited.

A seminal study by Christopher Jencks and his associates (1979) provides one of the few examinations of specific attitudes on occupational status and income. Jencks et al. found that "noncognitive" traits (especially industriousness and leadership) had some effect on occupational and income attainment. While family background produced the strongest overall effects in his study (accounting for about half of the total explained variation in occupational status and between 15 and 35% of the variation in income), taken together, attitudes and personality traits had effects about half as strong as family background and about as strong as measures of cognitive ability. No one attitude or trait in itself was found to be especially significant. Jencks et al. concluded that among the many attitudes and personality traits they examined, "industriousness" proved to be the best predictor of occupational status and "leadership" the best predictor of earnings.

However, it was not clear what exactly is being tapped by these individual measures. Jencks et al. note for instance, that "industriousness" was highly correlated with other attitude measures such as those for "cooperativeness," "dependability," and "emotional control." This highlights the problem of sorting out what is meant by "having the right attitude." Attitudes are related to other attitudes, and nuances of meaning among them tend to blend together, so pinpointing a particular combination of "right" attitudes for success becomes difficult. And, as Jencks et al. point out, a particular combination of attitudes and orientations might be "right" for success in one occupation but not for another (for instance, rigorously following rules might "work" for a successful accountant but might not "work" at all for the successful artist). Therefore, studies that attempt to link attitudes with success may be "of little help in determining the extent to which personality predicts success for the population in general" (Jencks et al. 1979, 124).

Some observers have suggested that "having the right attitude" is not necessarily related to cognitive abilities or job performance but may reflect employer preferences (Bowles and Gintis 1976, 2003). Employees who are more compliant or less demanding, for instance, may be preferred by employers irrespective of skill level, cognitive ability, or job performance.

Methodological problems in this area of research are particularly acute, often leading researchers to overinterpret findings. A particularly egregious example is the best-selling book *The Millionaire Mind* (2000), by Thomas Stanley. A former marketing professor, Stanley sent questionnaires to millionaires asking them to rate the importance of thirty "success" factors in terms of how important these factors were in explaining their economic success. The five most frequently selected factors among the millionaires surveyed were, in order of importance, (1) being honest with all people, (2) being well-disciplined (3) getting along with people, (4) having a supportive spouse, and (5) working harder than most people. These factors, as well as the others on the list, comprise what Stanley refers to as the "millionaire mind." As the title of the book implies, the message is that being a millionaire is a matter of having the right attitudes. The book, which rose to number 4 on the *New York Times* best-seller list, however, is riddled with methodological flaws and inconsistencies. First, there is no "control" group; that is, there is no statistical comparison between millionaires and nonmillionaires, so we don't know how unique the mind-set of the millionaire respondents really is. Many people, for instance, may report that they are "honest," but saying one is "honest" may be no more prevalent among millionaires than anyone else. Second, we don't even know how well this sample of millionaire respondents represents millionaires in general. The "response rate" for the survey among the targeted group of wealthy households was only 20%—low by social science standards. Finally, the perception of factors related to success was provided after the fact. Therefore, we don't know if these attitudes really "caused" wealth or whether wealthy people retrospectively simply attributed their success to attitudes their culture tells them are its source.

*The Millionaire Mind* is filled with anecdotes about people who purportedly embody these characteristics. In illustrating the importance of "getting along with other people," Stanley relates a story about a friend and former student who sells ladies' apparel. Stanley called on his friend to help set up a seminar with a top executive of a major corporation. In setting up the seminar, Stanley's friend called the secretary of the executive and asked her what size jeans the executive's wife wears. He was told a size 12. Stanley's friend sent a dozen pairs of jeans—all size 12 but marked size 8—to the executive as a gift for his wife. The executive exclaimed, "My God . . . my wife loves the blue jeans. She can't thank you enough. She feels a lot better about me giving up my Saturday when there are blue jeans involved. They fit her perfectly" (Stanley 2000, 43). In relating this story, Stanley was impressed by how good a salesman his friend is and how much empathy he has for people. Although "getting along with people" is the third most important success factor identified in *The Millionaire Mind*, in relating this story, Stanley evidently overlooked the most important success factor identified in his own data: "being honest with people."

*The Millionaire Mind* reflects an ideology of economic success that historian Richard Huber (1971) refers to as the "mind-power ethic." According to this ethic, success is a matter of mind over matter. Success can be acquired through sheer willpower. The mind-power ethic is a major theme running throughout American success self-help books of the twentieth century (Dunkleman 2000). Fueled by a tradition of Protestant individualism and later secularized and reflected in a fascination with psychology, the mind-power ethic peaked with the publication of Norman Vincent Peale's *The Power of Positive Thinking* (1952) and his success formula of "prayerize, picturize, and actualize." This ethic speaks especially to the notion that determination and persistence in the face of whatever obstacles may exist is the true secret of success. In this formulation, people may not be perceived as being responsible for being born poor as children, but they are perceived as responsible for staying poor as adults.

The position that success or failure is ultimately "all in your head" was also more recently echoed by anthropologists Charles Harrington and Susan Boardman in *Paths to Success* (1997). Using small samples, Harrington and Boardman compared a group of sixty "pathmakers" who achieved success despite coming from impoverished backgrounds, with a control group of forty other successful people from more privileged backgrounds. According to Harrington and Boardman, what most distinguished the pathfinders from other successful people is that the pathfinders had higher levels of perceived "internal locus of control."

Internal locus of control refers to the perception that people have control over what happens to them and to others. External locus of control, on the other hand, refers to the perception that forces beyond the control of individuals determine most of what happens to them. The problem is that we do not know if internal locus of control was a "cause" of beating the odds or the "result" of it. People can and do adjust their perceptions of the past to match their current circumstances, so we do not know what perceptions were operative at the time the mobility took place. Another study (Wang et al. 1999), which used a panel design in which the same individuals were surveyed at two different time points, did find real but quite small associations between both internal locus of control and self-esteem at age twenty-five and educational and occupational attainments at age thirty-two. However, by age twenty-five, educational and occupational trajectories are already somewhat established, so once again direction of causality is an issue. Also, the authors of this more recent study point out that it is not certain why this effect occurs, and it may be an artifact of other factors. Some people, for instance, may accept greater responsibility for positive outcomes than negative ones. Therefore, even if "pathfinders" do have higher internal locus of control than others, we cannot be certain that internal locus of control or high self-esteem is directly responsible for their upward mobility.

Other recent research using longitudinal panel data (same individuals interviewed at different points over an extended time period) shows links between the kinds of job values that people hold and their family background, cognitive ability, and gender (Halaby 2003). In this research, a comparison is made between those who hold "entrepreneurial" job values and " bureaucratic" job values. Those who have entrepreneurial orientations value high pay, esteem, discretion, autonomy, and variety. Those who have bureaucratic orientations particularly value job security, job training, pensions, and clean working conditions. In pursuit of jobs and careers, there is often a trade-off between risks and returns. Workers who adopt an "entrepreneurial" strategy may pursue jobs with high returns but also with higher risks. Those who adopt a "bureaucratic" strategy may be more likely to pursue jobs with lower returns but fewer risks. This research shows that males, individuals with higher levels of cognitive ability, and those from more privileged backgrounds more often adopt the higher risk "entrepreneurial" strategy, which may also be associated with greater prospects for rapid upward mobility. This research suggests that willingness to assume risk may have less to do with individual personality orientations and, instead, is more likely associated with the prospects of "fallback" options in the event of failure, which are much better for males (less subject to labor force discrimination), those from more privileged backgrounds (more insulated from downward mobility), and those with better cognitive capabilities (wider range of potential avenues for success).

It is not clear then, what specific attitudes are individually determinative of economic success as opposed to being merely associated with it or a consequence of it. It is also not clear which particular attitudes are associated with success in particular occupations or professions. Furthermore, it is not clear how to measure these attitudes or to distinguish their effects from other related factors such as family background. Much of what passes as the "right attitude," for instance, is likely to be at least partially the result of differential access to preferred forms of cultural capital (see chapter 4). Such intangibles as comportment, demeanor, and presentation of self to others (and interpreted by others as "attitude") may be more of a reflection of "upbringing" than uniquely personal or individual attitudes. These traits may be seen as desirable by persons in positions of authority even if such traits may not actually affect job performance.

## WORKING HARD OR HARDLY WORKING

In the formula for getting ahead, "hard work" ranks very prominently in most Americans' minds. Indeed, survey research shows that Americans mention "hard work" more frequently than any other single factor associated with "getting ahead" (Davis and Smith 1989; Dunkleman 2003). It is difficult to disentangle the effects of attitudes such as "motivation," "industriousness," "ambition," and so on from actual hard work. Attitudes alone, however, are likely not as important as actual behavior.

Americans nod their heads knowingly and approvingly whenever the importance of "hard work" is mentioned in association with the likelihood of success. But what does this really mean? Does it refer to the number of hours worked? Does it refer to the level of exertion expended in the conduct of work? How are these factors related to concrete measures of economic success, that is, wealth and income? As Barbara Ehrenreich (2001) discovered when she spent a year doing odd menial jobs in America in a participant observation study, often the hardest working Americans are those who get paid the least. It is the waitress with sore feet at the end of a day after several miles of trudging around between the kitchen and dining area taking orders, pouring drinks, and carrying dishes and heavy trays of food. It is the lowest paid member of the construction crew with aching muscles and a sore back at the end of a day after toting heavy loads of lumber and other construction materials on the work site. It is the secretary with carpal tunnel syndrome who literally works her fingers to the bone typing departmental reports. It is the janitor who moonlights as a housepainter and works over sixty hours a week because neither job pays enough to make ends meet. Individuals such as these represent the backbone of the American *working* class. Additional "hard work" of this kind is unlikely to result in any significant upward social mobility.

Conversely, those with high paying jobs may not be working any "harder" than those with less well-paying jobs in the same employing organizations. In most jobs in America, compensation is more directly related to levels of responsibility and authority than it is to "hard work" per se. Further, those who have the most may actually expend the least amount of effort. The really big money in America, as shown in the following chapter, does not come from working for a living at all but from ownership of property—especially the kind of property that produces additional wealth, such as stocks and bonds, real estate, businesses, and so on. Indeed, those who live off unearned income may not need to work at all. If one is wealthy enough, it is possible to hire small armies of accountants, lawyers, and brokers to manage one's holdings and still be among the wealthiest of all Americans.

Clearly "hard work" alone is neither a necessary nor a sufficient condition for receiving the most compensation for whatever it is that people do. When people cite "hard work" as a factor in getting ahead, what they really mean is hard work *in combination* with other factors—especially opportunity and acquired skills—both of which are more related to social background than individual capacities.

## MORAL CHARACTER

In addition to persistence in the face of adversity, another frequent theme in the American cultural folklore of meritocracy is that being made of the right stuff includes moral character and integrity. Moral fiber and character has been a constant theme in American "self-help" success books (Dunkleman 2000; Huber 1971; Hilkey 1997). The early advice manuals, in particular, echoed the twin pillars of the Protestant ethic: diligence and asceticism. In addition to working hard, the "truly" successful person was a person of honor and dignity. People should pursue wealth not for the purposes of self-gratification or personal indulgence but for the glory of God and to help others. In this formulation, success is taken as evidence of God's grace; successful people saw themselves as "moral people." There was always some tension, however, between materialism and idealism in the pursuit of wealth. As Richard Huber points out:

> The clash between materialism and idealism in the American spirit is expressed in the deep need to justify success. More than most societies, Americans yearn to justify their behavior in moral terms. In the nineteenth century success writers were always justifying the accumulation of wealth as socially, morally, and economically the right thing to do. It was not a rationalization but a justification based on a moral construct that making money was a good thing. It was what one ought to do. It was good, not only because it builds character within the individual, but also enabled the successful man to contribute funds to the general welfare of the community and the nation. (1971, 98–99)

Moreover,

> dishonesty and sinful behavior of any sort was considered not only ignoble but also an impractical way to make money. Pragmatically, it was not supposed to pay off. Those men who somehow amassed a fortune by crooked means were either scorned or unworthy exemplars of right conduct or ignored . . . businessmen and writers on the subject claimed that the justification for wealth was not climbing over the fallen bodies of others, but struggling against the evil in oneself and then going on to some kind of moral triumph. (1971, 98–99)

While honesty and integrity are certainly worthy goals in their own right, in the final analysis, do they help or hinder in the making of money? There is little direct evidence suggesting that these virtues help or hinder the prospects for social mobility. On the one hand, we have numerous testimonials of wealthy individuals who claim such virtues. Indeed, as already mentioned, "being honest with people" was listed as the number one factor responsible for success among self-reports of millionaires in *The Millionaire Mind*. On the other hand, we have much less frequent but occasional admissions of less than ethical practices among successful people who fell from grace. Among the latter include the personal account of the Watergate scandal by John Dean, who was then counselor to President Nixon, aptly titled *Blind Ambition* (1976). And we have one of the few glimpses of the inside workings of the corporate world, *On a Clear Day You Can See General*

*Motors* (1979), by deposed General Motors executive John DeLorean. More recently, we have revelations by inside whistle-blowers identifying alleged illegal or unethical business practices, including Sherron Watkins at Enron, Barron Stone at Duke Power, Marta Andreasen at the European Commission, and Cynthia Cooper at WorldCom ("The Whistle Blowers" 2003).

The only systematic evidence on the effect of integrity on success comes from *Who Gets Ahead* (Jencks et al. 1979, 154). Among the many "noncognitive" factors that they examined was "integrity," as measured by teachers' accounts of students' personalities longitudinally related to later mobility. They reported that, controlling for other factors, "integrity" produced a small *inverse* but statistically significant effect. That is, everything else being equal, integrity was associated with *less* upward mobility.

In the absence of other direct evidence, we suspect that the overall effect of integrity is to *suppress* rather than enhance upward mobility. We suspect that *not* cheating, *not* stealing, and choosing *not* to get ahead at the expense of others restricts social mobility and the accumulation of wealth. Wealth can be achieved by honest or dishonest means. The logic of this argument is that those who limit themselves to strictly honest means to get ahead have fewer opportunities to do so than those who do not limit themselves in this way. Direct evidence for the wealth-enhancing character of ruthless and unethical behavior comes from the history of industrial capitalism. Many of the wealthy industrialists of the last century earned notorious reputations as "robber barons" for their relentless and cutthroat pursuit of wealth and power. The indirect evidence for the wealth-enhancing character of unethical behavior comes from the extent of white-collar crime in America. Assuming that the amount of exposed white-collar crime represents only the tip of the iceberg of unscrupulousness, we would surmise, by extension, that the prospects for making money in America are often enhanced by less than impeccable moral standards.

It is difficult to estimate the full extent of white-collar crime in America. This type of crime has become more sophisticated and includes such practices as embezzlement, tax evasion, accounting fraud, restraint of trade and insider trading, price fixing, bribery, illegal competition, deceptive advertising, securities theft, illegal dumping of toxic waste, marketing unsafe products, occupational and safety violations—to name just a few. Attention is directed away from this type of crime since "crime in the suites" is less visible, less frequently detected, and less rigorously prosecuted than "crime in the streets." Conservative estimates are that white-collar crime costs society over $260 billion annually, which is forty times more than estimated losses from street crime (Simon 2002, 91). It is more difficult to detect white-collar crime since enforcement efforts of the criminal justice system are directed toward crimes committed by the poor rather than the rich (Reiman 2001), and people are often unaware that they have been victimized. When white-collar crime is exposed, the sums procured in the commission of these crimes is staggering—often totaling in the millions and sometimes even in the billions. Some examples include the notorious and illegal stock manipulations of Ivan Boesky (deal stocks), Michael Milken (junk bonds), and Charles Keating (savings and loan scandal) and a spate of alleged corporate ethics scandals at Enron, WorldCom, Arthur Andersen, Adelphia, Bristol-Myers Squibb, Duke Energy, Global Crossing, Xerox, and many others as well as recent allegations of misconduct in the vast mutual funds industry. Suffice it to say, at least some of the wealth of financiers, executives, and professionals has been gained through less than honest means. This is in addition to untold wealth realized from more conventional organized crime including drug trafficking, prostitution, pornography, racketeering, gambling, and the like, which itself is estimated to account for as much as 10% of the American economy (Schlosser 2003). In an ideal world, the virtuous succeed and the corrupt fail. But in the real world, too often it seems that this is not the case.

## A NOTE ON HUMAN CAPITAL

*Human capital* factors are often included in the "merit" formula for success. Human capital refers to whatever *acquired* skills, knowledge, or experience workers possess that they can exchange for income in open markets. Strictly speaking, however, acquired capacity is not the same as being inherently made of the right stuff, since opportunities to acquire skills and experience are independent of inherent capacity to do things. In human capital theory, wage laborers can "invest" in themselves through the accumulation of education and training, thus increasing their skills and presumably their productive capacities. But, as with investments in other forms of economic capital, investments in human capital require resources and entail an element of risk. Capacities to do things represent the "supply" side of the labor market; what specific capacities employers actually need represent the "demand" side of the labor market. The biggest returns on human capital investments are those in which the capacities acquired are both scarce and in high demand. It is possible, however, to invest in the "wrong" capacities. This can occur, for instance, when individuals are trained for jobs that become obsolete, sometimes even before the training period is complete. Or, too many individuals may invest in acquiring the same skills, glutting the market and reducing return on investment. In both cases, one could be very meritorious but also very unemployed. Although we explore the effects of human capital in greater detail in chapter 5 and the "demand" side of the equation in greater detail in chapter 6, the point here is that this type of "merit" alone does not guarantee success.

# THE MYTH OF THE *MOST* QUALIFIED

Defenders of meritocracy (and critics of affirmative action) will often proclaim that the issue of who should get what is simple and straightforward—just hire the *most* qualified. However, even ignoring the fact that the big money in America comes from economic investments and not from jobs for which people are hired, this is not as simple and straightforward as many presume. As William Ryan put it, "How would you know a meritocracy if you saw one?" (1984, 62). Ryan further asks:

> [D]o the best men and women really rise to the tops of the heaps that are important to us? Is it true that the smartest and most diligent of businessmen ascend straight and sure to the presidencies of General Motors and Exxon and IBM? Are the professors who sit in the most distinguished chairs at Harvard and Yale and Chicago and Stanford really the most able and learned scholars in our land? Are our state houses and the White House and the Untied States Capital populated by the wisest, most resourceful, and most far-sighted of our times? (1984, 62)

If merit were the sole cause of achievement, one would wonder why the vast amount of raw talent is found in white males, who clearly dominate leadership positions in key institutions in society. Even setting discrimination and differential access to opportunity aside, how, in fact, would one recognize the *most* qualified applicant for every position in America?

Let us take a somewhat extended example from our own profession. Combined, the authors of this book have nearly fifty years of experience in higher education. In addition to our own experience in the academic labor market, we have each been on literally scores of faculty hiring committees. For most of our careers, we have been employed in a rapid growth institution, and as a result we have hired numerous new faculty in our department. For most of that time, our department combined four disciplines—sociology, anthropology, criminal justice, and social work—so our experience goes beyond one discipline alone. We need to make two caveats. Hiring in academia is somewhat unusual compared to other sectors of the economy in that it is for the most part highly collegial; that is, the "decision" to hire is a collective one typically made jointly by the existing members of the faculty in a given department, subject to approval at higher levels. This joint decision-making process reduces the chance of capricious hiring based on the whims of any one person. Another unique quality of academic hiring is that faculty positions involve national searches; that is, job openings are advertised nationally, casting the widest possible net. All of this is intended to increase the chances of hiring the "best" person for the job.

Although the intent is to hire the "best" person for the job, as anyone who has ever participated in the process knows, the problem comes in figuring out what is "best" and who that "best" person might be. The first qualification for the job is to have a Ph.D. from an academically accredited institution in the discipline in which the faculty member will teach and do research. So far, so good. For a typical faculty position in our department, we might receive around 50 to 100 applications. Among these, 95% or more of the applicants will have a Ph.D. in the appropriate field. That is, only 5% of the applicants can be quickly eliminated as "unqualified."[3] Now what? The hiring committee then carefully reviews the remaining applications, which consist of a letter of application, an academic resume called a "vita," and three letters of recommendation. Together, these materials represent a "paper presentation of self" of the applicant to the committee.

After serving on a few of these committees, one realizes very quickly that some applicants are better at paper presentation of self than others. That is, holding experience, ability, and qualifications constant, some individuals are simply better than others at presenting their case on paper. Presenting a case on paper and actual ability to do the job are two different things. More on this later. Based on these paper presentations of self, the hiring committee will develop a "short list" of maybe ten individuals for closer review. The short list is generated based on all reasonable indicators of "merit"—teaching record and experience, research record and potential, and "goodness of fit" with the needs of the department. With respect to the latter quality, it should be noted that we often have applicants who are truly outstanding but do not "fit" the advertised position; that is, they may appear to be the most talented or meritorious person in the pool overall, but they do not have areas of specialization for the position as advertised (e.g., an applicant could be a great demographer, but what we were really looking for was a gerontologist). As with most academic hires at most universities, we are most often looking for "entry" level positions at the assistant professor level. This means that we will not usually consider the literally "best" in the field if such a candidate is a senior full professor with a proven track record because such a candidate would be too expensive for the institution to hire. In this sense, we are not looking for the *most* meritorious professor we can find; we are looking for the most meritorious new assistant professor we can afford in a specific area we need to fill.

In developing the short list, there are typically differences of opinion among members of the search committee. We try to reach a reasonable consensus, but perfect agreement rarely occurs. Majority sentiment prevails, but lack of consensus is itself an indicator of the difficulty of determining what "best" represents. We make a collective "best guess" as to whom the ten "best" applicants in the pool might be. In developing an initial short list, the committee may well have overlooked the candidate who was in fact, the "best" in the pool in terms of how that person ultimately could have done the job. Such a person, for instance, ultimately might have been the "best" for the job but poor in terms of presenting himself or herself on paper. We will never know. One could argue that how one presents oneself on paper is an indicator of merit. However, we also know that some candidates, especially new Ph.D.'s, are better "coached" than others, and paper presentation of self is often more a reflection of the good advice of senior mentors than of candidate skills. We now have ten or so "short listed" candidates but still only one position. The next step is to select three from among the top ten for "on campus" interviews.

Perhaps we would do a better job of screening for raw talent if we interviewed more candidates. But resources are limited, both the money kind that is required to pay for on-campus interviews and the time kind related to faculty who must also do all the other things faculty are supposed to do. Often, the short listed candidates seem indistinguishable in terms of merit. All appear excellent, and looking for distinctions can become an exercise in splitting hairs. Frequently, there is another twist to the hiring drama. A dilemma that frequently unfolds is related to the amount of experience a candidate has. Since we most often hire at the assistant professor level, this means that most of the applicants are new or relatively new Ph.D.'s. Relatively new Ph.D.'s present a comparison problem. If candidates are already assistant professors at other institutions, they have more teaching experience and typically more extensive research track records than new Ph.D.'s—but they are not necessarily "better" or more "meritorious." It is strictly a judgment call for a committee to decide whether potential exceeds track record in comparing new and almost-new Ph.D.'s—a source of more than one fierce debate in hiring committees we have been on.

At this point, other factors may come into play. Do we know any of the people who are writing letters of recommendation for the candidates? We may give more weight to candidates who have "big names" writing for them. Everything else being equal or indistinguishable, the prestige of the references might become a factor. The prestige of the institution where the candidates were trained may also become a factor. Here, some candidates may benefit from a "halo" effect of the glow of the institution from which they received their training, even though this in itself does not necessarily measure the merit of an individual.

Some of the most heated debates in hiring, however, have more to do with the faculty on the committee than the candidates. Hiring can become a political battle over which faction or which coalition will prevail. Factions might develop over methodological, theoretical, or substantive differences within the hiring committee. Everything else being equal (and sometimes even when it is not), faculty members will try to hire someone like themselves. Apart from strictly merit considerations, individual faculty may also be interested in promoting the power of their faction or in hiring someone who might be a personal asset to them.

When the dust of these debates clears, three warm bodies are brought to campus for an extended interview, usually lasting two or three full days.

During this time, candidates have one-on-one interviews with faculty and administrators, typically teach a class, and give a research presentation. There are also a number of opportunities for informal interaction at dinners, receptions, and community tours. We have been amazed over the years at how frequently the top three on paper do not end up being ranked in the same order after on-campus interviews, reflecting the differences we alluded to above between real and paper presentations of self. A final intangible screening factor is how well the candidates are liked. Here, interviewing skills may be more important than paper qualifications. How people present themselves in a job interview, however, may not reflect how they will actually perform on the job. Everything else being equal (and sometimes not so equal), the candidate who "gets along" best with the most influential members of the committee will triumph over others.

In the end, a job offer is made to one person. Although the hiring committee, the department, and the university may congratulate themselves for selecting the "*best*" person in the pool, the reality is that there is, in fact, no way to determine that with certainty. Do we routinely hire highly qualified candidates that are very meritorious? Absolutely. Have we always hired the *most* meritorious person for the job? Probably not, but we will never know for sure. The point of this extended example is to show that even within the professoriate, a profession in which qualifications and individual merit are highly extolled, there is no assurance that "the best" ultimately prevails. The hiring process is likely to be even more slippery for real estate agents, store clerks, janitors, and a host of other jobs for which the criteria for merit may be less agreed upon and more difficult to measure and which have far less rigorous screening processes. When it comes to hiring the "best" or "most qualified," there are many slips betwixt the cup and the lip.

## THE COSTS OF MEASURING UP

The American emphasis on merit and competition is not without its costs. In an insightful analysis of the American "performance ethic," sociologist John Mannon points out that in the "relentless quest to measure up to the innumerable standards of health, wealth, competence and so on, Americans are becoming less autonomous, less authentic, and less free" (1997, 1). Beginning with the Apgar Score for newborns, a numerical scale that indicates a baby's clinical vitality and well-being immediately after birth, Americans are subjected to a dizzying variety of "measures" purporting to indicate how they "rate" compared to others—IQ tests, standardized "aptitude" tests, achievement tests, "grades," athletic scores, the "thin to win" norms presented in women's magazines, incomes as yardsticks of worth, and so on. These measures are often of dubious reliability, validity, and relevance to real life.

In *The Competition Paradigm* (2003), Pauline Vaillancourt Rosenau explains how competition among individuals in the pursuit of these standards can often lead to a host of ill effects, ranging from irritability, insomnia, depression, impaired memory function, hypertension, cardiovascular disease, and diabetes, to lowered immunity. Rosenau distinguishes between destructive and constructive forms of competition. Constructive competition is associated with four characteristics:

> First, winning must not be so important that it generates the extreme anxiety that interferes with performance. Second, all participants in the competition must see themselves as having a reasonable chance to win and thus remain motivated to give it an honest try, their best effort. Third, the rules of competition need to be clear and fair as to procedures and criteria for winning. Finally, those competing should be able to monitor how they are doing compared to others. (2003, 9)

Destructive competition, by comparison, does not satisfy these conditions. Destructive competition creates negative unintentional side effects such as "cutting costs by polluting the environment, competing by reducing worker safety and protection measures, competing at misleading advertising, competing at socially irresponsible, damaging financial speculation" (Rosenau 2003, 13).

Unfortunately, much of the "competition" to get ahead in America is rigged and therefore falls into the destructive category, with all its attendant ill effects. The danger comes when a person's sense of self-esteem, inherent worth, and dignity are judged by societal standards that are often irrelevant by the rules of the game that are rigged. In short, if the race to get ahead is rigged and if individuals who do not get ahead are presumed to be personally deficient, however that is defined and to whatever ends, then devastating consequences can occur—both for individuals and society as a whole.

## SUMMARY

This chapter has explored the meritocratic formula for getting ahead in America—being talented, having the right attitude, working hard, and having high moral standards. We review the evidence linking these "individual" traits with life outcomes. With the exception of high moral standards, all of these traits have some bearing on getting ahead in America. That is, individual capacity, certain attitudes, and hard work all probably do help people get ahead. High moral standards, however, may actually have the opposite effect by reducing options available to get ahead. While being made of the "right stuff" in general helps people get ahead, the reality is that these qualities exist in greater quantity in the general population than is ever actually realized. Moreover, many individual traits often have social origins, and the effects of these traits are often much less than is presumed. By themselves, these traits are not typically enough to make the difference. It is not innate capacity alone, or hard work alone, or the proper frame of mind alone that makes a difference. Rather, it is the *combination* of opportunity and these factors that makes a difference.

Related to the issue of meritocracy, we call into question the presumption that people know merit when they see it. That is, it is a cardinal principle in meritocracy that the "most" qualified or "best" person should be hired for the job. Using an example from the process for hiring professors, however, we argue that it is often difficult or impossible to "know" who the "best" is. Finally, we discuss the costs of trying to "measure up" to sometimes artificial and irrelevant societal standards. In the frantic race to get ahead, the inherent value and dignity of all persons, regardless of their individual merit or lack of it, may get lost in the shuffle.

## NOTES

1. Between 1969 and 1961, a similar but much less publicized program for women pilots was conducted by the National Aeronautics and Space Administration. Thirteen of these women were selected after two rounds of the same testing that the Mercury male astronauts had passed earlier. The men were put through a third round of testing, but NASA prevented the women from taking the third round of tests and the program was suddenly dropped, essentially negating any prospect that any of the women would be included in NASA's space program regardless of their individual abilities (Ackmann 2003).

2. The phrase "the right stuff" was used by Tom Wolf in a 1979 book of the same title in reference to flight pioneers and the selection of NASA's first American astronauts. The book became the basis of a popular 1983 movie also of the same title.

3. Although most institutions list the Ph.D. as an absolute minimum requirement, the lack of this credential does not in itself mean that a candidate is "unqualified." Almost every academic field of study has at least a few cases of famous scholars who were giants in their fields of study but who never completed a Ph.D. In American sociology, three of the most famous such individuals are George Herbert Mead (1863–1931) at the University of Chicago, whose work was seen as the inspiration for the symbolic interactionist perspective in sociology; George Casper Homans (1910–1989) at Harvard University, who was a pioneer in the development of social exchange theory; and David Riesman (1909–2002), also of Harvard, who wrote the best-selling book of all time in the history of American sociology, *The Lonely Crowd*. Technically, Mead was a philosopher whose ideas attracted the attention of sociologists. Riesman was trained as a lawyer but became interested in social issues. Homans was trained as a sociologist but never earned a Ph.D., which he considered nothing more than a "status symbol." Despite the lack of this journeyman's credential, Homans became an important sociologist at America's most elite university and even served a term as president of the American Sociological Association.

# REFERENCES

Ackmann, Martha. 2003. *The Mercury 13: The Untold Story of Thirteen American Women and the Dream of Space Flight*. New York: Random House.

Auletta, Ken. 1982. *The Underclass*. New York: Random House.

Banfield, Edward C. 1970. *The Unheavenly City: The Nature and Future of Our Urban Crisis*. Boston: Little, Brown.

Barnes, Sandra L. 2002. "Achievement or Ascription Ideology? An Analysis of Attitudes about Future Success for Residents in Poor Urban Neighborhoods." *Sociological Focus* 35: 207–25.

Bowles, Samuel, and Herbert Gintis. 1976. *Schooling in Capitalist America*. New York: Basic Books.

———. 2003. "Does Schooling Raise Earnings by Making People Smarter?" Pp. 118–36 in *Meritocracy and Economic Inequality*, edited by Kenneth Arrow, Samuel Bowles, and Steven Durlauf. Princeton, N.J.: Princeton University Press.

Cawley, John, James Heckman, and Edward Vytlacil. 1999. "Meritocracy in America: Wages within and across Occupations." *Industrial Relations* 38, no. 3: 250–96.

Chambliss, William. 1989. "The Mundanity of Excellence." *Sociological Theory* 7: 70–86.

Coward, Barbara E., Joe R. Feagin, and Allen J. Williams Jr. 1974. "The Culture of Poverty Debate: Some Additional Data." *Social Problems* 21: 621–34.

Currie, Janet, and Duncan Thomas. 1999. "The Intergenerational Transmission of 'Intelligence': Down the Slippery Slopes of *The Bell Curve*." *Industrial Relations* 38, no. 3: 297–300.

Davis, James A., and Tom W. Smith. 1989. *General Social Surveys, 1972–1998*. Storrs, Conn.: The Roper Center for Public Opinion Research.

Dean, John W. 1976. *Blind Ambition: The White House Years*. New York: Simon & Schuster.

Della Fave, L. Richard. 1974. "The Culture of Poverty Revisited: A Strategy for Research." *Social Problems* 21: 609–21.

DeLorean, John. 1979. *On a Clear Day You Can See General Motors: John Z. DeLorean's Look inside the Automotive Giant*. Grosse Point, Mich.: Wright Enterprises.

Dunkleman, Allen J. 2000. "Our American Ideology of Success." Unpublished senior research project, University of North Carolina at Wilmington.

———. 2003. "The Perceived Determinants of Economic Success: Comparing the Perceptions of Students and Teachers." Master's thesis, Department of Sociology, East Carolina University.

Ehrenreich, Barbara. 2001. *Nickel and Dimed: On (Not) Getting By in America*. New York: Metropolitan Books.

Eitzen, D. Stanley. 1999. *Fair and Foul: Beyond Myths and Paradoxes of Sport*. Lanham, Md.: Rowman & Littlefield.

Farkas, George. 2003. "Cognitive Skills and Noncognitive Traits and Behaviors in Stratification Processes." Pp. 541–62 in *Annual Review of Sociology*, vol. 29, edited by Karen S. Cook and John Hagan. Palo Alto, Calif.: Annual Reviews.

Feldman, Marcus W., Sarah P. Otto, and Freddy B. Christiansen. 2000. "Genes, Culture, and Inequality" Pp. 61–85 in *Meritocracy and Economic Inequality*, edited by Kenneth Arrow, Samuel Bowles, and Steven Durlauf. Princeton, N.J.: Princeton University Press.

Fischer, Claude S., Michael Hout, Martin Sanchez Jankowski, Samuel R. Lucas, Ann Swidler, and Kim Voss. 1996. *Inequality by Design: Cracking the Bell Curve Myth.* Princeton, N.J.: Princeton University Press.

*Forbes.* 2003a. "The Celebrity 100." www.forbes.com/static_html/celebs/2003/index.shtml [accessed December 7, 2003].

———. 2003b. "The Forbes 400." 172, no. 7 (October 6): special issue.

Gilder, George. 1981. *Wealth and Poverty.* New York: Basic Books.

Gould, Mark, 1999. "Race and Theory: Adaptation to Discrimination in Wilson and Ogbu." *Sociological Theory* 17: 171–200.

Halaby, Charles. 2003. "Where Job Values Come From: Family and Schooling Background, Cognitive Ability, and Gender. *American Sociological Review* 68, no. 2: 251–78.

Harrington, Charles, and Susan K. Boardman. 1997. *Paths to Success: Beating the Odds in American Society.* Cambridge, Mass.: Harvard University Press.

Harris, Marvin. 1990. *Our Kind: Who We Are, Where We Came from and Where We Are Going.* New York: HarperCollins.

Herrnstein, Richard, and Charles Murray. 1994. *The Bell Curve: Intelligence and Class Structure in American Life.* New York: Free Press.

Hilkey, Judy. 1997. *Character Is Capital: Success Manuals and Manhood in Gilded Age of America.* Chapel Hill: University of North Carolina Press.

Huber, Richard. 1971. *The American Idea of Success.* New York: McGraw-Hill.

Inoue, Yukiko. 1999. *The Educational and Occupational Attainment Process: The Role of Adolescent Status Aspirations.* Lanham, Md.: University Press of America.

Jencks, Christopher, et al. 1979. *Who Gets Ahead? The Determinants of Economic Success in America.* New York: Basic Books.

Korenman, Sanders, and Christopher Winship. 2000. "A Reanalysis of *The Bell Curve*: Intelligence, Family Background and Schooling." Pp. 137–78 in *Meritocracy and Economic Inequality,* edited by Kenneth Arrow, Samuel Bowles, and Steven Durlauf. Princeton, N.J.: Princeton University Press.

Lewis, Oscar. 1959. *Five Families: Mexican Case Studies in the Culture of Poverty.* New York: Basic Books.

———. 1966. *La Vida: A Puerto Rican Family in the Culture of Poverty.* New York: Random House.

Mannon, James M. 1997. *Measuring Up: The Performance Ethic in American Culture.* Boulder, Colo.: Westview.

Maslow, Abraham. 1970. *Motivation and Personality.* 2d ed. New York: Harper & Row.

Morris, Michael. 1989. "From the Culture of Poverty to the Underclass: Analysis of a Shift in Public Language." *American Sociologist* 20: 123–33.

Murray, Charles A. 1984. *Losing Ground: American Social Policy, 1950–1980.* New York: Basic Books.

———. 1998. *Income Inequality and IQ.* Washington, D.C.: American Enterprise Institute Press.

Ogbu, John. 1974. *The Next Generation: An Ethnography of Education in an Urban Neighborhood.* New York: Academic Press

Oliver, Melvin, and Thomas Shapiro. 1995. *Black Wealth and White Wealth: A New Perspective on Racial Inequality.* New York: Routledge.

Peale, Norman Vincent. 1952. *The Power of Positive Thinking.* New York: Prentice-Hall.

Reiman, Jeffrey. 2001. *The Rich Get Richer and the Poor Get Prison: Ideology, Class, and Criminal Justice*. 6th ed. Boston: Allyn and Bacon.

Rodman, Hyman. 1963. "The Lower Class Value Stretch." *Social Forces* 42: 205–15.

Rosenau, Pauline Vaillancourt. 2003. *The Competition Paradigm: America's Romance with Conflict, Contest, and Commerce*. Lanham, Md.: Rowman & Littlefield.

Ryan, William. 1984. *Equality*. New York: Vintage.

Schlosser, Eric. 2003. *Reefer Madness: Sex, Drugs, and Cheap Labor in the American Black Market*. Boston: Houghton Mifflin.

Sewell, J. William, A. O. Haller, and G. W. Ohlendorf. 1970. "The Educational and Early Occupational Status Attainment Process: A Replication and Revision." *American Sociological Review* 35: 1014–27.

Simon, David R. 2002. *Elite Deviance*. Boston: Allyn and Bacon.

Stanley, Thomas. 2000. *The Millionaire Mind*. Kansas City, Mo.: Andrew McMeel Publishing.

Valentine, Charles. 1968. *Culture and Poverty*. Chicago: University of Chicago Press.

Wang, Li-ya, Edward Kick, James Fraser, and Thomas Jerome Burns. 1999. "Status Attainment in America: The Roles of Locus of Control and Self-Esteem in Educational and Occupational Outcomes." *Sociological Spectrum* 19: 281–96.

"The Whistle Blowers." 2003. *Business Week* 3815 (January 13): 90.

Wiley, Norbert. 1967. "The Ethnic Mobility Trap and Stratification Theory." *Social Problems* 15: 147–59.

Wilson, William Julius. 1980. *The Declining Significance of Race: Blacks and Changing American Institutions*. 2d ed. Chicago: University of Chicago Press.

———. 1996. *When Work Disappears: The World of the New Urban Poor*. New York: Alfred A. Knopf.

Winship, Christopher, and Sanders D. Korenman. 1997. "Does Staying in School Make You Smarter? The Effect of Education on IQ in *The Bell Curve*." Pp. 215–34 in *Intelligence, Genes, and Success: Scientists Respond to "The Bell Curve,"* edited by Bernie Develin, Stephen Fienberg, Daniel Resnick, and Kathryn Roeder. New York: Springer-Verlag.

Wolf, Thomas. 1979. *The Right Stuff*. New York: Farrar, Straus & Giroux.

Young, Michael 1961. *The Rise of the Meritocracy, 1870–2033: An Essay on Education and Inequality*. Baltimore: Penguin.

# 3

## The Silver Spoon: Inheritance and the Staggered Start

*To heir is human.*

—Jeffrey P. Rosenfeld (1980, 122)

A common metaphor for the competition to get ahead in life is the footrace. The imagery is that the fastest runner—presumably the most meritorious—will be the one to break the tape at the finish line. But in terms of economic competition, the race is rigged. If we think of money as a measure of who gets what of what there is to get, the race to get ahead does not start anew with each generation. Instead, the race to get ahead is more like a relay race in which we inherit a starting point from our parents. The baton is passed and, for a while, both parents and children run together. When the exchange is complete, the children are on their own as they position themselves for the next exchange to the next generation. Although each new runner may gain or lose ground on the competition, each new runner inherits an initial starting point in the race.

In this intergenerational relay race, children born to wealthy parents start at or near the finish line, while children born into poverty start behind everyone else. Those who are born close to the finish line do not need any merit to get ahead. They already are ahead. The poorest of the poor, however, need to traverse the entire distance to get to the finish line on the basis of merit alone. In this sense, meritocracy strictly applies only to the poorest of the poor; everyone else has at least some advantage of inheritance that places them ahead at the start of the race.

In comparing the effects of inheritance and individual merit on life outcomes, the effects of inheritance come first, *then* the effects of individual merit follow—not the other way around. Figure 3.1 depicts the intergenerational relay race to

*Start*                                                              *Finish*

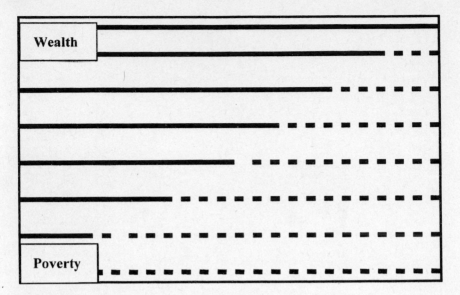

Solid lines = Effects of inheritance
Dotted lines = Potential effects of merit

**Figure 3.1.    The International Race to Get Ahead**

get ahead. The solid lines represent the effects of inheritance on economic outcomes. The dotted lines represent the potential effects of merit. The "distance"
each person needs to reach the finish line on the basis of merit depends on how
far from the finish line each person starts the race in the first place.

It is important to point out that equivalent amounts of merit do not lead to
equivalent end results. If each dash represents one "unit" of merit, a person
born poor who advances one unit on the basis of individual merit over a lifetime ends up at the end of her life one unit ahead of where she started but
still at or close to poverty. A person who begins life one unit short of the top
can ascend to the top based on an equivalent one unit of merit. Each person
is equally meritorious, but his or her end position in the race to get ahead is
very different.

Jennifer, Rory, and Phoebe Gates, heirs to the largest fortune in the world,
are starting life at the finish line. Barring the highly unlikely possibility of
parental disinheritance, there is virtually no realistic scenario in which they
end up destitute—regardless of the extent of their innate talent or individual
motivation. Their future is financially secure. They will grow up having the
best of everything and having every opportunity money can buy.

Most parents want the best for their children. As a result, most parents try to do everything they can to secure their children's futures. Indeed, that parental desire to provide advantages for children may even have biological origins. Under the "inclusive fitness-maximizing" theory of selection, for instance, beneficiaries are favored in inheritance according to their biological relatedness and reproductive value. Research shows that benefactors are much more likely to bequeath estates to surviving spouses and children than to unrelated individuals or institutions (Schwartz 1996). In other words, parents may invest in children through inheritance to ensure propagation of their genes in future generations. In a form of what might be called "reverse inheritance," parents may also invest in children to secure their own futures in the event that they become unable to take care of themselves. Finally, parents may invest in their children's future to realize vicarious prestige through the successes of their children, which may, in turn, be seen as a validation of their own genetic endowments and/or child-rearing skills.

Regardless of the source of parental motivation, it is clear that most parents wish to secure their children's futures. To the extent that parents are successful in passing on advantages to children, meritocracy does not operate as the basis for who ends up with what. Despite the ideology of meritocracy, the reality in America as elsewhere is inheritance first and merit second.

## INCOME AND WEALTH INEQUALITY

In considering how parents pass on advantages to children in the race to get ahead, researchers have usually looked at occupational mobility; that is, how the occupations of parents affect the occupations of children. The results of this research show that parental occupation has strong effects on children's occupational prospects. Some of this effect is mediated through education; that is, the prestige of parental occupation increases the educational attainment of children, which, in turn, increases the prestige of the occupations they attain. Looking at occupational prestige alone, however, underestimates the full extent of inequality in society and overestimates the amount of movement within the system. A fuller appreciation of what is at stake requires examination of the kind and extent of economic inequality within the system—who gets how much of what there is to get. Economic inequality includes inequalities of both income and wealth. Income is typically defined as the total flow of financial resources from all sources (e.g., wages and salaries, interest on savings and dividends, pensions, and government transfer payments such as social security, welfare payments, or other government payments) in a given time period, usually annually. Wealth refers not to what people "earn" but to what they "own." Wealth is usually measured as net worth that includes the total value of all assets owned (such as real estate,

**Table 3.1.   Share of Total Available Household Income and Total Net Worth**

| Income Group | Share of Income | Share of Net Worth |
|---|---|---|
| Top Fifth | 47.7% | 83.4% |
| Fourth Fifth | 22.9% | 11.9% |
| Third Fifth | 15.5% | 4.5% |
| Second Fifth | 9.7% | .8% |
| Bottom Fifth | 4.2% | -.6% |
| Total | 100.0% | 100.0% |

*Source*: Reprinted from Lawrence Mishel, Jared Bernstein, and Heather Bouchey, *The State of Working America 2002/2003*. Copyright © 2003 by Cornell University. Used by permission of the publisher, Cornell University Press.

trusts, stocks, bonds, business equity, homes, automobiles, banking deposits, insurance policies, and the like) minus the total value of all liabilities (e.g., loans, mortgage, credit card, and other forms of debt). For purposes of illustration, income and wealth inequalities are usually represented by dividing the population into quintiles and showing how much of what there is to get goes to each fifth, from the richest fifth of the population down to the poorest fifth. These proportions are illustrated in table 3.1.

In terms of income, in 2001 the richest 20% of households received a 47.7% share of all income, compared to only 4.2% received by the bottom 20%. As income increases, so does the level of concentration. The top 15% alone accounts for 26.7% of the total, and the top 5% alone accounts for 21% of the total. Moreover, income has great staying power over time. That is, the same households that are at the top income group now were very likely to have been at the top of the income group in previous years. Using longitudinal data and comparing income quintiles between 1969 and 1994, Mishel et al. (2003) note that most households in 1994 had remained at or near where they were in 1969. Forty-one percent of those in the lowest income group in 1969 remained in the lowest income fifth twenty-five years later, while 39% of those who were in the top income fifth remained there twenty-five years later. With regard to movement over the twenty-five year period, Mishel and his associates note that large intragenerational transitions are uncommon:

> Only 5.8% of those who began the period in the first fifth ended up in the top fifth, while only 9.5% fell from the top fifth to the lowest fifth. Those transitions that do occur are most likely to be a move up or down to the neighboring fifth. For example among the middle three-fifths, slightly less than two thirds of the transitions were to the neighboring fifths. (2003, 76–77)

When wealth is considered, the disparities are much greater. In 1998, the richest 20% of American households accounted for 83.4% of total net household wealth. The bottom 40% combined, by contrast, held *less than one-half of 1%* of all available net worth. At the bottom end of the wealth scale, 18%

of households had zero or negative net worth (Mishel et al. 2003, 285). In other words, a significant number of Americans either own nothing or owe more than they own.

As MIT economist Lester Thurow has observed, "Even among the wealthy, wealth is very unequally distributed" (1999, 200). In 1998, for instance, the top 1% of all wealth holders alone accounted for 38.1% of all net worth. Additional evidence shows that 78% of the wealth held by the richest 1% is owned by a scant one-half of 1% of all households (Mishel et al. 2003, 286).

In short, the degree of economic inequality in the United States is substantial by any measure. In fact, the United States now has a greater economic inequality than all industrial countries in Western Europe (Hacker 1997; Mishel et al. 2003; Wolff 2002). Moreover, the extent of this inequality is increasing. One standard measurement of the extent of inequality is the Gini Ratio, which measures the extent of discrepancy between the actual distribution of income and a hypothetical situation in which each quintile of the population receives the same percentage of income. Values of the Gini Ratio range between 0 and 1, where 0 indicates complete equality and 1 indicates complete inequality. Thus the higher the number, the greater the degree of inequality. The U.S. Census Bureau (2003) reports that the Gini Ratio has steadily and incrementally increased from .399 in 1975 to .460 in 2000—representing a 17% increase over a twenty-five-year span. An Internal Tax Revenue study (Balkovic 2003) further shows that the 400 American taxpayers with the highest adjusted gross income in 2000 accounted for 1.6% of all income in the United States, more than double their corresponding share in 1992. The average income of these 400 taxpayers was $174 million, nearly quadruple the average in 1992. These top 400 American taxpayers increased their incomes at fifteen times the rate of the bottom 90% of Americans. These figures actually underestimate the true amount of inequality, because adjusted gross income does not include nontaxable income earned on municipal bonds and other tax shelters. These data clearly show that the rich in America are getting richer. Another indication of income inequality is revealed by a comparison of pay for the chief executive officers of major corporations with that of rank-and-file employees. CEO pay as a ratio of average worker pay increased from 26 to 1 in 1965 to 310 to 1 in 2000, with much of the compensation package for CEOs coming in the form of stock options (Mishel et al. 2003).

Increases in wealth inequality are also dramatic. The percentage of net worth held by the richest 1% of Americans nearly doubled between 1976 and 1997, from approximately 20% to 35% (Wolff 2002, 83). In short, the gap between those who live off investments and the large majority of people who work for a living has considerably widened in recent decades.

Consideration of wealth as opposed to just income in assessing the total amount of economic inequality in society is critical for several reasons. First, the really big money in America comes not from wages and salaries but from owning property—particularly the kind of property that produces more wealth. If it "takes money to make money," those with capital to invest have a distinct advantage over those whose only source of income is wages. Apart from equity in owner-occupied housing, assets that most Americans hold are the kind that tend to *depreciate* in value over time—cars, furniture, appliances, clothes, and other personal belongings. Many of these items end up in used car lots, garage sales, and flea markets selling at prices much lower than their original cost. The rich, however, have a high proportion of their holdings in the kinds of wealth that *increase* in value over time. In 1998, for instance, the top 1% of households held 67.7% of all business equity, 50.8% of all financial securities, 54% of all trusts, 49.4% of all stocks and mutual funds, and 35.8% of all nonhome real estate (Wolff 2002, 26).

Second, wealth is especially critical with respect to inheritance. When people inherit an estate, for instance, they inherit accumulated assets—not incomes from wages and salaries. Inheritance of estates, in turn, is an important nonmerit mechanism for the transmission of privilege across generations. In strictly merit terms, inheritance is a form of getting something for nothing. Since only very large estates are taxed, there is no systematic accounting of the transfer of wealth across generations. As a result, data on the flow of these resources are skimpy. There are several factors that contribute to the lack of data on wealth transfers. Because wealth is highly concentrated, only a small percentage of Americans own great wealth. Since the number is small, wealthy people tend not to be sampled on random national surveys—the primary tool used in mobility research. In addition, the rich often conceal the full extent of their assets both for tax purposes and to avoid public scrutiny. Even when interviewed on surveys, most people are not fully aware of the current value of their assets and liabilities. In some studies, the lack of systematic and reliable data on wealth is addressed through the use of complex simulation models that take what wealth data are available and "fill in the gaps" with empirically derived estimates (see Keister 2000; Gokhale et al. 2001).

Despite these limitations, there is strong evidence that a substantial amount of accumulated wealth is passed on through inheritance. One source of information on wealth is the annual list of the 400 wealthiest Americans published by *Forbes* magazine. An early study of the *Forbes* list, for instance, showed that at least 40% of the 1982 *Forbes* list inherited at least a portion of their wealth, and the higher on the list, the greater the likelihood that wealth was derived from inheritance (Canterbery and Nosari 1985). A more recent study of the 1997 *Forbes* list showed that the majority of individuals on the list (56%) inherited a fortune of at least $50 million (Collins 1997). Among the ten wealthiest Americans on the 2003 *Forbes* list, five (ranked 4–8 respectively) are direct descendants of Sam Walton, founder of the Wal-Mart empire. The five Walton heirs have a combined estimated net worth of $102.5 billion (*Forbes* 2003).

Although there is some movement over time into and out of the *Forbes* list of the richest 400 Americans, this does not mean that those who fall off the list have lost or squandered their wealth. Most likely, when wealthy individuals fall off the *Forbes* list they have not lost wealth at all but rather have not gained it as fast as others. Although those who fall off the 400 list may have lost ground relative to others, they typically still have vast amounts of wealth and most likely remain within the upper 1% of the richest Americans. The richest 400 Americans represent less than two ten-thousandths of 1% of the total American population, but in 2001 they collectively accounted for 2.3% of all personal wealth (Kennickell 2003, 3). The top 1% of wealth holders represents approximately 2.9 million Americans—a considerable number but still far less than one-tenth of the approximately 33 million Americans living below the official poverty line.

Examining the population as a whole, the evidence suggests that as with income shares, shares of wealth ownership are very stable over long periods of time. Using a wealth simulation model spanning the period from 1975 to 1995, sociologist Lisa Keister reports that:

> The results indicate that there was little movement among wealth percentiles, even over a 20 year period. Sixty percent of those who started in the bottom 25% in 1975 were in the bottom 25% of wealth owners in 1995. Only 21% had moved to the second quartile, and 12% had moved to the third quartile. There was no movement over these 20 years from the bottom of the distribution to the very top, among these households. Downward movement was also rare. (2000, 79)

In short, most of those starting in the top of the wealth distribution remained there, with a few sliding down marginally. Continuity of income and wealth within households over time is not the same thing as continuity of wealth across generations. Unfortunately, the longitudinal data required to track transfers of wealth across specific parent–child households are not yet available. However, given that we know there is a high level of concentration of wealth in the United States and that wealth has great staying power over time, it is reasonable to assume that a substantial amount of concentrated wealth is available for transfer across generations. One study, for instance, estimates that sums in excess of $10 trillion will be available for transfer intergenerationally between 1990 and 2040 (Shapiro 1994). It is unlikely that these vast amounts of wealth simply evaporate between generations.

In the absence of longitudinal data on individual intergenerational wealth transfers, one team of university and private sector economists led by Jagadeesh Gokhale recently created an empirically derived simulation model of the transmission of wealth inequality through inheritance (Gokhale et al. 2001). This model, although sensitive to necessary assumptions built into it, shows high degrees of stability of wealth across generations. In this model, Gokhale and his associates estimate that nearly one-half of children whose parents are in the upper 20% of wealth holders at age sixty-six will themselves end up at age sixty-six in that bracket as well. At the other end of the wealth scale, children whose parents are in the bottom 6% of wealth holders have a 47% chance of remaining in the bottom 6% of wealth holders as adults. They have an additional 47% of ending up between the bottom 6% and 18% of wealth holders. In other words, 95% of children born to parents in the bottom 6% of wealth holders will end up poor as adults. Children who start out life born to parents in the bottom 6% of wealth holders have only one-half of 1% chance of ending up even in the upper half of wealth holders as adults. In short, this model, which simulates the intergenerational transmission of wealth—consistent with patterns of intragenerational income and wealth inequality—shows very little movement from rags to riches or riches to rags. Most people stay at or very close to where they started, with most of the movement occurring between immediately adjacent categories.

Despite the evidence of wealth stability over time, much is made of the investment "risks" that capitalists must endure as a justification for returns on such investments. And to some extent, this is true. Most investments involve some measure of risk. The superwealthy, however, protect themselves as much as possible from the vicissitudes of "market forces"—most have diversified investment portfolios that are professionally managed. As a result, established wealth has great staying power. In short, what is good for America is, in general, good for the ownership class. The "risk" endured, therefore, is minimal. Instead of losing vast fortunes overnight, the more common scenario for the superrich is for the *amount* of their wealth to fluctuate with the ups and downs of the stock market as a whole. Given the very high levels of aggregate and corporate wealth concentration in the economy, the only realistic scenario in which the ownership class goes under is one in which America as a whole goes under.

## THE CUMULATIVE ADVANTAGES OF WEALTH INHERITANCE

Inheritance is more than bulk estates bequeathed to descendants; more broadly defined, it refers to the total impact of initial social class placement at birth on future life outcomes. Therefore, it is not just the superwealthy who are in a position to pass advantages on to children. Advantages are passed on—in varying degrees—to all of those from relatively privileged backgrounds. Even minor initial advantages may accumulate during the life course. In this way existing inequalities are reinforced and extended across generations. As Harvard economist John Kenneth Galbraith put it in the opening sentence of his well-known book, *The Affluent Society*: "Wealth is not without its advantages and the case to the contrary, although it has often been made, has never proved widely persuasive" (1958, 13). Specifically, the cumulative advantages of wealth inheritance include the following.

## Childhood Quality of Life

Children of the privileged enjoy a high standard of living and quality of life regardless of their individual merit or lack of it. For the privileged, this not only includes high-quality food, clothing, and shelter but also extends to luxuries such as entertainment, toys, travel, family vacations, enrichment camps, private lessons, and a host of other indulgences that wealthy parents and even middle-class parents bestow on their children. Children do not "earn" a privileged life style—they inherit it and benefit by it long before their parents are deceased.

## Knowing with Which Fork to Eat

Cultural capital refers to what one needs to know to function as a member of the various groups to which one belongs. (We address the issue of cultural capital more fully in chapter 4.) All groups have norms, values, beliefs, ways of life, and codes of conduct that identify the group and define its boundaries. The culture of the group separates insiders from outsiders. Knowing and abiding by these cultural codes of conduct is required to maintain one's status as a member in good standing within the group. By growing up in privilege, children of the elite are socialized into elite ways of life. This kind of cultural capital has commonly been referred to as "breeding," "refinement," possessing the "social graces," having "savoir faire" or simply "class" (meaning upper class). Although less pronounced and rigid than in the past, these distinctions persist into the present. In addition to cultivated tastes in art and music ("high brow" culture), cultural capital includes—but is not limited to— manners, etiquette, vocabulary, and demeanor. Those from more humble backgrounds who aspire to become elites must acquire the cultural cachet to be accepted in elite circles, and this is no easy task. Those born to it, however, have the advantage of acquiring it "naturally" through inheritance, a kind of social osmosis that takes place through childhood socialization.

## Having Friends in High Places

Everybody knows somebody else. Social capital refers to the "value" of who you know. (We review the importance of social capital on life outcomes more fully in chapter 4.) For the most part, rich people know other rich people, and poor people know other poor people. Another nonmerit advantage inherited by children of the wealthy is a network of connections to people of power and influence. These are not connections that children of the rich shrewdly foster or cultivate on their own. The children of the wealthy travel in high-powered social circles. These connections provide access to power, information, and other resources. The difference between rich and poor is not in knowing people; it is in knowing people in positions of power and influence who can do things for you.

## Early Withdrawals on the Family Estate

Children of the privileged do not have to wait until their parents die to inherit assets from their parents. Inter vivos transfers of funds and "gifts" from parents to children can be substantial, and there is evidence suggesting that such transfers account for a greater proportion of intergenerational transfers than lump-sum estates at death (Gale and Scholz 1994). Inter vivos gifts to children provide a means of legally avoiding or reducing estate taxes. Currently, an individual can transfer $10,000 per recipient tax-free each year. In this way, parents can "spend down" their estates during their lives to avoid estate and inheritance taxes upon their deaths. In 2001, however, the federal government enacted legislation that will ultimately phase out the federal estate tax. Many individual states have also reduced or eliminated inheritance taxes. The impact of these changes in tax law on intergenerational transfers is at this point unclear. If tax advantages were the only reasons for inter vivos transfers, we might expect that parents would slow down the pace of inter vivos transfers. But it is unlikely that the flow of such transfers will be abruptly curtailed because they serve other functions. Besides tax avoidance, parents also provide inter vivos transfers to children to advance their children's current and future economic interests—especially at critical or milestone stages of the life cycle. These milestone events include going to college, getting married, buying a house, and having children. At each event, there may be a substantial infusion of parental capital—in essence an early withdrawal on the parental estate. One of the most common current forms of inter vivos gifts is paying for children's education. (We address education more fully in chapter 5.) A few generations ago, children may have inherited the family farm or the family business. With the rise of the modern corporation and the decline of family farms and businesses, inheritance increasingly takes on more fungible or liquid forms, including cash transfers. Indeed, for many middle-class Americans education has replaced tangible assets as the primary form by which advantage is passed on between generations.

## What Goes Up Doesn't Usually Come Down

If America were truly a meritocracy, we would expect fairly equal amounts of both upward and downward mobility. Mobility studies, however, consistently show much higher rates of upward than downward mobility. There are two key reasons for this. First, most mobility that people have experienced in America in the past century—particularly occupational mobility—

was due to industrial expansion and the rise of the general standard of living in society as a whole. Sociologists refer to this type of mobility as "structural mobility," which has more to do with changes in the organization of society than with the merit of individuals. (We discuss the effects of social structure on life outcomes in more detail in chapter 6.) A second reason why upward mobility is more prevalent than downward mobility is that parents and extended family networks insulate children from downward mobility. That is, parents frequently "bail out" or "rescue" their adult children in the event of life crises such as sickness, unemployment, divorce, or other setbacks that might otherwise propel adult children into a downward spiral. In addition to these external circumstances, parents also rescue children from their own failures and weaknesses, including self-destructive behaviors. Parental rescue as a form of inter vivos transfer is not a generally acknowledged or well-studied benefit of inheritance. Indirect evidence of parental rescue may be found in the recent increase in the number of "boomerang" children—adult children who leave home only to later return to live with parents. Demographers report that in 1980, one in thirteen adults between the ages of twenty-five and thirty-four lived with parents; by 1990, one in eight did (Edmondson and Waldrop 1993). The reasons for adult children returning to live at home are usually financial—adult children may be between jobs, between marriages, or without other viable means of self-support. Such living arrangements are likely to increase during periods of high unemployment, which in 2003 topped 6% of the civilian labor force.

If America operated as a "true" merit system, people would advance solely on the basis of merit and fail when they lack merit. In many cases, however, family resources prevent or at least reduce "skidding" among adult children. One of the authors of this book recalls that when he left home as an adult, his parents took him aside and told him that no matter how bad things became for him out there in the world, if he could get to a phone, they would wire him money to come home. This was his insurance against destitution. Fortunately, he has not yet had to take his parents up on their offer, but neither has he forgotten it. Without always being articulated, the point is that this informal familial insurance against downward mobility is available—in varying degrees—to all except the poorest of the poor, who simply have no resources to provide.

## Live Long and Prosper

From womb to tomb, the more affluent one is, the less the risk for injury, illness, and death (Cockerham 2000; National Center for Health Statistics 1998, Smith 1999). Among the many nonmerit advantages inherited by those from privileged backgrounds is higher life expectancy at birth and greater chances of better health throughout life. Data from the Internal Revenue Service show that those who file estate tax returns have on average lived three years longer than the average life expectancy for the general population as a whole, which is itself likely to be much higher than the life expectancy of those living below the poverty line (Johnson and Mikow 1999). In addition to longer life expectancy, the wealthier are also healthier throughout their lives. Americans who report that they are in excellent health have 74% more wealth than those who report being in fair or poor health (Smith 1999). There are several possible reasons for the strong and persistent relationship between socioeconomic status and health. Beginning with fetal development and extending through childhood, increasing evidence points to effects of "the long reach of early childhood" on adult health (Smith 1999). Prenatal deprivations, more common among the poor, for instance, are associated with later life conditions such as retardation, coronary heart disease, stroke, diabetes, and hypertension. Poverty in early childhood is also associated with increased risk of adult diseases. This may be due in part to higher stress levels among the poor. There is also evidence that cumulative wear and tear on the body over time occurs under conditions of repeated high stress. Another reason for the health–wealth connection is that the rich have greater access to quality health care. In America, access to quality health care is still largely for sale to the highest bidder. Under these conditions, prevention and intervention are more widely available to the more affluent. Finally, not only does lack of income lead to poor health, poor health leads to reduced earnings. That is, if someone is sick or injured, he or she may not be able to work or may have limited earning power.

Overall, the less affluent are at a health disadvantage due to higher exposure to a variety of unhealthy living conditions. As medical sociologist William Cockerham points out:

> [P]ersons living in poverty and reduced socioeconomic circumstances have greater exposure to physical (crowding, poor sanitation, extreme temperatures), chemical and biochemical (diet, pollution, smoking, alcohol, and drug abuse), biological (bacteria, viruses) and psychological (stress) risk factors that produce ill health than more affluent individuals. (1998, 55)

Part of the exposure to health hazards is occupational. According to the Department of Labor, the occupations with the highest risk of being killed on the job are—listed in order of risk—fishers, timber cutters, airplane pilots, structural metal workers, taxicab drivers, construction laborers, roofers, electric power installers, truck drivers, and farmworkers. With the exception of airline pilots, all the jobs listed are working-class jobs. Since a person's occupation is strongly affected by family background, the prospects for generally higher occupational health risks are in this sense at least indirectly inherited. Finally, although homicides constitute only a small proportion of all causes of death, it is worth noting that the less affluent are at higher risk for being victims of violent crime, including homicide.

Some additional risk factors are related to individual behaviors, especially smoking, drinking, and drug abuse—all of which are more common among the less affluent. Evidence suggests that these behaviors, while contributing to poorer health among the less affluent, are responsible for only one-third of the "wealth–health gradient" (Smith 1999, 157). These behaviors are also associated with higher psychological as well as physical stress. Indeed, the less affluent are not just at greater risk for physical ailments; research has shown that the less affluent are at significantly higher risk for mental illness as well (Cockerham 2000). Intriguing new evidence suggests that—apart from material deprivations—part of the link between wealth and health may be related to the psychological stress of relative deprivation, that is, the stress of being at the bottom end of an unequal social pecking order, especially when the dominant ideology attributes being at the bottom to individual deficiencies.

Despite the adage that "money can't buy happiness," social science research has consistently shown a tendency for happiness and subjective well-being to be related to the amount of income and wealth people possess (Frey and Stutzer 2002). This research shows that people living in countries that are wealthier (and more democratic) tend to be happier and that rates of happiness are sensitive to overall rates of unemployment and inflation. In general, poor people are less happy than others, although greater amounts of income beyond poverty only slightly increase levels of happiness. Beyond a certain threshold, additional increments of income and wealth are not likely to result in additional increments of happiness. Thus, although money may not *guarantee* a long, happy, and healthy life, a fair assessment is that it aids and abets it.

## YOU CAN'T TAKE IT WITH YOU

Whatever assets one has accumulated in life that remain at death represent a bulk estate. Bequests of such estates are what is usually thought of as "inheritance." Because wealth itself is highly skewed, so are bequests from estates. Beyond personal belongings and items of perhaps sentimental value, most Americans at death have little or nothing to bequeath. There is no central accounting of small estates, so reliable estimates on total number and size of estates bequeathed are difficult to come by. Only about 20% of all households report ever having received a bequest (Joulfaian and Wilhelm 1994; Ng-Baumhackl et al. 2003). As the wealth of households increases, however, so does the likelihood of reporting having received a bequest. When bequests are made, they often involve substantial amounts. Recent data from the IRS show that less than 2% of all estates are subject to the federal estate tax (Johnson and Eller 1998). To be subject to federal estate tax, estates had to have a value of over $600,000 after allowable deductions and exemptions. In short, although few are likely to inherit great sums, bequests from estates are nevertheless a major mechanism for the transfer of wealth across generations (McNamee and Miller 1989, 1998; Miller et al. 2003).

Some may argue that those who receive inheritances often deplete them in short order through spending sprees or unwise investments and that the playing field levels naturally through merit or lack of it. Although this may occur in isolated cases, it is not the general pattern—at least among the superwealthy. Although taking risks may be an appropriate strategy for acquiring wealth, it is not common strategy for maintaining wealth. Once secured, the common strategy is to protect wealth by playing it safe—to diversify holdings and to make safe investments. The superwealthy usually have teams of accountants, brokers, financial planners, and lawyers to "manage" portfolios for precisely this purpose. One of the common ways to prevent the quick spending down of inheritances is for benefactors to set up "bleeding trusts" or "spendthrift trusts," which provide interest income to beneficiaries without digging into the principal fund. Despite such efforts to protect wealth, estates may, in some families, be gradually diminished over generations through subdivision among descendants. The rate at which this occurs, however, is likely to be slow, especially given the combination among the wealthy of low birthrates and high rates of marriage within the same class. Even in the event of reckless spending, poor financial management, or subdivision among multiple heirs, the fact remains that those who inherit wealth benefit from it and are provided opportunities that such wealth provides—for as long as it lasts—regardless of how personally meritorious they may or may not be.

## WHAT IS IT LIKE TO BE BORN RICH?

In a 1926 short story, "The Rich Boy," F. Scott Fitzgerald wrote, "Let me tell you about the very rich. They are different from you and me." By the very rich, we mean the 1% or so of Americans who own nearly 40% of all the net worth in America. Most of the very rich either inherited their wealth outright or converted modest wealth and privilege into larger fortunes. How different are they? By the sheer volume and type of capital owned, this group is set apart from other Americans. This group is further distinguished by common lifestyles, shared relationships, and a privileged position in society that produces a consciousness of kind (Domhoff 2002). In short, they are a class set apart in both economic and social terms. Using surveys and simulations, sociologist Lisa Keister has created a demographic profile of the wealthiest 1% of Americans. Compared to all households, the wealthiest 1% are much more likely to be white (96% for the top 1% compared to 82% for the general population), between forty-five and seventy-four years of age (73% for the top

1% compared to 41% for all households), and college educated (68% for the top 1% compared to 22% for all households). As one might expect, the upper class is about equally divided between men and women, but men have historically played a more dominant role within the upper class. Besides being almost exclusively white, the inner circle of the upper class has historically been predominantly Protestant and of Anglo-Saxon heritage. The acronym WASP (for white Anglo-Saxon Protestant) was first coined by sociologist E. Digby Baltzell, himself a member of the upper class, to describe its social composition. Although the upper class is gradually becoming less exclusively WASP, there is still a strong association of upper-class status and WASP background. Beyond these demographic characteristics, how else are the rich different from most other Americans?

## Exclusive

An important defining characteristic of the upper class is that it is exclusive. Wealth in America is highly concentrated. Money alone, however, does not grant full admission into the highest of elite circles. Full acceptance requires the cultural capital and cachet that only "old money" brings. And "old money" means inherited money. The exclusiveness of the old money is exemplified by the *Social Register*, a list of prominent upper-class families first compiled in 1887. The list has been used by members of the upper class both to recognize distinction and as a guide for issuing invitations to upper-class social events. For years separate versions of the *Social Register* were published in different cities throughout the United States. But since the Malcolm Forbes family took over the publication in 1976, the *Social Register* has been consolidated into one national book. To be listed, a potential member must have five letters of nomination submitted by those already on the list. There is great continuity across generations among the names included in these volumes. One study (Broad 1996), for instance, shows that of the eighty-seven prominent founders of family fortunes listed in the 1940 *Social Register*, 92% had descendants listed in the 1977 volume. The percent of descendants of these prominent families included in the 1995 volume—fifty years later—dipped only slightly to 87%. Highlighting connections to the past, almost half those listed in 1995 use serial numbers attached to surnames, such as II, III, IV, V, VI, and so on. Another common practice among upper-class families is to use maternal surnames as first names or middle names. The use of these "recombinant" names highlights connections to prominent families on both sides as well as patterns of intraclass marriage. Almost 50% of those listed in 1995 had such recombinant names. Most social clubs of the upper class also show connections to the past—if only because they have been in existence for a long time and their membership shows intergenerational continuity.

It is not mere coincidence that the upper class has great reverence for the past. In a highly meritocratic culture, it is an ongoing challenge for those who inherit great wealth to justify their claim to it. The past, therefore, is a source of the justification of wealth for the upper class and a claim to status. Nelson W. Aldrich Jr., himself born into the upper class and a chronicler of the upper-class traditions, put it this way:

> Time has always had to carry a large part of the rhetorical burden of justifying the key institution that makes Old Money possible—the inheritance of wealth. Inherited wealth is an especially egregious, because wholly unearned, source of inequality. Even in the purest most abstract condition, where it does nothing for its inheritor but make him or her more money, wealth confers a certain superiority. At the very least, it confers an invidious distinction. (1988, 31)

The children of the wealthy in America are not immune to the ideology of meritocracy that pervades the culture as a whole. Dealing with guilt for having inherited wealth is a prevalent theme among those who were born into wealth (Schervish et al. 1994). As one inheritor of an oil fortune put it, "The feelings of guilt put me through much agony. For a long, long, long time, it gave me low self-esteem: who am I to deserve all of this good fortune?" (Schervish et al. 1994, 118). Unlike the children of European aristocrats who felt entitled to privilege as a matter of birthright, American children of great wealth are victims of an ideology that, through no fault of their own, essentially invalidates them.

## Isolated

Although exclusive, the upper class in America is relatively anonymous and hidden from the public view. A second defining characteristic of the upper class in America is that it is isolated. The upper class is separated from the mainstream of society into a world of privacy—remote private residences, private schools, private clubs, private parties, and private resorts. With the exception of service staff, upper-class individuals from womb to tomb interact mostly with people like themselves. The geography of the upper class shows a distinct pattern of isolation, intentionally maintained and reinforced through land use strategies that include incorporation, zoning, and restrictive land covenants (Higley 1995). Houses and mansions are tucked away in exclusive communities. Individual residences within these communities, often with long and meandering driveways, are typically set back from the public roads that connect them with the larger world. Once approached, the residences are fortresses of security, complete with fences, gates, guard dogs, and sophisticated electronic surveillance. Children raised within these confines are isolated as well, separated from the outside world by a series of private nannies, private tutors, private preparatory boarding schools, and private elite Ivy League colleges. Even travel within the upper class is often isolated—in private planes, private limos, and private yachts. And even when resorting to more commercial forms of transportation, there is always the more isolated and pampered option of traveling "first class."

The tendency of the upper class to geographically isolate themselves from the rest of society has been emulated by the upper middle classes. The creation of "white flight" suburbs in the post–World War II era began a trend that has now extended to the rising popularity of "gated" communities (Blakely and Snyder 1997). Once restricted to the superwealthy and some retirement villages, gated communities are now for the "merely affluent."

One reason for this self-imposed isolation is security. Those who have more have more to lose. Keeping potential criminals out, however, also has the effect of keeping the rich in. In addition to concerns about property theft or vandalism, the superwealthy are also concerned about the potential for kidnapping, which is a real concern for those of great wealth who might be targeted for ransom.

## Endogamous

Beyond security concerns, however, all indications are that—like those of all classes—the rich simply prefer to be among themselves. One aspect of this self-segregation is the high tendency toward class endogamy or marriage within the group. People draw marriage partners from within their social circles of acquaintances. Beyond the increased likelihood of such unions as a result of social isolation, marriage within the upper class has the added advantage of "keeping money in the family." Upper-class social institutions such as the debutante ball, at which young upper-class women are first "presented" to "society," certainly increase these probabilities. As E. Digby Baltzell, a sociologist and himself a member of the upper class, put it, "the debutante ritual is a *rite de passage* which functions to introduce the post-adolescent into the upper-class adult world, and to insure upper-class endogamy as a normative pattern of behavior, in order to keep important functional class positions within the upper class" (1992, 60). Other upper-class institutions with this function include the elite boarding prep school, the elite social clubs, and the elite summer resorts—all of which provide settings and organized activities that bring upper-class young adults together.

## Distinctive Lifestyle

At the beginning of the twentieth century, America entered "the Gilded Age," so named for its opulent and even ostentatious displays of great wealth. Romanticized in such novels as *The Great Gatsby*, the Gilded Age was one in which the rich were in competition with one another to flaunt their wealth. It was during this time that some of the great mansions were built, including George Vanderbilt's Biltmore Estate in Asheville, North Carolina, a 175,000 square foot, 250-room Renaissance-style chateau completed in 1895 and still the largest private house ever built in America (Frank 1999, 14). In some ways, America's wealthy of this period were insecure about their status and envious of the more established European aristocracy. As a result, the new-found industrial wealth in the United States patterned itself after everything old and European. As the Great Depression deepened, such displays were no longer considered in good taste. In subsequent decades, more subdued forms of luxury were preferred. Nevertheless, a lifestyle organized around formal parties; exclusive resorts and clubs; and such upper-class leisure activities as golf, tennis, horseback riding, and yachting persisted. Some segments of the upper class indulge themselves in support of the arts—theater, opera, orchestra, and other highbrow forms of cultural consumption. Recently, some observers of upper-class life have noted a surge in luxury spending, including luxury cars, boats, and homes as well as items such as premium wines, fancy home appliances, and even cosmetic surgery (Frank 1999, 14–32, Brooks 2000; Taylor 1989). It should be noted, however, that the rich are not all alike in their consumption behavior. One of the advantages of being rich is that you can choose to appear not to be rich. Sam Walton, founder of the Wal-Mart empire, for instance, was known to ride around in his hometown of Bentonville, Arkansas, in a beat-up Ford pickup (Packard 1989). For the most part, however, the consumption patterns of the wealthy set them apart as a distinct social class. As Domhoff points out:

[T]he more extravagant social activities of the upper class—the expensive parties, the jet-setting to spas and vacation spots all over the world, the involvement with exotic entertainers—may seem like superfluous trivialities. However, these activities play a role both in solidifying the upper class and in maintaining the class structure. Within the upper class itself, these occasions provide an opportunity for members to show each other that they are similar to each other and superior to the average citizen. (2002, 46)

## Politically Powerful

In a substantial sense, the upper class in America is also a ruling class. Despite the ideology of democracy in which everyone has an equal say in deciding what happens, the reality is that those who have the most economic resources wield the most power. In *Gospels of Wealth: How the Rich Portray Their Lives*, sociologists Paul Schervish, Platon Coutsoukis, and Ethan Lewis describe the power of the wealthy to make things happen (and other things not happen) as "hyperagency":

In the broadest terms of the empowerment of the wealthy can be described as the capacity to exercise hyperagency. This is the ability to determine the conditions and circumstances of life instead of merely living within them. . . . If agency means ferreting out the best possible path within the institutionally given constraints imposed by others, hyperagency means being able to construct a self and a world that transcend the established institutional limits and, in fact, create the limits for others. As one real estate magnate [interviewed in their study] declares, wealth grants him the "power to get through time and red-tape barriers. I can pick up the phone and call a congressman who's heard my name and I can have the impact of one million votes on the issue with a phone call." (1994, 8)

To the extent that it is possible to convert wealth into political power, the upper class can exert influence on political outcomes far beyond their numbers alone. The specific mechanisms by which this influence is exerted have been well documented (Domhoff 2002; Phillips 2003; Perrucci and Wysong 1999; Useem 1984). Beyond direct forms of influence such as substantial campaign contributions and direct participation of economic elites holding government positions, indirect but no less important forms of influence are also exerted through the corporate community, the policy planning network comprising foundations, think tanks and lobbies, and the media—all of which are dominated by propertied interests.

Included in this power is the power to protect claims to property and to justify the kind and extent of inequality that exists in society. A recent example of the exercise of this power is the elimination of the federal estate tax (known as the "death tax" by its critics)—a measure that stands to directly benefit only the 2% of those Americans whose estates were large enough to be subject to the tax. Among the advantages of the wealthy, therefore, is the capacity—through control of the flow of economic resources in society—to make some things happen and other things not happen. For all of the key measures of political power as identified by sociologist G. William Domhoff—who decides policy, who wins in disputes, and who benefits from political outcomes—the interests of the upper class usually prevail.

It should be pointed out, however, that the upper class does not act as a political monolith. That is, as with all large groups, there are always internal differences of opinion. On the estate tax issue, for instance, two very prominent members of the upper class—William Gates II (Bill Gates's father) and Warren Buffett (financier and second richest American)—have been outspoken critics of proposals to abolish estate taxes. Both maintain that it is entirely appropriate for the government to heavily tax recipients of large estates as a form of unearned income.

The power of the upper class, while considerable, falls short of complete control. Labor unions, environmental groups, civil rights groups, consumer groups, and others chip away at the edges of the system of privilege on behalf of their constituencies. But in the final analysis, although these groups and the general public as a whole win some of the battles, propertied interests continue to win the class wars—even to the point of denying the existence of the classes altogether.

## SUMMARY

The United States has high levels of both income and wealth inequality. In terms of the distribution of income and wealth, America is clearly not a middle-class society. Income and especially wealth are not evenly distributed, with a few families better off at one end and a few families worse off at the other. Instead, the overall picture is one in which the bulk of the available wealth is concentrated in a narrow range at the very top of the system. In short, the distribution of economic resources in society is not symmetrical and certainly not bell-shaped—the poor who have the least greatly outnumber the rich who have the most. Moreover, in recent decades, by all measures, the rich are getting richer and the gap between the very rich and everyone else has appreciably increased.

The greater the amount of economic inequality in society, the more difficult it is to move up within the system on the basis of individual merit alone. Indeed, the most important factor in terms of where people will end up in the economic pecking order of society is where they started in the first place. Economic inequality has tremendous inertial force across generations. Instead of a race to get ahead that begins anew with each generation, the race is in reality a relay race in which children inherit different starting points from parents. Inheritance, broadly defined as one's initial starting point in life based on parental position, includes a set of cumulative nonmerit advantages for all except the poorest of the poor. These include enhanced childhood standard of living, differential access to prestigious cultural capital, differential access to social networks of power and influence, infusion of parental capital while parents are still alive, greater health and life expectancy, and the inheritance of bulk estates when parents die.

At the top of the system are members of America's ownership class—roughly the 1% of the American population who own nearly 40% of all the available net worth. The upper class is set apart from other Americans not only by the amount and source of wealth held but by an exclusive, distinctive, and self-perpetuating way of life that reduces opportunities for merit-based mobility into it.

## REFERENCES

Aldrich, Nelson W., Jr. 1988. *Old Money: The Mythology of America's Upper Class.* New York: Alfred A. Knopf.

Balkovic, Brian. 2003. "High-Income Tax Returns for 2000." *SOL Bulletin* (Spring): 10–62.

Baltzell, E. Digby. 1992. *The Philadelphia Gentlemen: The Making of a National Upper Class.* New Brunswick, N.J.: Transaction.

Blakely, Edward J., and Mary Gail Snyder. 1997. *Fortress America: Gated Communities in the United States.* Washington, D.C.: Brookings Institute Press.

Broad, David. 1996. "The Social Register: Directory of America's Upper Class." *Sociological Spectrum* 16: 173–81.

Brooks, David. 2000. *Bobos in Paradise: The New Upper Class and How They Got There.* New York: Simon & Schuster.

Canterbery, E. Ray, and Joe Nosari. 1985. "The Forbes Four Hundred: The Determinants of Super-Wealth." *Southern Economic Journal* 51: 1073–83.

Cockerham, William. 1998. *Medical Sociology.* 7th ed. Upper Saddle River, N.J.: Prentice Hall.

———. 2000. *Medical Sociology.* 8th ed. Upper Saddle River, N.J.: Prentice Hall.

Collins, Chuck. 1997. *Born on Third Base: The Sources of Wealth of the 1997 Forbes 400.* Boston: United For A Fair Economy.

Domhoff, William G. 2002. *Who Rules America?* 4th ed. *Power and Politics.* Boston: McGraw-Hill.

Edmondson, Brad, and Judith Waldrop. 1993. "Married with Grown Children." *American Demographics* 15: 32.

*Forbes.* 2003. "The Forbes 400." 172, no. 7 (October 6): special issue.

Frank, Robert H. 1999. *Luxury Fever: Why Money Fails to Satisfy in an Era of Excess.* New York: Free Press.

Frey, Bruno S., and Alois Stutzer. 2002. *Happiness and Economics: How the Economy and Institutions Affect Well-Being.* Princeton, N.J.: Princeton University Press.

Galbraith, James. 1998. *Created Unequal: The Crisis in American Pay.* Reading, Mass.: Addison Wesley.

Galbraith, John Kenneth. 1958. *The Affluent Society.* New York. Mentor Press.

Gale, William G., and John Karl Scholz. 1994. "Intergenerational Transfers and the Accumulation of Wealth." *Journal of Economic Perspectives* 8: 145–60.

Gokhale, Jagadeesh, Laurence J. Kotlikoff, James Sefton, and Martin Weale. 2001. "Simulating the Transmission of Wealth Inequality Via Bequests." *Journal of Public Economics* 79: 93–128.

Hacker, Andrew. 1997. *Money: Who Has How Much and Why.* New York: Touchstone.

Higley, Stephen R. 1995. *Privilege, Power and Place: The Geography of the American Upper Class.* Lanham, Md.: Rowman & Littlefield.

Johnson, Barry E., and Martha Britton Eller. 1998. "Federal Taxation of Inheritance and Wealth Transfers." Pp. 61–89 in *Inheritance and Wealth in America,* edited by Robert K. Miller Jr. and Stephen J. McNamee. New York: Plenum Press.

Johnson, Barry W., and Jacob M. Mikow. 1999. "Federal Estate Tax Returns, 1995–1997." *Internal Revenue Service, Statistics of Income Bulletin* 19, no. 1: 69–129.

Joulfaian, D., and M. O. Wilhelm. 1994. "Inheritance and Labor Supply." *Journal of Human Resources* 29: 1205–34.

Keister, Lisa A. 2000. *Wealth in America: Trends in Wealth Inequality.* Cambridge, U.K.: Cambridge University Press.

Kennickell, Arthur. 2003. *A Rolling Tide: Changes in the Distribution of Wealth in the U.S., 1989–2001.* Washington, D.C.: Federal Reserve Board.

Levy, Frank. 1998. *The New Dollars and Dreams: American Incomes and Economic Change*. New York: Russell Sage Foundation.

McNamee, Stephen J., and Robert K. Miller Jr. 1989. "Estate Inheritance: A Sociological Lacuna." *Sociological Inquiry* 38: 7–29.

———. 1998. "Inheritance and Stratification." Pp. 193–213 in *Inheritance and Wealth in America*, edited by Robert K. Miller Jr. and Stephen J. McNamee. New York: Plenum Press.

Miller, Robert K., Jr., Jeffrey Rosenfeld, and Stephen J. McNamee. 2003. "The Disposition of Property: Transfers between the Living and the Dead." Pp. 917–25 in *Handbook of Death and Dying*, edited by Clifton D. Bryant. Thousand Oaks, Calif.: Sage.

Mishel, Larence, Jared Bernstein, and Heather Boushey. 2003. *The State of Working America, 2002/2003*. Ithaca, N.Y.: Cornell University Press.

National Center for Health Statistics. 1998. *Health, United States, 1998 with Socioeconomic Status and Health Chartbook*. Hyattsville, Md.: National Center for Health Statistics, U.S. Department of Health and Human Services.

Ng-Baumhackl, Mitj, John Gist, and Carlos Figueiredo. 2003. *Pennies from Heaven: Will Inheritances Bail Out the Boomers?* Washington, D.C.: American Association of Retired Persons Public Policy Institute.

Packard, Vance. 1989. *The Ultra Rich: How Much Is Too Much?* Boston: Little, Brown.

Perrucci, Robert, and Earl Wysong. 1999. *The New Class Society*. Lanham, Md.: Rowman & Littlefield.

Phillips, Kevin. 2003. *Wealth and Democracy: A Political History of the American Rich*. New York: Random House.

Rosenfeld, Jeffrey P. 1980. *Legacy of Aging: Inheritance and Disinheritance in Social Perspective*. Norwood, N.J.: ABLEX.

Schervish, Paul G., Platon E. Coutsoukis, and Ethan Lewis. 1994. *Gospels of Wealth: How the Rich Portray Their Lives*. Westport, Conn.: Praeger.

Schwartz, T. P. 1996. "Durkheim's Prediction about the Declining Importance of the Family and Inheritance: Evidence from the Wills of Providence, 1775–1985." *Sociological Quarterly* 26: 503–19.

Shapiro, H. D. 1994. "The Coming Inheritance Bonanza." *Institutional Investor* 28: 143–48.

Smith, James P. 1999. "Healthy Bodies and Thick Wallets: The Dual Relation between Health and Economic Status." *Journal of Economic Perspectives* 13: 145–66.

Taylor, John. 1989. *Circus of Ambition: The Culture of Wealth and Power in the Eighties*. New York: Warner Books.

Thurow, Lester C. 1999. *Building Wealth: The New Rules for Individuals, Companies and Nations in a Knowledge-Based Economy*. New York: HarperCollins.

U.S. Census Bureau. 2003. Table H-4, "Gini Ratios of Households, by Race and Hispanic Origin of Householder: 1967–2000." In *March Current Population Survey*. Washington, D.C.: U.S. Government Printing Office.

Useem, Michael. 1984. *The Inner Circle: Large Corporations and the Rise of Business Political Activity in the U.S. and U.K.* New York: Oxford University Press.

Wolff, Edward N. 2002. *Top Heavy: The Increasing Inequality of Wealth in America and What Can Be Done about It*. New York: The New Press.

# 4

## It's Not What You Know But . . . : Social and Cultural Capital

*It's not what you know but who you know.*

—Anonymous

We now turn our attention to two additional nonmerit factors, *social capital* and *cultural capital*. *Social capital* refers essentially to whom you know—which is another type of nonmerit resource that individuals can exploit to advance their position in society. All individuals are embedded in networks of social relations; that is, everybody knows somebody. Social capital focuses attention on differential access to opportunities through social connections. Individual and family social connections mediate access to educational, occupational, and economic opportunity.

*Cultural capital* refers to knowledge of the norms, values, beliefs, and ways of life of the groups to which people belong. It is information, often esoteric, specialized, costly, and time-consuming to accumulate, that like social capital, mediates access to opportunity. It is a factor in social mobility because as people move into different segments of society, they need to acquire the cultural wherewithal to travel in different social circles. In essence, cultural capital is a set of cultural credentials that certify eligibility for membership in social and economic groups. To "fit in" and "look and know the part" is to possess cultural capital; to "stick out like a sore thumb" is to be without the cultural cachet necessary to blend in.

In this chapter we discuss these forms of capital and how they are related. We also examine the related phenomenon of social climbing or deliberate attempts to enhance one's social standing by conspicuously displaying particular forms of social or cultural capital.

## WHO YOU KNOW

Americans have a love/hate relationship with social capital. We love it when it works for us and we hate it when it works against us. If we "get a foot in the door" because we have a "contact" on the inside, we are grateful. Indeed, job placement counselors encourage and coach job applicants to cultivate personal ties and to "network." If, however, we are bypassed for a job (or a promotion) for someone we perceive to be less qualified but who knows someone higher up in the food chain than we do, we are outraged.

Anyone who has ever filled out a job application knows that whom you know matters. Almost all job applications have a space for "references." References not only provide testimony to an applicant's character and ability, they also signal a connection to the applicant. Apart from the merit of the candidate, applicants whose references are well known, prestigious, or powerful have an advantage over applicants whose references are none of those things. In some cases, interest in a job candidate by an employer may reflect the merit of the applicant's references more than the candidate's. Particularly in the professions, but also in other jobs, mentor–protégé relationships are critical—not just for training, but when the time comes for job placement as well. Good mentors go to bat for their protégés and often risk their own stock of prestige and credibility to do so. Who you know may become especially important when the quality of candidates is unknown or indistinguishable, which for neophytes just starting out with little or no track record is often the case.

The social science community is just beginning to catch up to the folk wisdom on this issue. The first systematic modern analysis of social capital was produced in the 1980s by the French sociologist Pierre Bourdieu (1986, 248). Bourdieu focuses attention on the benefits that accrue to individuals from their participation in groups and deliberate attempts by individuals to foster social relations for the purpose of creating this resource. Despite people's efforts to draw on social networks to enhance their power, wealth, or status, Bourdieu points out that these investment strategies do not always work. Further, those strategies that are successful, that is, those that produce valuable social capital, are not necessarily attributable to individual merit, especially in cases in which investments are made by others (parents) or involve substantial economic capital that is inherited or otherwise unearned. Through social capital, individuals can get access to economic resources such as desirable jobs, subsidized loans, investment tips, protected markets, and the like. They can increase their cultural capital through contacts with experts or individuals of refinement. In addition, they can affiliate with institutions that confer valued credentials, such as diplomas or degrees.

James S. Coleman (1988), an American sociologist, has also contributed much to the understanding of social capital and the examination of its effects. Coleman emphasizes the point that social capital is not a characteristic of persons but is embedded in *relations* among persons. The networks of these relations, in turn, have characteristics in and of themselves. These characteristics include the level of trust within the network, the extent of obligations and expectations of reciprocity among individuals within the network, the degree to which the network facilitates the exchange of information within it, and the type of sanctions used to enforce norms of sociability within the network. Since the source of social capital ultimately resides in groups and not individuals per se, individuals benefit not by "owning" social capital but by tapping into it. Thus social capital is available only in and through relationships and the groups in which these relationships occur.

One reason that social capital is dependent on the larger social context in which it occurs is that neither of its critical components, resources or access, is distributed evenly. What is more, simply having more ties to others or more diverse ties does not necessarily increase an individual's likelihood of accessing resources of various kinds. Such a view glosses over the enormous differences that different sorts of ties and network positions, and the resources they give access to, can make. For resources such as "insider information" to be converted into social capital, individuals must perceive that some specific resource is present within their social field and have some form of social relationship that provides access to those resources. Individuals can thus be said to have social capital when resources are present and accessible. Finally, there can be no presumption that individuals utilize their social capital all the time, or that they use it equally well or with equal effectiveness.

With these qualifications in mind, a rapidly growing body of empirical research confirms what most people already suspect based on their own observations: connections matter. That is, social capital enhances the likelihood of a person attaining educational, occupational, and entrepreneurial success.

With respect to education, for instance, research shows that social capital matters, especially in the form of parental and kin levels of social support, for the development of academic aspirations among adolescents, school achievement, and reduced rates of dropping out (Coleman 1988; Parcel and Menaghan 1990, 1994; McLanahan and Sandefur 1994; Teachman, Paasch, and Carver 1996). The more social support students can draw upon from their immediate social circles, the better they do in school. To the extent that social capital contributes to academic success and educational attainment, it also increases chances for later adult success.

A substantial body of research also confirms the effects of social capital directly on adult success (cf. Lin 1999, 2000a, 2000b; Portes 1998). Social capital affects access to employment opportunities, mobility through occupational ladders, promotions, earnings, and entrepreneurial success. In one classic study of job placement, sociologist Mark Granovetter (1974) showed that 56% of all job applicants found out about the job through a personal contact. An additional 19% of job applicants found out about the job through third-party contacts such as advertisements, employment agencies, university placement services, professional associations, or other formal means. Only 18% of the respondents in this study directly applied for a job without either a personal contact or third-party intervention. Many jobs are never advertised. The only way applicants even know there may be openings is through an informal "grapevine." Indeed, it is often the case, especially in the private sector, that only those jobs that are unattractive or are difficult to fill are publicly advertised. The underlying principle, in many but clearly not all cases, is that whom you know does make a difference.

Social capital is not simply social networks but rather networks and the resources that access to and use of such networks provide. In this context, it is important to understand that different types of networks contribute to different forms of occupational success. Granovetter (1983), for instance, makes an important distinction between "strong ties" and "weak ties." Strong ties are those in which a person knows someone very well; weak ties, by contrast, represent more casual acquaintances. Maintaining close friendships (strong ties) requires time and energy. One cannot be "best friends" with a large number of people. The closer you are to a few people, the fewer people you can be close to. The disadvantage of such groups is that no one in the group is likely to know anyone else that the others within the group don't already know. Information flows within such groups, therefore, tend to be redundant. Unlike the strong ties that bind cliques of individuals who share mostly within-group information, weak ties are sources of new information because they bridge different cliques. That is, you may know someone who knows someone else whom you do not know who, in turn, knows someone else that neither of you know, and so on. Thus, the more weak ties an individual has in his or her network, the more valuable the network is as a source of new information. In terms of having access to new sources of information, it is often better to have a larger number of casual acquaintances than to know just a few people very well. In short, weak ties serve as an informal employment referral system, tapping people "into the loop" about jobs that come up and people who can help. Numerous follow-up studies (Granovetter 1974; Lin, Vaughn, and Ensel 1981; Lin, Ensel, and Vaughn 1981; Lin 1982; Lin and Dumin 1986; DeGraaf and Flap 1988) demonstrate that weak ties are "strong" in facilitating occupational attainment.

Other research, however, suggests that the "strength of weak ties" may only be valid for individuals in high social strata (Wegener 1991, 69). While those with high prestige jobs advance by employing weak intimate ties, those with low occupational prestige advance by using strong intimate ties. This is true because most networks are heterogeneous, and job searchers of relatively low social standing can contact persons of higher prestige *within their own network*. They are thus able to exploit strong intimate ties. For individuals who occupy high prestige positions in a network, this is not possible because they must reach beyond the bounds of their network to contact persons of even higher prestige, and this can only be done by employing weak intimate ties. Thus in heterogeneous networks, the "strength of weak ties" depends on an individual's current status.

It is not just whom you know that counts but whom you do not know. Individuals derive unique information from a particular person to the extent that the person is disconnected from others in the individual's network. One sociologist used the term *structural hole* to indicate the absence of direct connections among those in the network, arguing that the more structural holes surrounding an individual, the more conducive the individual's network is to mobility (Burt 1992). Networks full of structural holes enhance career opportunities for individuals competing for promotions within an organization.

Other studies, on the other hand, have demonstrated that in some situations density of networks can be a resource, especially among minority and immigrant populations. Dense networks are ones in which people within the network are highly concentrated within a given area, such as an ethnic enclave in a big city. Studies of immigrant and ethnic entrepreneurship consistently identify dense networks and the social capital that flows through them as a key resource for the successful creation of small businesses. Dense networks, for instance, have been shown to be an important source for pooling capital among Asian immigrant firms in the United States (Light 1984). Several studies of ethnic business enclaves have also demonstrated the importance of community networks as social capital. Enclaves are dense concentrations of immigrant or ethnic firms, a significant proportion of whose employees are coethnic, that develop a distinctive physical presence in urban places.

Numerous studies highlight the role of kin and ethnic community networks as a source of vital resources for ethnic firms, including start-up capital, tips about business opportunities, access to markets, and docile and disciplined labor forces (Portes 1987; Portes and Stepick 1985; Perez 1992; Light and Bonacich 1988; Nee, Sanders, and Sernau 1994).

Finally, ethnic niches emerge when a group is able to colonize a particular sector of employment in such a way that members have privileged access to new job openings, while restricting that of outsiders. Mobility opportunities through niches are network-driven: Members find jobs for others, teach them necessary skills, and supervise their performance (Doeringer and Moss 1986; Bailey and Waldinger 1991; Waldinger 1996; Stepick 1989).

Although the research on social capital has tended to emphasize the advantages of connections (at least for those who benefit), there are distinct disadvantages as well. What is good for the goose is not always good for the gander. Connections that bring benefits to members of one group typically discriminate against others, sometimes unintentionally. If positions within a group are filled primarily on the basis of social contacts, then the group will tend to replicate its own social and demographic profile. One study showed how social connections utilized by white ethnics in the construction trades and the fire and police unions of New York effectively kept racial minorities out (Waldinger 1995, 557). Ultimately, such informal networks reduce organizational efficiency, since otherwise qualified applicants for positions are never considered.

Another disadvantage of social capital is that in the private sector (or in public sectors that rely on patronage), individuals in positions of power may be constantly deluged by the demands of job and loan-seeking kinsmen. This can give rise to a massive free-riding problem, as less diligent members enforce on the more successful all kinds of demands backed by expectations of familial loyalty.

Yet another disadvantage of social connections is that strong associations within the group may restrict opportunity outside the group. This often occurs among groups that have experienced long histories of discrimination. In such groups, there is safety in numbers, since isolated members of the group can often become the most vulnerable targets for exploitation and oppression. This circumstance contributes to a heightened sense of in-group solidarity grounded in the common experience of subordination. Along with a heightened sense of in-group solidarity, long histories of oppression can also generate a sense of out-group hostility and suspicion. Within some segments of the African American community, for instance, academic success may be looked at suspiciously as "acting white," effectively cutting off opportunities for advancement in the dominant mainstream of society.

The lack of social connections or truncated networks in areas of concentrated poverty such as inner cities contribute to occupational problems for their inhabitants. Everyday survival in poor urban communities frequently depends on close interaction with kin and friends in similar situations. Since such ties seldom reach beyond the inner city, the inhabitants are deprived of sources of information about employment opportunities elsewhere and ways to attain them (Stack 1974). This problem is compounded by the departure of middle-class families from black inner-city areas, which has depleted the social capital of the remaining population and contributed to high levels of unemployment and welfare dependency (Wacquant and Wilson 1989; Wilson 1987, 1996).

Access to regular jobs and participation in deviant activities are both network mediated (Sullivan 1989). Teenagers seldom find jobs; instead jobs come to them through the mediation of parents and other adults in their immediate community. If such networks are weak because of the scarcity of adults employed in good jobs, teenagers have less social capital and receive less information about jobs. Left to their own resources, minority adolescents are seldom able to compete successfully for good regular jobs. The result is high rates of teenage unemployment and greater involvement in alternative forms of income earning. Dense but truncated networks of inner-city black families not only cut off members from information about the outside world; they simultaneously support alternative cultural styles that make access to mainstream employment more difficult (Fernandez-Kelly 1995).

There appears to be disagreement about the relative advantages and disadvantages of social connections. Sociologist Nan Lin (2000a) has recently developed a theory of group or aggregate inequality in social capital that explains many of the apparently contradictory findings regarding effects of social capital. He points out the need to examine whether different social groups possess different qualities or quantities of social capital; whether they gain different returns from what social capital they have; and finally, whether it is possible for members of disadvantaged groups to overcome such deficiencies. Using females as an example, Lin offers three observations. First, females, traditionally socialized for roles outside the workplace in society, may not always use or mobilize their social capital in the labor market. Or the appropriate social ties are mobilized, but for a variety of reasons, these contacts are reluctant to expend their own capital on the female's behalf. Finally, there may be biased responses from the labor market structure itself. Employers may respond differently to male and female job or promotion candidates even if they present similar types of social capital. In this way, the return on investment of social capital may be less for females than for males.

Lin also suggests an explanation for the interesting finding that those with friends in high places are not more likely than those with friends in lower places to actively mobilize personal contacts in job search, and that non-searchers (those who do not actively mobilize social resources) seem to do as well or even better compared to searchers who use informal methods in getting higher income or better jobs (Granovetter 1973; Lin, Vaughn, and Ensel 1981; Campbell and Rosenfeld 1985; DeGraaf and Flap 1988). Having friends in high places increases the likelihood of receiving useful information in routine exchanges without actively seeking such information. Persons having networks yielding access to substantial job information will be more apt to be presented with opportunities to change jobs without an active search. Having friends in high places is associated with the routine flow of useful information—*the invisible hand of social capital*. Only when such useful information is not available and not forthcoming would mobilization of social contacts become necessary. Those with friends in lower places, however, must more often call upon whatever contacts they have to actively seek useful information (Lin 2000a, 792). This explains why strong ties are less effective for minority group members and why cross-gender ties are more useful for females than for males.

Thus, it is clear that not all individuals or social groups uniformly acquire social capital or receive expected returns from their social capital. Social groups (class, status, gender, racial, and ethnic) have different access to social capital because of their advantaged or disadvantaged structural positions and associated social networks. Individuals with better socioeconomic origins are more likely to access better social resources in social networks and/or find contacts with better social standings. Others, occupying inferior positions in the social hierarchy and accessing worse resources in social networks, attain lower status in their careers. People in lower socioeconomic status groups tend to be members in resource-poor networks that share a relatively restricted variety of information and influence. They tend to use local ties, strong ties, and family and kin ties. Since these ties are usually homogeneous in resources, this networking tendency reinforces poor social capital. People in higher socioeconomic status groups tend to be embedded in resource-rich networks that are characterized by relative richness not only in quantity but also in *kind*—resource heterogeneity (Lin 1982, 2000a; Lin and Dumin 1986; Campbell, Marsden, and Hurlbert 1986).

## A NOTE ON NEPOTISM

The most blatant form of advantage through social capital is *nepotism,* often defined as the undue preference for close kin or friends where open merit-based competition should prevail. The beneficiaries of nepotism possess social capital—parents, siblings, other close kin, and friends—that is activated on their behalf and is quite independent of their individual merit or qualifications. In his recent *In Praise of Nepotism: A Natural History* (2003), Adam Bellow (son of the famous author and Noble laureate, Saul Bellow) argues that nepotism has a biological basis (enhancing chances for survival by maximizing inclusive fitness). According to Bellow, nepotism is based on the "natural" preference for close kin and is found in one form or another in all human societies. He emphasizes that America is no exception, that despite its meritocratic ideology, nepotism is American as apple pie, has been endemic throughout its history, and is actually resurgent in a new form that he calls the "new nepotism." Bellow documents the pervasiveness of nepotism in America from colonial times to the present, correctly pointing out that many of the exemplars of the "self-made man" were in fact beneficiaries of significant nepotism.

Nepotism then, is a form of inherited and unearned advantage, based on social capital that is independent of individual merit and that varies by social class. The most privileged classes tend to have the most valuable social capital. For the privileged, nepotism provides considerable advantage and is an important means by which privilege is transferred from one generation to the next, enabling the formation of dynasties of wealth and power. For the privileged, nepotism takes the forms of essentially unearned access to high appointive or elective office, as well as high income and authority occupations.

Nepotism operates in all social classes, but potential benefits decline as one moves down the social class ladder. Thus members of the working class are also recipients of nepotism, but its payoffs are less valuable simply because the working class tends to have lower social capital. Nepotism in the working class tends to be limited to access to apprenticeships, unions, or the more "desirable" working-class occupations. For example, in the capitalist class, a son may be placed in an upper echelon position in the family business; in the working class, a son may get access to union membership or a "good" job running one of the machines at the mill where his father has worked for twenty years.

One of Bellow's least compelling arguments is that the "new nepotism" in America is compatible with principles of merit. Bellow contends that although one might *initially* secure a position through nepotism, today the recipient must continually display merit to *keep* the position, often working harder to demonstrate competence and hence worthiness. The problem with this line of reasoning is that although nepotism and meritocracy can coexist in a social system, they ultimately represent zero-sum principles of distribution. That is, the *more* nepotism operates, the *less* merit operates, and there is no nuanced argument that can escape this fundamental contradiction. The initial advantage of placement, for instance, is a crucial one that summarily denies access to opportunity for others regardless of their level of merit. Further, contrary to Bellow, there is precious little evidence that the beneficiaries of nepotism are at a competitive disadvantage once placed in positions of power and privilege. Instead, they tend to "get the benefit of the doubt" and operate in what might be called a "climate of positive expectations" that produces self-fulfilling prophecies that legitimate the nepotism.

In sum, the operation of nepotism and variations in the quantity and quality of social capital provide unequal access to educational, occupational, and entrepreneurial success. These effects are independent of individual merit and are related to a great extent to the class-based social circles that people travel in. Beyond one's social milieu, some people may have better social skills than others and may be better able to cultivate social capital. The advantage of the social capital itself, however, is independent of a person's ability to perform certain tasks; that is, someone may be good at making friends and use those friends to help get a job that itself has nothing to do with the ability to make friends. In short, social connections matter beyond a person's ability to do the job.

## FITTING IN

The importance of something is sometimes most dramatically revealed by its absence. The lack of cultural capital, for instance, has been the gist of several

comic moments on film. The musical comedy *My Fair Lady* was a story about
the efforts of a stuffy professor played by Rex Harrison—on a bet—to coach
a young London cockney girl played by Audrey Hepburn to "pass" as a British
socialite. A similar theme was at work in the popular American film *Pretty
Woman*, in which a wealthy businessman played by Richard Gere befriends
a hooker played by Julia Roberts who, with some crash course coaching from
the manager of the Beverly Hills Wilshire Hotel, attempts, with limited success, to "pass" as his dignified and refined escort. In one particularly reveal-
ing restaurant scene, Julia Robert's character begins to eat the salad at the beginning of the dinner only to be told that the salad comes at the end of the
meal. Her exasperated response, "But that is the fork I knew!" exposes her
lack of cultural capital. The lack of cultural capital was especially sharply
drawn in the 1960s TV show *The Beverly Hillbillies*. In this situation comedy,
a family of Tennessee hillbillies becomes instant millionaires. Although the
hillbillies were portrayed as having enormous sums of economic capital, they
were without upper-class cultural capital and wildly out of place among the
rich and famous in Beverly Hills. These are, of course, exaggerated and fic-
tionalized accounts, but they serve to illustrate what sociologists refer to as
"cultural capital."

Social inequality is not just about wealth and power but about culture as
well. Claims that one group's culture ranks higher in social standing than
others can be based on almost anything—tastes in music, leisure, food,
fashion—in short, anything that creates invidious status distinctions (Weber
1968; Veblen 1953). What is required is a claim of superiority and getting others to accede to it. French sociologist Pierre Bourdieu (1986) has explored
this dimension of inequality at length. For Bourdieu, cultural capital is cultural property, or more specifically, the possession of knowledge and arti-
facts associated with groups. The source of cultural capital is located in and
transmitted through what Bourdieu calls *habitus*, the whole panoply of practices, dispositions, and tastes that organizes an individual's participation
within the culture of a group.

The process of acquiring culture requires an investment of time and effort.
Like the acquisition of a muscular physique or a suntan, others cannot do it
for you. Knowledge of the ways of life of a group cannot be transmitted in-
stantaneously by gift or bequest, purchase, or exchange. It is acquired over
time through the process of socialization. In this sense, it is a form of hereditary transmission that is heavily disguised. Because the social conditions of
its transmission and acquisition are more disguised than those of economic
capital, it is likely to be unrecognized as a form of inherited capital and instead be claimed as individual competence. That is, the possession of cultural capital is generally claimed as "evidence" of individual merit, while its
fundamental dependence on differential opportunities for its inheritance
goes unrecognized. Like other forms of capital, its value is based on the fact

that not everyone possesses it. The logic of scarcity secures material and symbolic advantages for those who possess it. That is, any given cultural competence derives a scarcity value from its position in the distribution of cultural capital and yields profits of distinction for its owner (e.g., being able to read in a world of illiterates).

The initial accumulation of cultural capital, the precondition for the fast, easy accumulation of every kind of useful cultural capital, starts at the outset, without delay, without wasted time, only for the offspring of families endowed with strong cultural capital. Indeed, the transmission of cultural capital through socialization is the most valuable hidden form of hereditary transmission of privilege. Cultural capital, therefore, receives proportionately greater weight in justification of privilege (presumed merit) because more direct and visible forms of transmission (e.g., inheritance of economic capital) tend to be more strongly censored and controlled (e.g., getting something for nothing).

Cultural capital can also be objectified in material objects and media such as writings, paintings, and the like, and is transmissible in its materiality. Thus, a collection of paintings can be transmitted as easily as economic capital. But what is transmissible is legal ownership and not what constitutes the precondition for specific appropriation, namely, the possession of the means of "consuming" the paintings. Owning a Rembrandt, for instance, presupposes knowing who Rembrandt was and why he is considered a talented artist. Bourdieu argues that cultural capital can be certified in the form of academic qualifications and serve as a testimony of cultural competence for its bearer. This objectification, he says, is what makes the difference between the capital of the self-educated person, which may be called into question at any time, and the cultural capital academically sanctioned by legally guaranteed qualifications formally independent of the bearer. With the academic qualification, a certificate of cultural competence confers on its holder a conventional, constant, legally guaranteed value with respect to culture. By conferring institutional recognition on the cultural capital possessed, the academic qualification also makes it possible to compare qualification holders and even to exchange them (by substituting one for another in succession). Furthermore, it makes it possible to establish conversion rates between cultural capital and economic capital by guaranteeing the monetary value of a given academic capital (e.g., the "going" starting salary for an MBA from the Wharton School of Business).

DiMaggio and Mohr (1985, 168) further suggest that it is useful to distinguish between cultural capital at the national level and the many kinds of cultural competence that help people get ahead in local settings. While such local cultural resources may well be more important than national cultural capital to the life chances of individuals in particular communities, networks, or organizations, they are unlikely to play a consistent role from place to place. DiMaggio and Mohr note, for example, that command of IBM's corporate culture (a local cultural resource) may be more important than more generalized forms of cultural capital in getting ahead at IBM but may be an impediment if one moves to Apple. They emphasize that it is precisely because cultural capital is institutionalized as legitimate and valuable at the societal level that it enables persons to form ties across local boundaries.

In this regard, different kinds of cultural capital work like the different kinds of social capital: Some network forms constitute resources for mobility among groups, organizations, or communities, while other network forms are resources for mobility within groups, organizations, or communities.

Until very recently, most of the literature on cultural capital and its effects was conceptual and theoretical, and empirical research was based on ethnographic studies that were limited in their generality by small or unrepresentative samples. While considerable empirical research has been conducted on how the possession of social capital contributes to upward social mobility, there has been less work on how the possession of cultural capital contributes to success in its various dimensions. According to Bourdieu, the intergenerational transmission of cultural capital, especially through educational systems, is an important mechanism of social class reproduction. While the direct intergenerational transmission of cultural capital in the United States appears to be relatively weak, the effects of cultural capital on schooling and other adult outcomes are relatively strong (DiMaggio and Mohr 1985). Evidence suggests that the contribution of cultural capital to socioeconomic success, independent of socioeconomic background and individual merit factors, is substantial, and occurs primarily through its strong net effects on educational outcomes. Student cultural capital is a significant net predictor of school success (Aschaffenburg and Maas 1997), including grades, college and postgraduate attendance and completion, educational attainment of one's spouse (DiMaggio 1982; DiMaggio and Mohr 1985; Farkas 1996), and subsequent adult success (Persell, Catsambis, and Cookson 1992). Further, recent research reveals that the integration of blacks into high-status culture has contributed to black–white convergence in schooling and suggests that cultural capital may serve as a route to upward mobility for blacks and other minority groups (Kalmijn and Kraaykamp 1996).

Research on the upper class consistently demonstrates the importance of cultural capital in distinguishing "old money" from "new money." Outside of the upper class, however, cultural capital does not appear to be strongly determined by parental socioeconomic status. There are relatively small correlations between cultural capital and conventional measures of parental socioeconomic status, and the explanatory power of parental socioeconomic background decreases little after cultural capital measures are introduced into explanatory models. Thus it appears that initial deficits in cultural capital can be closed though education, which is a much better predictor of cultural capital than economic background per se. Recent research (Mohr and DiMaggio 1995; Egerton 1997) also suggests that household cultural climate varies according to parents' level of formal education and the employment situation of the father. In those families in which the father is employed in an occupation for which cultural capital is recognized as important for success (e.g., professionals), there is investment in cultural resources in the home, and such investment leads to children's acquisition of cultural capital. Thus, occupational groups dependent for their authority on cultural rather than economic capital invest more in legitimate culture in their homes and transmit cultural capital more effectively to their children, and occupational effects are evident beyond the impact of family income and parents' education. Under these conditions, a form of cultural capital reproduction across generations occurs.

The reproduction of cultural capital has occurred with enough frequency to have generated commonplace stereotypes of subcultural differences among occupational groups, status groups, and social classes. Even within social classes, subcultural differences are manifest. For example, within the upper class, the *upper*-upper class with its "old money" (dynastic wealth) and its cultural capital displayed as refined manners, styles, and tastes, is contrasted to the *lower*-upper class, the *nouveau riche*, who may possess as much or even more economic capital but are "betrayed" by lack of cultural capital, as indicated by deficiencies in *savoir faire*, unrefined manner, lack of style, and pedestrian tastes.

Research suggests that parents may influence children's cultural capital in three ways: Children may acquire cultural skills "frictionlessly" by living in a home where parents possess considerable cultural capital; they may acquire it effortlessly in their friends' homes, whether or not their own parents are so oriented; or parents may invest strategically in cultural goods to improve their children's life chances (Mohr and DiMaggio 1995, 179). What is more, young adults may, independent of their families, seek out cultural capital to escape their socioeconomic origins or to reject that which their family has provided.

From this, we can conclude several things. First, while the possession of cultural capital is related to social class background, that correlation is far from perfect. The privileged do tend to have more cultural capital than those of lower socioeconomic status, but there are many cases that do not fit this pattern. Second, while the possession of cultural capital may be viewed as evidence of individual merit, it is in fact acquired in ways that can hardly be attributable to individual effort or merit as conventionally defined. That is, much cultural capital is the result of familial socialization—cultural capital is often "frictionlessly" and effortlessly inherited. In this sense, the acquisition of cultural capital is best conceptualized as a process of differential cultural inheritance, not one of differential achievement. Third, strategies of mobility and reproduction are constrained but not wholly determined by social class. Thus, cultural resources enter into individual and familial strategies for advancement in a variety of ways. For some, investment in cultural capital is conscious and purposeful effort or strategy, either for one's own mobility or for that of one's children. Fourth, cultural capital contributes directly to the acquisition of education. Educational credentials (cultural capital in its institutionalized form) then become criteria for access to occupational opportunity (eligibility requirements for hiring and promotion).

## GEORGE WALKER BUSH

George Walker Bush, the forty-third president of the United States, exemplifies the advantages of social and cultural capital. A self-admitted mediocre student, George Walker Bush nevertheless ascended to prominence and power aided considerably by pedigree and social connections.

The Bushes trace their immediate ancestry to wealthy New England established families. George Walker Bush's paternal grandfather, Prescott Sheldon Bush, was a graduate of Yale University, a wealthy banker and financier, and U.S. senator from Connecticut. George Walker Bush's father, George Herbert Walker Bush, was the forty-first president of the United States. Consistent with a practice in which upper-class families often use maternal surnames as first or middle names, George Herbert Walker Bush was named after his maternal grandfather, George Herbert Walker. Prior to becoming president, George H. W. Bush held other political positions, including member of the U.S. House of Representatives, U.S. ambassador to the United Nations, chairman of the Republican National Committee, chief of the U.S. Liaison Office in the People's Republic of China, director of the Central Intelligence Agency, and vice president of the United States.

George H. W. Bush grew up in Greenwich, Connecticut, one of the most prestigious upper-class communities in America. He attended a private elementary day school in Greenwich and completed prep school at Phillips Andover Academy in Andover, Massachusetts, one of the most elite upper-class boarding schools in America. He graduated, as his father did, from Yale University. While at Yale, George H. W. Bush was a member of the Skull and Bones Society, the most elite upper-class men's club on campus. After graduating from Yale, George H. W. Bush launched a career in the oil business in Texas, aided by connections and financial backing from his father and some of his own friends from the Yale Skull and Bones Society (Parmet 1997).

George W. Bush's mother, Barbara Pierce Bush, also comes from a prominent upper-class family. Her father, Marvin Pierce, was president of McCall Publishing Company, most noted as publishers of *McCall* and *Redbook* magazines. The Pierce family heritage includes Franklin Pierce, the fourteenth president of the United States. Barbara's mother, Pauline Robinson Pierce, was the daughter of an Ohio Supreme Court justice (Parmet 1997). Barbara grew up in Rye, New York, but later attended the Ashley Boarding School in Charleston, South Carolina, an upper-class boarding school for girls. She then attended Smith College, one of the upper-class "seven sisters," elite colleges for women, but dropped out to marry George H. W. Bush upon his return from wartime service as a World War II fighter pilot in the Pacific.

George Walker Bush was born on July 6, 1946, in New Haven, Connecticut, where his father was then a student at Yale. In many respects, his upbringing and career closely parallel those of his father. Like his father, "W" went to Phillips Andover Academy, went on to Yale, joined the Skull and Bones Society, and became a fighter pilot. "W" also got into the oil business, got involved in politics, and became president of the United States. But there were key differences as well.

Unlike his New England father, "W" grew up mostly in Texas during his father's oil days, although he did spend summers, as his father did, in the family summer home in Kennebunkport, Maine. Unlike his father, who graduated Phi Beta Kappa and was captain of the Yale baseball team, "W" was a mediocre student who did not play on any Yale teams but was a cheerleader. He was also very active in his college fraternity. Unlike his father, "W" did not fly fighter planes during wartime but was in the reserves at the height of the Vietnam conflict. Notably, it has been alleged that "W" gained a scarce and highly coveted spot in the Texas Air National Guard during wartime through family connections or at least indirectly through deference paid to the Bush family name by Texas authorities (if so, this would be an example of "the invisible hand of social capital") (Ivins and Dubose 2000, 9). During this period, the Texas Air National Guard included so many sons of prominent Texas families—including, besides "W," Lloyd Bentsen III, son of a U.S. senator and future vice-presidential candidate, and William Connally III, son of the U.S. secretary of the Treasury and former governor of Texas—that it was informally referred to as "the Champagne Unit" (Minutaglio 1999, 121).

After graduation from college in 1968, "W" entered a phase of his life sometimes described as "the lost years." Helped by his father's connections, "W" held jobs during this period including working on GOP political campaigns, working for a family friend first in the oil business and then in agribusiness, and working in an inner-city development program in which his father had served as honorary chairman (Minutaglio 1999, 137–53). After a few years, "W" decided to return to school, and despite being a C student at Yale, was admitted into the elite MBA program at the Harvard Business School in 1973 and completed the MBA two years later. In 1977 "W" married Laura Welch, a librarian and daughter of a house builder. That same year, "W" made an unsuccessful bid for a seat in the House of Representatives. The following year, "W" established his own oil and gas company. Once again, family and upper-class connections were used to attract investors. At the time the company was getting established, "W's" father was either running for president or was vice president under Ronald Reagan. In short, "Bush" was a well-known name, not only in Texas oil circles but also nationwide.

In 1989, while his father was vice president and a candidate for president, "W" shifted his interest from oil to baseball. "W" put together a deal attracting big time investors to purchase the Texas Rangers. Unlike his father, who was a college baseball player, "W" became a major league baseball team owner. "W" invested $606,000 of his own money, which amounted to 2% interest in the team. The rest was secured through investors. As part of the deal, if the investors made their money back, "W's" interest would increase to 11%. The franchise did well, and "W" sold his 11% interest ten years later for $15.4 million (Minutaglio 1999, 322).

In 1994 "W" again ventured into politics, this time running successfully for governor of Texas. His father, who had been defeated for reelection to the presidency the year before, had settled into the role of retired statesman. The Bush name still went a long way, especially in Texas, a state in which his father had previously served as a member of Congress. The Bush legacy was also enormously beneficial to "W" in his bid for the presidency. "W" was able to profit from his father's insider advice as well as the web of political contacts his father had established in his long career in Washington political circles. As president, "W" has surrounded himself with many of his father's political advisors. Most prominent among them is Vice President Dick Cheney, who served as his father's secretary of defense and commanded the Pentagon during the Persian Gulf War. Colin Powell, chairman of the Joint Chiefs of Staff under his father and during the Gulf War, is now "W's" secretary of state. James Baker III, Bush family friend and secretary of state under "W's" father, was "W's" point man and one of his chief counsels during the legal battles surrounding "W's" disputed presidential election.

In short, George Walker Bush is awash in social and cultural capital. Throughout his life "W" has benefited from the social capital of friends, relatives, and contacts in high places. Despite his famous lapses in syntax, he has profited from ample amounts of cultural capital, including prestigious academic credentials. He is well known for his considerable charm and social skills. Reared in the midst of big business and big government, he is comfortable traveling in these high-powered circles.

"W" is not alone in this regard. There have been a number of dynastic political families in the United States, including the Adamses, the Roosevelts, the Rockefellers, and the Kennedys—all of whom had progeny whose careers were enhanced by their upper-class origin and the economic, social, and cultural capital that goes along with it.

George "W." Bush, himself a son of privilege, is apparently not averse to helping other sons and daughters of privilege to government office. For example, "W" appointed J. Strom Thurmond Jr., the son of the late Republican Senator Strom Thurmond, as U.S. attorney for South Carolina. Eugene Scalia, son of Supreme Court Justice Antonin Scalia, was appointed as chief counsel for the Department of Labor. Among others given posts in the Bush administration are Michael Powell, son of Secretary of State Colin Powell, who is chairman of the Federal Communications Commission, and Elizabeth Cheney, daughter of Vice President Cheney, who is deputy assistant secretary of state. "W" also picked Janet Rehnquist, daughter of Chief Justice William Rehnquist, to be inspector general at the Department of Health and Human Services. Ms. Rehnquist previously served as associate White House counsel for "W's" father.

In and of themselves, connections alone do not diminish or demean the individual accomplishments of the sons and daughters of the rich and powerful. Such individual accomplishments, however, must be understood within the larger social context of differing advantages in which they occur. Certainly through no fault of their own but equally through no merit of their own, the sons and daughters of the rich and powerful inherit, along with the family name, disproportionate access to prestigious and influential forms of social and cultural capital.

## SOCIAL CLIMBING

*Social climbing* and *snobbery* have long been stock material for novelists and are part of the American folklore of social ranking and mobility. The very existence of these terms reflects a cultural recognition of unequally ranked socioeconomic groups or social classes and individual efforts to move upwardly among them. In general discourse, the terms *social climber* and *snob* tend to be used interchangeably. Both snobs and social climbers engage in activities that exclude and usurp. Essentially, social climbing may be defined as strategies and activities used to achieve upward social mobility that come to be defined negatively because they are seen as violating accepted rules for the acquisition and use of social and cultural capital. To the extent that efforts for upward social mobility involve the inappropriate deployment of social and cultural capital, they run the risk of negative labeling as social climbing.

Social climbers, within the limits set by their economic capital, systematically cultivate social capital, then attempt to deploy it in the pursuit of upward social mobility. They cultivate social relationships and engage in those social activities that provide access to members of the group to which they seek membership. Such activities include the conscious construction of social networks that have a status appreciably higher than that of the networks of nonclimber peers. Climbers may carefully select organizational memberships (the "right" clubs, churches, charities, boards, and the like), develop social relations, and cultivate friendships among members of the target group. They use numerous strategies, including "name-dropping," segregating audiences when deemed necessary (Mills 1956; Goffman 1951, 1959, 1967), and refusing to associate with members of lower ranked groups. They may even use their children as sources of social contacts or as symbols of attainment. The placement of children in exclusive preparatory schools and the selection of their children's friends and activities are means of translating economic capital into social capital.

Social climbers hope that by associating with people of higher status, some of the higher status will "rub off" on them. Those who associate with social climbers, however, risk having their own status lowered by such associations. In this regard, Vance Packard, in his influential book *The Status Seekers* (1959), makes a useful distinction between *status lending* and *status declassing*. Climbers may attach themselves to status lenders, individuals who voluntarily confer their status by association with lower status individuals and organizations. Status declassing, however, reflects efforts by higher status individuals to take on characteristics of lower status individuals with whom they are interacting. Higher status individuals may "declass," as in professing a "we're just plain folks" perspective, if it is deemed socially useful for them to do so. Climbers, however, must recognize and avoid higher status individuals who declass as a strategy to avoid evaluating the climber's status claims. Similarly, climbers must avoid individuals who employ strategies of condescension. By temporarily but ostentatiously abdicating dominant status to "reach down," the higher status individuals may profit from this relation of domination, which continues to exist, by denying it.

Social climbers also attempt to develop and use cultural capital in the pursuit of upward social mobility. But one impediment to social climbing lies in the very nature of cultural capital. Components of cultural capital can usually be acquired only through extended and informal socialization within the group. While it is possible for the climber to acquire cultural capital formally, as through education or systematic training, such formal acquisition is economically costly and typically results in a tense, subtly imperfect mastery that is always marked by the conditions of its acquisition (e.g., Julia Roberts's character in *Pretty Woman* not knowing which fork to use). The resulting uneasy, practiced, unnatural, or even stilted displays are easily detected by members of the target group and thus betray the climber as a *poseur*—as not truly "one of us."

Status competition within groups may lead to changes in what status pacesetters define as prestigious. This is most evident in the fickle nature of what is considered currently "fashionable" within elite circles. The constantly changing nature of status symbols suggests the source of yet another impediment to social climbing. Self-assured and long-established members of any group come to feel that adherence to its own standard canons is beneath them. Their status is so secure that to indulge in those observances would only lower them. They can best announce and display their unassailability by changing the canons. They have adopted an apparently noninvidious way of life for the quintessentially invidious purpose of showing that they are above taking part in a game played by "lessers." Such changes in cultural capital increase the difficulty of its acquisition and penetration of the target group by climbers. It is more difficult to hit a moving cultural target than a stationary one.

Social climbing elicits negative reactions for a variety of reasons. For some, the evidence of single-minded, obsessive preoccupation with status or the transparent, crudely instrumental efforts to deploy social and cultural capital are simply annoying. What is more, the actions of social climbers can make individuals acutely aware of their own cultural and social capital deficiencies. The American Dream encourages individuals to maintain or, if possible improve, their social positions by acquiring social, cultural, and economic capital and using them to their advantage. But such activity is governed by generally understood and accepted rules, and the social climber's actions challenge or violate them. Violating the rules is sufficient basis for negative labeling and exclusion. "Not knowing" the rules is no excuse, because knowing and adhering to the rules is a nonsubstitutable criterion of eligibility.

Further, the instrumental acquisition and deployment of social and cultural capital as a strategic means for the achievement of upward social mobility violates meritocratic notions. According to meritocratic ideology, individual merit is the only legitimate basis for mobility. Hence, the purposeful use of social and cultural capital as a means of social mobility is suspect to the extent that it is not the product of individual merit or that it is viewed as being a substitute for individual merit.

From another perspective, the actions of social climbers challenge the legitimacy of group ranking and the unequal distribution of social and cultural capital, and lay bare class-based resentments and hostilities. Rejection and exclusion of the climber by the target group constitutes an exercise of power. In fact, the climber's own group may experience a threat to its status and attempt to impose sanctions on the climber, because at least by implication, the climber's actions constitute a negative evaluation of that group and therefore a threat to its status claims and solidarity.

In sum, the actions of social climbers run counter to the individualistic and meritocratic components of the American Dream and the normative structure that underlies it. Climbing behavior also calls attention to inequalities among groups in the distribution of various forms of capital. Social climbers highlight the social and cultural insecurities of those with whom they interact. For all these reasons, the actions of social climbers tend to be viewed, especially by those of higher status, as fraudulent and shameful.

## SUMMARY

This chapter reviewed the evidence on the importance of "whom you know" (social capital) and "fitting in" (cultural capital) for getting and staying ahead in America. Social capital and cultural capital are ultimately resources. As with the possession of wealth, the possession of social and cultural resources is not necessarily evidence of "individual merit." Wealth can be converted into social and cultural capital providing distinct nonmerit advantages that can be transferred to the children of the rich and powerful. We explored the related phenomenon of social climbing. Conscious construction and use of social networks, conspicuous and invidious consumption, name-dropping, and the pretense of highbrow culture are some of the techniques employed by social climbers in their attempts to attain higher status. Instead of gaining the prestige and rank that they desire, however, social climbers are often viewed as snobs within their own groups and as impostors by those in the groups to which they aspire to gain membership.

## REFERENCES

Aschaffenburg, Karen, and Ineke Maas. 1997. "Cultural and Educational Careers: The Dynamics of Social Reproduction." *American Sociological Review* 62: 573–87.

Bailey, T., and R. Waldinger. 1991. "Primary, Secondary, and Enclave Labor Markets: A Training System Approach." *American Sociological Review* 56: 432–45.

Becker, Gary S. 1964. *Human Capital*. Chicago: University of Chicago Press.

Bellow, Adam. 2003. *In Praise of Nepotism: A Natural History*. New York: Doubleday.

Bourdieu, Pierre. 1973. "Cultural Reproduction and Social Reproduction." Pp. 71–112 in *Knowledge, Education, and Cultural Change*, edited by Richard Brown. London: Tavistock.

———. 1986. "The Forms of Capital." Pp. 241–58 in *Handbook of Theory and Research for the Sociology of Education*, edited by John G. Richardson. New York: Greenwood Press.

Bourdieu, Pierre, and Jean Claude Passeron. 1977. *Reproduction: In Education, Society and Culture*. Translated by R. Nice. Beverly Hills, Calif.: Sage.

Briggs, Xavier de Souza. 1998. "Brown Kids in White Suburbs: Housing Mobility and the Many Faces of Social Capital." *Housing Policy Debate* 9: 177–221.

Burt, Ronald S. 1992. *Structural Holes: The Social Structure of Competition*. Cambridge, Mass.: Harvard University Press.

———. 1997. "The Contingent Value of Social Capital." *Administrative Science Quarterly* 42: 339–65.

———. 2001. "Structural Holes versus Network Closure as Social Capital." In *Social Capital: Theory and Research*, edited by N. Lin, K. Cook, and R. S. Burt. Boulder, Colo.: NetLibrary.

Campbell, Karen E. 1988. "Gender Differences in Job-Related Networks." *Work and Occupations* 15: 179–200.

Campbell, Karen E., Peter V. Marsden, and Jeanne S. Hurlbert. 1986. "Social Resources and Socioeconomic Status." *Social Networks* 8: 97–117.

Campbell, Karen E., and Rachel A. Rosenfeld. 1985. "Job Search and Job Mobility: Sex and Race Differences." *Research in the Sociology of Work* 3: 147–74.

Coleman, James S. 1988. "Social Capital in the Creation of Human Capital." *American Journal of Sociology* 94: S95–S120.

———. 1990. *The Foundations of Social Theory*. Cambridge: Belknap.

Coleman, James S., Thomas S. Hoffer, and Sally Kilgore. 1982. *High School Achievement: Public, Catholic, and Private Schools Compared*. New York: Basic Books.

Collins, Randall. 1979. *The Credential Society: An Historical Sociology of Education*. New York: Academic Press.

DeGraaf, Nan Dirk, and Hendrik Derk Flap. 1988. "With a Little Help from My Friends." *Social Forces* 67: 452–72.

DiMaggio, Paul. 1979. "Review Essay on Pierre Bourdieu." *American Journal of Sociology* 84: 1460–74.

———. 1982. "Cultural Capital and School Success: The Impact of Status-Culture Participation on the Grades of U.S. High School Students." *American Sociological Review* 47: 189–201.

DiMaggio, Paul, and John Mohr. 1985. "Cultural Capital, Educational Attainment, and Marital Selection." *American Journal of Sociology* 90: 1231–61.

Doeringer, P., and P. Moss. 1986. "Capitalism and Kinship: Do Institutions Matter in the Labor Market?" *Industrial and Labor Relations Review* 40: 48–59.

Egerton, Muriel. 1997. "Occupational Inheritance: The Role of Cultural Capital and Gender." *Work, Employment and Society* 11: 263–82.

Farkas, George. 1996. *Human Capital or Cultural Capital? Ethnicity and Poverty Groups in an Urban School District*. New York: Walter de Gruyter.

Fernandez-Kelly, M. P. 1995. "Social and Cultural Capital in the Urban Ghetto: Implications for the Economic Sociology of Immigration." Pp. 213–47 in *The Economic Sociology of Immigration,* edited by Alejandro Portes. New York: Russell Sage.

Fischer, Claude. 1977. "Network Analysis and Urban Studies." Pp. 19–37 in *Networks and Places*, edited by Claude S. Fischer et al. New York: Free Press.

Foley, Michael W., and Bob Edwards. 1999. "Is It Time to Disinvest in Social Capital?" *Journal of Public Policy* 19, no. 2: 141–73.

Goffman, Erving. 1951. "Symbols of Class Status." *British Journal of Sociology* 2: 294–304.

———. 1959. *The Presentation of Self in Everyday Life*. Harmondsworth, U.K.: Pelican.

———. 1967. *Interaction Ritual*. New York: Pantheon.

Granovetter, Mark S. 1973. "The Strength of Weak Ties." *American Journal of Sociology* 78: 1360–80.

———. 1974. *Getting a Job: A Study of Contacts and Careers*. Cambridge, Mass.: Harvard University Press.

———. 1983. "The Strength of Weak Ties: A Network Theory Revisited." *Sociological Theory* 1: 201–33.

———. 1985. "Economic Action and Social Structure: The Problem of Embeddedness." *American Journal of Sociology* 91: 481–510.

Ivins, Molly, and Lou Dubose. 2000. *Shrub: The Short but Happy Political Life of George W. Bush*. New York: Vintage.

Jencks, C., et al. 1979. *Who Gets Ahead: The Determinants of Economic Success in America*. New York: Basic Books.

Jencks, C., J. Crouse, and P. Muesser. 1983. "The Wisconsin Model of Status Attainment: A National Replication with Improved Measure of Ability and Aspiration." *Sociology of Education* 56: 3–19.

Kalmijn, Matthijs, and Gerbert Kraaykamp. 1996. "Race, Cultural Capital, and Schooling: An Analysis of Trends in the United States." *Sociology of Education* 69: 22–34.

Lamont, Michelle, and Marcel Fournier, eds. 1992. *Cultivating Differences: Symbolic Boundaries and the Making of Inequality*. Chicago: University of Chicago Press.

Lamont, Michelle, and Annette Lareau. 1988. "Cultural Capital: Allusions, Gaps and Glissandos in Recent Theoretical Developments." *Sociological Theory* 6: 153–68.

Lang, Robert E., and Steven B. Hornburg. 1998. "What Is Social Capital and Why Is It Important for Social Policy?" *Housing Policy Debate* 9: 1–16.

Light, Ivan. 1984. "Immigrant and Ethnic Enterprise in North America." *Ethnic and Racial Studies* 7: 195–216.

Light, Ivan, and Edna Bonacich. 1988. *Immigrant Entrepreneurs: Koreans in Los Angeles 1965–1982*. Berkeley: University of California Press.

Lin, Nan. 1982. "Social Resources and Instrumental Action." Pp. 131–45 in *Social Structure and Network Analysis*, edited by Peter V. Marsden and Nan Lin. Beverly Hills, Calif.: Sage.

———. 1990. "Social Resources and Social Mobility: A Structural Theory of Status Attainment." Pp. 247–71 in *Social Mobility and Social Structure*, edited by Ronald Breiger. Cambridge: Cambridge University Press.

———. 1999. "Social Networks and Status Attainment." *Annual Review of Sociology* 23: 467–88.

———. 2000a. "Inequality in Social Capital." *Contemporary Sociology* 29: 785–95.

———. 2000b. *Social Capital: A Theory of Structure and Action*. Cambridge: Cambridge University Press.

Lin, Nan, and Mary Dumin. 1986. "Access to Occupations through Social Ties." *Social Networks* 8: 365–85.

Lin, Nan, Walter M. Ensel, and John C. Vaughn. 1981. "Social Resources and the Occupational Status Attainment." *Social Forces* 58: 1163–81.

Lin, Nan, John C. Vaughn, and Walter M. Ensel. 1981. "Social Resources and Strength of Ties: Structural Factors in Occupational Attainment." *American Sociological Review* 46: 393–405.

Loury, Glen C. 1977. "A Dynamic Theory of Racial Income Differences." Pp. 153–87 in *Women, Minorities, and Employment Discrimination*, edited by P. A. Wallace and A. M. LaMond. Lexington, Mass.: Heath.

Marsden, Peter V., and Karen E. Campbell. 1984. "Measuring Tie Strength." *Social Forces* 63: 482–501.

Marsden, Peter V., and Jeanne S. Hurlbert. 1988. "Social Resources and Mobility Outcomes: A Replication and Extension." *Social Forces* 66: 1038–59.

McLanahan, Sara, and Gary D. Sandefur. 1994. *Growing Up with a Single Parent: What Hurts, What Helps*. Cambridge, Mass.: Harvard University Press.

Menaghan, Elizabeth G., and Toby L. Parcel. 1991. "Determining Children's Home Environments: The Impact of Maternal Characteristics and Current Occupation and Family Conditions." *Journal of Marriage and the Family* 53: 417–31.

Mills, C. Wright. 1956. *White Collar*. New York: Oxford University Press.

Minutaglio, Bill. 1999. *First Son: George W. Bush and the Bush Family Dynasty*. New York: Three Rivers Press.

Mohr, John, and Paul DiMaggio. 1995. "The Intergenerational Transmission of Cultural Capital." *Research in Social Stratification and Mobility* 14: 167–99.

Nee, Victor, J. Sanders, and S. Sernau. 1994. "Job Transitions in an Immigrant Metropolis: Ethnic Boundaries and the Mixed Economy." *American Sociological Review* 59: 849–72.

Packard, Vance O. 1959. *The Status Seekers*. New York: David McKay.

Parcel, Toby L., and Mikaela J. Dufur. 2001. "Capital at Home and at School: Effects on Student Achievement." *Social Forces* 79: 881–912.

Parcel, Toby L., and Elizabeth G. Menaghan. 1990. "Maternal Working Conditions and Child Verbal Ability: Studying the Transmission of Intergenerational Inequality from Mothers to Young Children." *Social Psychology Quarterly* 53: 132–47.

———. 1994. "Early Parental Work, Family Social Capital, and Early Childhood Outcomes." *American Journal of Sociology* 99: 972–1009.

Parkin, F. 1979. *Marxism and Class Theory: A Bourgeois Critique*. New York: Columbia University Press.

Parmet, Herbert S. 1997. *George Bush: The Life of a Lone Star Yankee*. New York: Scribner.

Perez, L. 1992. "Cuban Miami." Pp. 83–108 in *Miami Now*, edited by G. J. Grenier and A. Stepick. Gainesville: University of Florida Press.

Persell, Caroline, Sophia Catsambis, and Peter W. Cookson Jr. 1992. "Family Background, School Type, and College Attendance: A Conjoint System of Cultural Capital Transmission." *Journal of Research on Adolescence* 2: 1–23.

Portes, Alejandro. 1987. "The Social Origins of the Cuban Enclave Economy of Miami." *Sociological Perspectives* 30: 340–72.

———. 1998. "Social Capital: Its Origins and Applications in Modern Sociology." *Annual Review of Sociology* 24: 1–24.

———. 2000. "The Two Meanings of Social Capital." *Sociological Forum* 15: 1–12.

Portes, Alejandro, and Patricia Landolt. 1996. "The Downside of Social Capital." *The American Prospect* 26: 18–21.

Portes, Alejandro, and Julia Sensenbrenner. 1993. "Embeddedness and Immigration: Notes on the Social Determinants of Economic Action." *American Journal of Sociology* 98: 1320–50.

Portes, Alejandro, and Alex Stepick. 1985. "Unwelcome Immigrants: The Labor Market Experiences of 1980 (Mariel) Cuban and Haitian refugees in South Florida." *American Sociological Review* 50: 493–514.

Schultz, Theodore W. 1961. "Investment in Human Capital." *American Economic Review* 51: 1–17.

Stack, Carol. 1974. *All Our Kin*. New York: Harper & Row.

Stepick, A. 1989. "Miami's Two Informal Sectors." Pp. 111–34 in *The Informal Economy: Studies in Advanced and Less Developed Countries,* edited by A. Portes, M. Castells, and L. A. Benton. Baltimore: Johns Hopkins University Press.

Sullivan, M. L. 1989. *Getting Paid: Youth Crime and Work in the Inner City.* Ithaca, N.Y.: Cornell University Press.

Swartz, David. 1977. "Pierre Bourdieu: The Cultural Transmission of Social Inequality." *Harvard Educational Review* 47: 545–55.

Teachman, Jay D., Kathleen Paasch, and Karen Carver. 1996. "Social Capital and Dropping Out of School Early." *Journal of Marriage and the Family* 58: 773–83.

———. 1997. "Social Capital and the Generation of Human Capital." *Social Forces* 75, no. 4: 1343–60.

Veblen, Thorstein. [1899] 1953. *The Theory of the Leisure Class*. New York: Modern Library.

Wacquant, Lois, and William Julius Wilson. 1989. "The Cost of Racial and Class Exclusion in the Inner City." *Annals of the American Academy of Political and Social Sciences* 501: 8–26.

Waldinger, Roger. 1995. "The 'Other Side' of Embeddedness: A Case Study of the Interplay between Economy and Ethnicity." *Ethnic and Racial Studies* 18: 555–80.

———. 1996. *Still the Promised City? African-Americans and New Immigrants in Post-Industrial New York*. Cambridge, Mass.: Harvard University Press.

Weber, Max. 1968. *Economy and Society*, translated and edited by Guenther Roth and Claus Wittich. Berkeley: University of California Press.

Wegener, Bernd. 1991. "Job Mobility and Social Ties: Social Resources, Prior Job and Status Attainment." *American Sociological Review* 56: 1–12.

Wilson, Kenneth L., and Alejandro Portes. 1980. "Immigration Enclaves: An Analysis of the Labor Market Experiences of Cubans in Miami." *American Journal of Sociology* 86: 295–319.

Wilson, William Julius. 1987. *The Truly Disadvantaged: The Inner City, the Underclass, and Public Policy*. Chicago: University of Chicago Press.

———. 1996. *When Work Disappears: The World of the New Urban Poor*. New York: Alfred A. Knopf.

Woolcock, Michael. 1998. "Social Capital and Economic Development: Toward a Theoretical Synthesis and Policy Framework." *Theory and Society* 27: 151–208.

# 5

# Making the Grade:
# Education and Mobility

*To those of you who received honors, awards, and distinctions, I say, well done. And to the C students, I say you too can be president of the United States.*

—George W. Bush, Yale commencement address,
thirty-three years after his graduation

According to the American Dream, education identifies and selects intelligent, talented, and motivated individuals and provides educational training in direct proportion to individual merit. The amounts and kinds of education attained are taken as measures of merit and are used as criteria of eligibility for occupations and the material awards attached to them. In the American Dream, education is the "engine" of meritocracy. Most Americans believe that education is the key to success: to get ahead in life you need a "good education."

A radically different view of the role of education sees education not as a cause but as an effect of social class. Working-class children get working-class educations, middle-class children get middle-class educations, and upper-class children get upper-class educations. In each case, children from these different class backgrounds are groomed for different roles that they will likely fill as adults. In this way, education largely reproduces existing inequalities across generations.

In America, as in all contemporary industrial societies, education has come to play an important role in selecting people for positions in the occupational structure. The overall relationship between education and future income is clear—the more education, the greater the chances of higher income (see table 5.1).

**Table 5.1.   Median Annual Income for All Workers Eighteen Years and Over by Educational Attainment, 2001**

| Education Level | Median Income ($) |
|---|---|
| Professional degree | 71,606 |
| Doctorate degree | 63,952 |
| Master's degree | 49,324 |
| Bachelor's degree | 37,203 |
| Associate degree | 28,563 |
| Some college, no degree | 21,658 |
| High school graduate, including GED | 19,900 |
| Not high school graduate | 11,864 |

*Source*: Adapted from U.S. Census Bureau, *Current Population Survey, Detailed Tables PPL-169*, Table 8 (Washington, D.C.: U.S. Government Printing Office, 2002).

The close connection between "getting ahead" and education, however, is relatively recent. In the mid-nineteenth century, the United States was a nation of small property owners, farmers, and shopkeepers. Many could read and write but most had little formal education. Although opportunity has been an essential part of the American Dream since its beginnings, it meant the possibility for a person to grow to full potential, unfettered by the limits of class background or older feudal relations. The beliefs had important noneconomic as well as economic connotations, referring to opportunities to develop competence, character, and satisfying social ties, as well as to attain material well-being. The idea of opportunity as the chance to "move up" in the world gradually became a part of the American Dream, but it did not become very important until later in the nineteenth century. Thus at first opportunity was not associated with upward social mobility, much less with upward mobility through education.

During the second half of the nineteenth century, the ideal of the "self-made man" emerged and became an increasingly important component of the American Dream. But at first, it was business not education that was seen as the main road to opportunity. The "self-made man" started and grew his business or farm through intelligence and hard work, not by getting more education than his competitors.

The expansion of schooling was the result of major changes in the structure of occupational opportunities. With continuing industrialization, technological change, the rise of giant corporations, and the closing of the frontier, by the end of the nineteenth century opportunities for becoming a "self-made man" had declined precipitously (see chapter 7). America was no longer a nation of small-scale entrepreneurs, farmers, and shopkeepers. More people were becoming employees in increasingly large, bureaucratically structured work organizations. These new conditions generated the development of new pathways to success.

At first education seemed an unlikely avenue. Businessmen, many of whom were "self-made men" with little formal schooling, graduates of the "school of hard knocks"—typically thought that schooling made young people unfit for the "real world" or at least didn't prepare them very well for it. Gradually, however, education increasingly came to be viewed as a replacement for the faltering promise of the family farm or business entrepreneurship. Andrew Carnegie, for example, believed that schools and colleges should be made into "ladders upon which the aspiring can rise" (1899, 663). But at the end of the nineteenth century, America's schools hardly constituted a well-organized ladder to success. It was during the first few decades of the twentieth century that the patchwork of American schooling was reorganized into the ladder structure that people like Andrew Carnegie advocated, thereby providing a mechanism to keep the American promise of opportunity at the very time when fundamental changes in the economy were threatening to destroy it (Brint and Karabel 1989, 3–6).

Between 1900 and 1940, the proportion of white-collar jobs in the American labor force almost doubled—from one out of six at the turn of the century to almost one out of three by 1940. Between 1940 and 1970, the proportion of professional and managerial jobs increased from one out of seven to almost one out of four. These massive changes in the occupational structure created increasing incentives for investment in education and led first to increasing high school enrollments and subsequently to higher graduation rates (see table 5.2).

Since World War II, growth in corporate size and concentration have continued, and opportunities for upward mobility through various forms of entrepreneurship have continued to decline. As this occurred, young people began to see diplomas and degrees as an alternate and less risky means to upward mobility as tickets to the newer white-collar jobs that had proliferated. This view was reflected in public support for the building of secondary

**Table 5.2. Educational Level Completed by Persons Age Twenty-Five and Over, 1910–2001**

| Year | High School | B.A. or Higher |
|------|-------------|----------------|
| 1910 | 13.5% | 2.7% |
| 1920 | 16.4% | 3.3% |
| 1930 | 19.1% | 3.9% |
| 1940 | 24.5% | 4.6% |
| 1950 | 34.3% | 6.2% |
| 1960 | 41.1% | 7.7% |
| 1970 | 55.2% | 11.0% |
| 1980 | 68.6% | 17.0% |
| 1990 | 77.6% | 21.3% |
| 2001 | 84.3% | 26.1% |

*Source*: Adapted from U.S. Department of Education, *Digest of Education Statistics, 2002*, Table 8 (Washington, D.C.: National Center for Education Statistics, 2002).

**Table 5.3. College Enrollment Rates of High School Graduates, 1960–2001**

| Year | Percent of High School Graduates Enrolled in College |
|------|------|
| 1960 | 45.1 |
| 1965 | 50.9 |
| 1970 | 51.8 |
| 1975 | 50.7 |
| 1980 | 49.3 |
| 1985 | 57.7 |
| 1990 | 59.9 |
| 1995 | 61.9 |
| 2001 | 61.7 |

*Source*: Adapted from U.S. Department of Education, *Digest of Education Statistics, 2002*, Table 184 (Washington, D.C.: National Center for Education Statistics, 2002).

schools and colleges and for provision of financial aid for those who wanted to attend college but lacked the economic means.

Between the end of World War II and today, the proportions of students attending and graduating from college have increased significantly (see table 5.3). Higher education has not completely replaced entrepreneurship as an avenue to economic success. However, building one's own business is an arduous task with high risk for failure. Given the uncertainties of entrepreneurship, even many business people prefer that their children pursue the less risky path of professional training rather than following in their footsteps as entrepreneurs.

These and similar data show that more Americans are enrolled in higher education today than ever before, and their numbers are growing. For example, from 1985 to 1998, enrollments increased 20%, and enrollments are projected to increase another 20% by 2010, with equal rates of increase in two-year and four-year institutions. Also from 1985 to 1998, the number of associate and bachelor's degrees granted increased 20%, and master's and doctoral degrees granted increased 49 and 41%, respectively (U.S. Department of Education 2000).

## THE PAPER CHASE

Over the past century, educational requirements for entry to jobs have spread to a wide range of occupations, keeping step with advances in educational attainment. The desire for more opportunity may be enough to increase the numbers of students seeking higher levels of schooling, but it does not in itself increase the probability that such hopes will be realized. Only a tightening link between educational qualifications and jobs can do that. An important facet of the school's changing role in social selection has to do with the rise of what Randall Collins (1979) has called *credentialism*, the monopolization of access to the more rewarding jobs and economic opportunities by the holders of education degrees and certificates.

In the process of credentials inflation, higher education degrees come to be required even for some jobs that may not be very intellectually demanding or for which an advanced degree would hardly seem necessary. For example, a college degree may not actually be needed to manage a video store. But if the pool of applicants for such a position comes to include holders of college degrees, they will tend to be selected over those without degrees, and soon a college degree will become a requirement. Once credentials are established as a requirement for hiring, inflationary pressures are strong, because students and their families have a strong interest in obtaining resources—in this case educational credentials that promise them greater opportunities. In short, the aspiration for upward mobility can "ratchet up" credential requirements above what they might otherwise be, producing credentials inflation. The result has been the proliferation of specialized occupational jurisdictions that are off-limits to anyone without the accepted educational credentials. Professional associations, governments, and educational institutions have each played a role in constructing occupations and carving the structure of occupations into a maze of occupational jurisdictions controlled by the holders of specialized credentials; all have a stake in the expansion of the "credential society" (Collins 1979; Brown 2001).

A related argument is that the growth of credentialism has been fueled primarily by the growth of large organizations and the incentives of those in positions of authority in these organizations to find efficient ways to process people and to fill positions. Those making hiring decisions can hardly have a deep knowledge of each of perhaps hundreds of applicants' job-relevant characteristics. Some "shorthand" is needed—objective "evidence" that can be presumed to indicate potential for success. Organizations have come to use educational credentials as an important component of this shorthand—as signals that their holders are more likely than other people to behave in organizationally valued ways. Thus, educational credentials have proven to be a cost-effective way to limit the pool of eligibles and to aid in the hiring of people who are presumed to have qualities that organizations value. For example, educational credentials may "signal" the ability of a job applicant to concentrate in a disciplined way on assigned problems, something that students must do repeatedly if they are to succeed in school. Other traits include reliability (simply showing up every day on time and in a work-ready state), the ability to handle nonroutine or self-directed work, and the ability to conform to the direction and desires of superiors. From the employers' point of view, it is a good bet that those who have survived all the paper writing and examinations of a college education have developed these qualities to a greater degree than those who have not.

Furthermore, as one moves up organizational hierarchies, the qualities that schooling selects may be even more important (Bourdieu 1984; Bourdieu and Passeron 1990). According to Blackburn and Mann, organizational careers are "fundamentally an apprenticeship in cooperation. . . . The essential point about jobs at the top of the hierarchy is not an unusual degree of skill but the costliness to management of error and the likelihood of error being made" (1979, 108). Therefore employers are often less concerned with possession of specific information and technical skills than with possession of cultural capital (arbitrary knowledge, manners and decorum, styles and tastes representative of privilege) and "noncognitive" characteristics such as discipline, steadiness, and responsibility.

Today, higher educational credentials are required for professional, technical, and managerial occupations and for most other nonclerical white-collar jobs in large private and public sector work organizations. These jobs represent a very large proportion of the most prestigious and best-paying jobs available. Even in the less credentialized sphere of business management, credentialism has grown rapidly. Almost no one is promoted up the ranks into top management today without a college degree, and an MBA from a top-ranked business school has become an important ticket of admission to the executive suite.

However, the widespread practice of using educational credentials as proxies for skills needed to do certain jobs is imperfect. Beyond literacy and basic computational skills, most of what people need to know to perform most work tasks is learned on the job, not in the classroom. Educational credentials are only an indirect means of assessing a person's capacity to perform such tasks. To the extent that educational "signals" used as convenient screening devices for job placement are inaccurate, true meritocracy is compromised. In such cases, education does not act as a vehicle of upward social mobility for the most deserving; instead, the *lack* of particular credentials operates as an artificial barrier to mobility.

Although credentialism has increased tremendously during the past century, certain spheres of the job structure have been affected less than others. For example, some people without educational qualifications continue to start and run successful farms and small businesses, and these continue to be handed down within families. In addition, access to jobs in numerous skilled trades (plumber, electrician) is regulated more by family networks and informal training than by formal education. However even here, state licensure, based on passing formal competency tests, is becoming the norm, and taken together, these represent a declining proportion of job opportunities in modern America.

## EDUCATION AND MOBILITY

The expansion of formal education and the rise of credentialism have substantially increased the importance of schooling in the process of social selection. In modern corporate America, with increasingly complex and bureaucratized work structures, educational credentials have become an important determinant of an individual's life chances. According to the American Dream, the educational system provides substantial opportunities for able and hardworking children from lower status families to move up, while requiring children from higher status families to at least prove themselves in school if they want to maintain their advantages. Among those who take this view, schools are likened to an elevator in which everyone gets on at the same floor but, depending on how well he or she does in school, gets off at a different floor corresponding to a particular level of occupational prestige and income.

James Bryant Conant, while president of Harvard University, wrote two articles (1938, 1940) that specified his view of the role of education in the process of social selection. He argued that democracy does not require a "uniform distribution of the world's goods" or a "radical equalization of wealth." What it requires instead is a "continuous process by which power and privilege may be automatically redistributed at the end of each generation" (Conant 1940, 598). He and other "meritocrats" considered schools to be the primary mechanism of redistribution. They doubted that talent was concentrated at the top of the social class structure but was instead rather evenly distributed throughout. By giving every student—from the most humble to the most privileged—an equal educational opportunity at the beginning of life, society would be in a position to select those most qualified by intelligence and hard work to occupy the command posts at the top. In this way, an "aristocracy of talent" would be re-created fresh in every generation. The argument neatly combines a principle of an "aristocracy" based on merit with a principle of democratic selection, or equality of opportunity.

In this view, the meritocratic foundation of the American Dream is its educational system—the primary engine of equality of opportunity. The educational system recognizes and rewards with diplomas and certificates those who work hardest, have the most ambition and perseverance, and possess the most talent and intelligence. These credentials in turn constitute the only legitimate basis for access to desirable jobs and other rewards of society. In short, the educational system recognizes and rewards the meritorious, regardless of the circumstances into which they are born, thus reducing inequalities based on nonmerit factors like birth or inheritance. To the extent that this notion of meritocracy is true, we should expect that (1) there should be little or no correlation between social class background and educational achievement and (2) educational achievement should be strongly and positively related to occupational rewards (prestige, authority, and income).

Two widely held social scientific theories imply meritocratic arguments. In sociology, the technical-functional theory of education suggests that one of the important functions of educational systems in modern society is to prepare people to become independent, economically productive adults. This means providing training and skills needed to fill occupations in America's modern and changing industrial economy. The educational requirements of jobs in industrial society constantly increase as a result of technological change. The proportion of jobs that require low skill declines while the proportion that requires high skill increases. What is more, the same jobs are continually upgraded in their skill requirements. The result is educational expansion: educational requirements for employment continually rise and more and more people are required to spend longer and longer periods in school. The most obvious meritocratic aspect of this theory is its clear claim that the opportunity to acquire training and skills is directly proportional to individual merit: talent and ability. By implication, educational expansion should reduce socioeconomic inequality, since educational opportunity is apportioned on the basis of individual merit, which is distributed equally among the social classes.

In economics, human capital theory (Schultz 1961; Becker 1993) suggests that human resources are a form of capital. Humans can invest in themselves to increase their capital, thereby increasing their productivity and their earnings. In modern society, the education system is the most important means through which individuals can invest in their "human capital" (skills and knowledge). In short, education increases productive capacities and thus earnings. The argument has considerable appeal: The worker is no mere "wage-earner" who holds no property and controls neither the work process nor the product of his labor, but instead is transformed into a capitalist. In this view, the worker is a holder of capital—human capital—and has the capacity to invest in himself through education.

## SOCIAL CLASS AND EDUCATION

Meritocracy requires equality of educational opportunity. The schooling system, however, provides the most privileged in society with greater opportunities to succeed and fewer chances to fail than it does for those from less privileged backgrounds. This is so because it frequently fails to identify and reward the potential and achievements of those who do not inherit the social, cultural, and economic capital of the privileged classes.

French sociologist Pierre Bourdieu emphasized that schools are instruments of social and cultural reproduction, which are means of social class reproduction (Bourdieu 1973; Bourdieu and Passeron 1990). According to Bourdieu, schools do not produce cultural capital or even the means to appropriate it. Instead, they recognize it, reward the possession of it, and certify its possession by differentially awarding educational credentials in proportion to the amount of cultural capital possessed. Children from lower classes with less cultural capital are eliminated from the system because of their cultural capital deficits, or self-eliminate as they come to recognize their low objective chances of success within the system. Thus, school tends to reinforce the cultural capital inequalities based on differences in family socioeconomic status.

While social reproduction theory began in Europe as a critique of the social class biases of the schooling system (cf. Bernstein 1961; Bourdieu 1973; Bourdieu and Passeron 1990), perhaps the most famous American example of reproduction theory is Samuel Bowles and Herbert Gintis's *Schooling in Capitalist America* (1976). They showed that while cognitive skills are important in the economy and in predicting individual success, the contribution of schooling to individual economic success can be explained only partly by the cognitive development fostered in schools. They argued that schools prepare children for adult work rules by socializing them to function well and without complaint in the hierarchical structure of the modern corporation. Schools accomplish this by what they called the "correspondence principle," namely, by structuring the social relations of school—interactions and individual rewards to replicate the environment of the workplace—the social relations of production. Bowles and Gintis (1976, 2002) focus attention not on the explicit curriculum but on the socialization implied by the structure of schooling, and demonstrate that the contribution of schooling to later economic success is explained only in part by the cognitive skills learned in school.

Finally, a good case can be made that although it might be at least theoretically possible for schools to select people on strictly meritocratic grounds, it is not possible for market economies to do the same. This is because markets do not reward according to the same merit criteria as schools but according to the economic value of the services/talents offered, which can vary as demand for them changes (see chapter 6).

To the extent that social reproduction theory is correct, we would expect to see a high level of status transmission through the education system. If cultural and social reproduction is a primary function of schooling, cognitive ability should count less than socioeconomic background, family-based possession of social and cultural capital, and noncognitive "personality" traits as predictors of who gets ahead in both school and jobs.

## STATUS ATTAINMENT RESEARCH

Although there were prior studies of "who gets ahead" in America, sociologists Peter Blau and Otis Dudley Duncan's *The American Occupational Structure*, published in 1967, produced an avalanche of research on the subject of social mobility—the overall amounts and patterns of movement in the occupational structure as well as what has come to be called status attainment, the process whereby a set of interrelated factors operate to determine which individuals "get ahead" educationally and occupationally. The latter research has produced the "Wisconsin School," so named because the Department of Sociology at the University of Wisconsin became the most important site devoted to the elaboration and extension of Blau and Duncan's initial work. The Wisconsin School, which has dominated the formulation of the questions and methods used to address the issue of status attainment, uses complex multivariate statistical techniques to examine an ever-increasing number of individual-level psychological and attitudinal characteristics that would seem to make a difference in the levels of education, status of occupations, and incomes that people eventually attain. These "status attainment" studies develop and test models that measure the independent effects of various attributes, such as socioeconomic background (parental education, occupation, income), measured mental ability (IQ for example), educational and occupational aspirations, and the influence of significant others on these aspirations, by statistically holding other variables in the model constant.

In a nutshell, these studies indicate that there is a mixture of merit or "achieved" and nonmerit or "ascribed" factors that help explain variations in educational, occupational, and income attainment. Family background (socioeconomic status) is an important ascribed factor that indirectly affects educational attainment through its effects on "significant others" and aspirations. In turn, educational attainment has a sizable effect on occupational attainment, but it is important to remember that educational attainment is itself influenced by ascribed factors, some of which are not included in these models.

While these studies seem to do a good job explaining educational attainment, one very important finding is that most of the variation in people's adult occupational status and income cannot be predicted by the individual-level "merit" characteristics included. In fact, measures of family socioeconomic status, cognitive ability, and educational attainment together leave the majority of the variation in adult occupational status and income unexplained. Thus, neither educational attainment nor family socioeconomic status do a very good job of accounting for variations in adult success as measured by occupational status and income.

Both family socioeconomic status (SES) and measured cognitive ability do show up as important explanatory factors for that part of the variation in people's adult attainments than can be explained, primarily because they both influence the likelihood that a person will obtain high-level educational credentials. Children with high cognitive test scores are more likely to end up with good educational credentials, even if they were not born into a privileged family. Conversely, growing up in a privileged family means that children are likely to end up with good educational credentials, even if they do not have especially high test scores or superior academic performance.

These studies of status attainment report that for recent cohorts, especially for recent cohorts of men, cognitive ability is more important than family background in predicting educational attainment. Grades and cognitive test scores are the best single predictors of educational attainment (measured as number of years of schooling or highest degree earned). Even so, family background never disappears as an explanatory factor because it helps to predict test scores, and it also has a modest direct effect on how much schooling a person attains, regardless of test scores.

Other factors that have been found to have an independent effect on educational attainment once family background and cognitive ability are statistically controlled include having an intact two-parent household, having families and friends who value education (social capital), taking academic courses (especially courses in math and science), having a father whose occupation depends on high educational attainment (cultural capital), and having strong personal aspirations to succeed.

Clearly, high-level education credentials are an important key to obtaining prestigious and well-paid jobs, and research suggests that people who finish higher level degrees have a "leg up" in the labor market even if they are not otherwise advantaged. This is because the people who tend to move up are those who have the same habits and skills that brought them success in school: they show up regularly and on time, are diligent, and have good reasoning abilities.

Recently, an important weakness of status attainment research, the inability to adequately examine the process of occupational attainment across the course of individuals' lives, has been addressed. Sociologists John Robert Warren, Robert Hauser, and Jennifer Sheridan used data from the Wisconsin Longitudinal Study to examine changes with age in the consequences of family background, gender, educational attainment, and cognitive ability for occupational attainment. They report that

> family background variables affect occupational standing only indirectly, through their effects on education and cognitive ability. The effects of education decline substantially with age. . . . In general, the total effect of years of education on current or last occupation is about two-thirds of its effect on the standing of first occupation. . . . Education has a powerful effect on the standing of first occupation, first occupation has a powerful effect on the standing of second occupation, and so forth. There are positive, direct effects of cognitive ability on occupational standing throughout the life course . . . however, these effects are substantively small at all observed points in the occupation career. These effects appear to remain stable between first and current or last occupations. (2002, 450)

## THE LIMITATIONS OF STATUS ATTAINMENT RESEARCH

While status attainment studies have made important contributions to our understanding of "who gets ahead," this essentially individualistic perspective has produced results that are incomplete and sometimes misleading. Individual-level psychological, attitudinal characteristics, and "human capital" resources of people—intelligence, aspirations, and the like are assumed by these models to be the most important factors relevant to the attainment of education, occupational status, and income.

Status attainment models, however, have tended to underestimate the effects of ascriptive factors, but more important, they neglect the effects of impersonal economic forces structures of occupational and industrial opportunity ("demand-side" variables)—that are beyond the control of individuals and have a role in determining the payoff of human capital resources (see chapter 6).

Occupations can be ranked in terms of numerous characteristics, including status or prestige, complexity, technical skill, authority, and property divisions. Status attainment research, however, has focused on only one aspect of occupational success—occupational status or prestige—and has not done a very good job explaining that.

Status attainment models underestimate the effects of family background (socioeconomic status) because the measures of family background used are typically incomplete (often including only measures of father's [and sometimes mother's] education, income, or occupational status) and suffer problems of measurement validity. Other aspects of family background may have substantial effects if included in these models. Differences in wealth (Conley 1999), differences in amounts and kinds of inter vivos inheritance (Miller and McNamee 1998), and differences in amounts of social and cultural capital provided by the family (see chapter 4) have all been shown to independently account for additional variation in educational, occupational, and income attainment.

Discrimination on the basis of any number of ascribed characteristics, including race and ethnicity, gender, age, sexuality, disability status, and even "looks," can affect educational, occupational, and income attainment (see chapters 8 and 9). A substantial body of research documents the persistence of such discrimination as well as its deleterious effects.

At best, the status attainment models account for only about half of the variance in occupational attainment and only about 40% of the variance in income. Over the past two decades, it has become increasingly clear that some of the unexplained variation in life fates simply has nothing to do with individual-level characteristics. Instead, it has everything to do with the effects of societal-level variables, including demand side factors like the ups and downs of local markets, companies, industries, regions, the national, and even the global economy (see chapter 6). Economic returns for identical jobs that require identical levels of educational attainment, for instance, vary widely depending on where the work is done (e.g., location and sector of the economy) and for whom (type of employing organization). In short, individuals are subject to complex and shifting structures of demand, the vicissitudes of history, accident, employers' decisions (rational and nonrational), and their own decisions (good and bad). While some of the unexplained variation in "who gets ahead" no doubt has to do with "being in the right place at the right time" and similar factors of good or bad fortune, we must remember that these are actually individual-level reflections of structurally based demand for talents, skills, and experience. It thus seems clear that much of the variance in occupation and income left unexplained in the status attainment models is accounted for by structural-level variables.

## THE SOCIAL CONSTRUCTION OF "INDIVIDUAL" MERIT

Education certifies individual skills, knowledge, and other competencies in the form of diplomas, certificates, and degrees. These certifications are not merely purchased or assigned; individuals must demonstrate competencies through examination and other forms of assessment. Such certifications therefore are widely regarded as evidence of personal achievement and individual merit. The opportunity to acquire such competencies, however, is socially constructed. In this way, education performs a dual role in both certifying individual achievement and reproducing existing inequalities (Aschaffenburg and Mass 1997; Bourdieu and Passeron 1990).

There are several ways in which the social construction of individual merit occurs. Children from privileged families, for instance, are more likely to be the beneficiaries of home environments that promote cognitive development and provide the social and cultural capital needed to do well in school. Therefore, privileged children are already ahead of the less privileged in cognitive ability, social skills, and cultural capital when they enter school. They are also more likely to attend "good" schools that are staffed by competent and experienced teachers, provide an academic college preparatory curriculum, and are populated by other privileged students. Once in school, teacher expectations build on these initial advantages: Teachers expect more of children from higher class backgrounds, and differential treatment based on these expectations leads to better performance among these children (Rosenthal and Jacobson 1968; Rist 1970; Good and Brophy 1987).

Another practice that jeopardizes equality of educational opportunity is tracking. Approximately five out of six U.S. public schools use some form of tracking in which children are placed in different groups or tracks that prepare some for college and others for vocational skills that do not lead to college. There has been much research on the factors that influence track placement and the outcomes of such placement, but conclusions are complex because of the variety of tracking systems in use. One early study showed that all factors that could conceivably be taken to measure cognitive ability and academic performance *together explain less than half of the variation in track placement.* So much for the argument that individual "merit" measured by cognitive ability and academic performance is the primary determinant of track placement. While many studies do show that measured intellectual skills are factors most directly responsible for track placement (Jencks et al. 1972, 35; Heyns 1974), recall that cognitive skills and academic performance are influenced by family SES. In short, tracking has tended to separate children by class background and race.

The outcomes of tracking are also fairly clear. First, track mobility is typically low: Once placed in a low track, it is difficult to "move up," and for those placed in a high track, it is difficult to do poorly enough to "move down." In short, tracking affects teacher expectations, access to quality teachers, and access to courses needed for college eligibility. Tracking produces self-fulfilling prophecies. Children in higher college preparatory tracks tend to improve in academic achievement over the years, while those in lower tracks tend to perform at levels that make them ineligible for higher education. Children in higher tracks are less likely to drop out of school, have higher educational aspirations, and are more likely to attend college. In short, tracking works to reinforce class differences and has an independent effect of further differentiating children in terms of family background (Alexander, Cook, and McDill 1978, 57; Gamoran and Mare 1989).

There is a vast body of research on the effects of school quality on educational attainment, but the findings are contradictory and not easy to sort out. At first, it seemed unnecessary to demonstrate that sizable differences in school quality "obviously" produce inequality of educational opportunity. However, early research by Coleman (1966) and Jencks et al. (1972) seemed to show that a number of measures of school quality did *not* show significant relationships with outcomes such as test scores and later college attendance. These surprising findings did not deter those whose intuition and experience convinced them that school quality does, in fact, affect educational attainment. The findings of more than thirty-five years of research are mixed: Some differences in educational, occupational, and income attainment are attributable to school quality, but the net effects of school quality are relatively small.

Perhaps the best conclusion is that school quality does, in fact, affect educational and subsequent attainments. However, the net effects of school quality are difficult to determine because school quality is partially the product of the socioeconomic composition of student bodies. First, it is clear that however measured, school quality does vary considerably, not only across school districts but also among schools within the same district. It is also clear that among the schools available in a given locale, children from higher-income families tend to attend what are generally acknowledged as the "better" schools because their parents can either afford to live in areas where the public schools are better or can afford to send their children to private schools that provide valued high-prestige credentials. The public schools attended by children from higher-income families are better because a significant portion of school funding comes from local property taxes (U.S. Department of Education 2000, Table 160 and Figure 11), which produce more revenue in privileged residential areas.

But this is only part of the story. Schools in these areas are "better" for reasons other than amount of economic resources spent on students. High-income families, living in high-income residential areas, not only provide a strong tax base that can be tapped to fund quality schools; such families also have the political clout needed to more effectively demand quality education for their children. Further, as noted above, the children of high-income families bring considerable cognitive ability as well as social and cultural capital with them to the schools. Finally, the socioeconomic composition of the student body contributes to the formation of school climates or cultures that can prove beneficial or harmful to academic and subsequent occupational attainment. For example, students benefit from peers and "significant others" who exhibit high educational and occupational aspirations because they contribute to educational and occupational attainment. Thus, school quality not only varies by amounts and kinds of economic inputs; it also varies by social, cultural, and intellectual composition of the students, and these vary by family SES.

Finally, it is clear that parents believe that there are real differences in school quality and that school quality affects their children's chances for future academic and occupational success. Thus, parents are willing to pay the higher costs of housing in residential areas served by "quality" schools. But of course, variation in income means that not all parents can equally afford these higher housing costs. As a result, many parents go into considerable debt to advance their children's futures (Warren and Warren Tyagi 2003). In fact, one of the main causes of personal bankruptcy is defaults on mortgages. We suggest that a sizable but unknown number of these bankruptcies represent cases of family attempts to procure quality education for their children.

## HAS EDUCATIONAL EXPANSION LED TO GREATER SOCIAL MOBILITY?

By now it should be clear that some Americans do "get ahead." However, we have also shown (see especially chapter 3) that the extent of such mobility has been exaggerated and that the forces that reproduce inequalities across generations are strong.

Have advantages of the privileged been reduced by the expansion of education? If we examine the correlation between family background and educational attainments over time (Isheda et al. 1995), we see that differences among socioeconomic groups have not narrowed despite the vast expansion of schooling. This is because high-status parents continue to have greater

economic, social, and cultural resources to provide better educational opportunities for their children than do lower-status parents.

What is more, school systems have responded to increased demand for
credentials in ways that have not reduced class advantages. Educational expansion has been accompanied by the development of an elaborately differentiated structure of tiers and quality levels. Lower-status children tend to
be limited to the lower tiers of the system and channeled into the lower quality sectors within tiers, while upper-status children are more likely to make
it into the higher tiers and enjoy the advantages of the higher quality sectors
within each tier. In short, educational expansion has simply led to segregation within tier and the transfer of class differences to higher levels of the system. For example, when working-class children became better represented
in high school, college became the key to higher social status. When work-
ing- and lower-middle-class children began to enter college in larger numbers, the system shifted again to a higher point, and graduate or professional
school has become the key to higher social status. Thus, increases in educational attainment are completely compatible with stable levels of social inequality and class reproduction.

Most studies have found declining correlations between father's status and
children's educational attainments over the course of the century. But this decreasing correlation doesn't necessarily mean that class inequality has been
reduced at the highest levels of the system where credentials are most valuable. Instead, this lower correlation largely reflects the decreasing variation in
the amount of schooling children receive and the higher average levels of
schooling in the population. Blossfeld and Shavit (1993) conclude that educational expansion is compatible with little movement toward greater equality across socioeconomic groups in the distribution of the most valuable years
of schooling or the most valuable degrees. In short, the odds of receiving the
most school or the most valuable degrees are still highest for students of high-
status families. Privileged families continue to successfully convert economic
advantages into social and cultural advantages that help their children go further in school than others usually do, and then reconvert school credentials
into economic (occupational, income, and wealth) advantages.

## FAMILY BACKGROUND AND HIGHER EDUCATION

Access to good jobs and most other forms of opportunity has become increasingly dependent on educational attainment, and credentials inflation has
made a college degree a requirement for most of the desirable white-collar
jobs. Most of the family background factors and their correlates discussed
above are also important in college admissions and attendance, but much of
the effect of family background on college admissions and attendance is indi-

rect. Parents with high socioeconomic status are more likely to encourage their children to go to college, provide role models leading to higher educational aspirations, and create a social environment for their children in which their peer groups are composed of other privileged children. In short, having privileged parents and privileged peers promotes educational aspirations and attainment.

If college admissions and attendance were based mostly on cognitive ability or intelligence, there would be much less class reproduction. But as we have noted, socioeconomic inequality operates to weaken the relationship between cognitive ability and college attendance. Family background differences in college completion are also striking. Even at the height of the equal opportunity era in the United States—roughly from the end of World War II until 1980—bright children whose fathers had blue-collar occupations were less likely than other children to obtain a college degree. Using General Social Survey data, sociologists Hout, Raftery, and Bell (1993, 46) found that unskilled blue-collar workers' children who had high IQs (top 14% on a word recognition test) who reached college age in the 1950s and early 1960s had slightly more than a 50% chance of completing college. This was significantly lower than the 80% chance of graduating enjoyed by high IQ children who had professional or managerial fathers. And it was not even as good a chance as the 70% completion rate enjoyed by children of all IQ levels who were lucky enough to have been born into families in the top tenth of the occupational hierarchy. In short, controlling for cognitive ability, children from privileged backgrounds are more likely to attend college, to start college right out of high school, to go to a four-year institution, to go to a "quality" college or university, and to graduate on time.

Interestingly, college attendance seems to provide significant occupational and income rewards only for those who graduate. On average, those who have completed "some college" (one to three years) do not earn much more than those who have only completed high school (see table 5.1). This strongly suggests that it is the *credential*, and not the increments of information or skill provided by each additional year, that counts.

For those who do begin college, family background is not a very strong predictor of ultimate college completion. This is primarily because the socioeconomic backgrounds of college students are relatively homogeneous. Thus, after a considerable proportion of the working class sorted out into technical or community colleges and most of the middle class moves on to four-year colleges and universities to collect their degrees, family background doesn't seem to account for much variation in measures of college achievement (GPA or even college completion). This should not be surprising, because constants—in this case family background (most students who begin college at four-year schools are middle or upper-middle class) can't account for differences in anything! And the converse is also true: no variable can account for phenomena that show little variation. That is, no variable can

explain a constant. There is actually not that much variation in most measures of college academic achievement. College grade point average is an
excellent example. Students who have GPAs of less than 2.00 are usually required to leave, and very few students have perfect 4.0 GPAs. This leaves an
effective range of less than 2.0. Grade inflation and the use of college "re-
tention rates" as a measure of excellence has reduced that range further:
most GPAs fall between 2.5 and 3.5. Now, if more than 80% of those who begin eventually graduate, and most have averages between 2.5 and 3.5, there
is very little variation in college academic performance to explain. Thus, it is
not surprising that research has shown that what is essentially a constant individual academic "merit" (as measured by college GPA) shows only a weak
relationship to something that does vary widely: later income attainment.

Finally, research seems to show that type or quality of college attended
has only a weak net effect on later occupational or income attainment
(Jencks et al. 1979, 226; Sewell and Hauser 1975, 141). We should expect this
for two important reasons. First, in 1998 there were approximately 4,064 institutions of higher education in the United States (U.S. Department of Education 2000, Table 246). Despite their posturing and claims of "excellence,"
except for their names, locations, and other secondary characteristics, the
majority of these institutions are essentially indistinguishable in terms of
"quality." The top fifty "national universities" and the top fifty "national liberal arts colleges" as identified by U.S. News and World Report's *America's
Best Colleges, 2001 Edition* (2000), constitute *less than 2.5%* of all colleges
and universities and grant an even smaller proportion of the degrees. Their
effects are simply statistically "drowned out" by the vast numbers graduated
by the other 3,964 "non-elite" colleges and universities. For example,
Swarthmore College, ranked first among the top fifty "national liberal arts
colleges," has an enrollment of less than 1,700 and typically graduates fewer
than 400 students per year. By contrast, in 1997, *each* of the 100 largest colleges and universities had an enrollment over 21,000. What is more, the total enrollment for the ten largest institutions was over 465,000, and *each* had
an enrollment over 40,000 (U.S. Department of Education 2000, Table 219).
Second, while the incomes of graduates of "elite" or "highly selective" colleges and universities are higher, the *net* effect, or "value added," of such institutions may be low simply because all their students are privileged, have
high cognitive ability, or both. In short, after the effects of family background
and cognitive ability are factored out, there is not much variation left for
"school quality" to explain.

We conclude that education in America, including higher education, is not
governed by strict principles of meritocracy, but instead reflects, legitimizes,
and reproduces class inequalities. Those from privileged families (top quarter
of an index of socioeconomic status composed of parents' education, income,
and occupation) are three times as likely as those from less privileged fami-

lies to be admitted to elite highly selective colleges and universities (Sacks 2003, 7). This is because all the advantages of class that we have already discussed—inherited familial economic resources (which translate into "quality education" and high educational aspirations), social capital (which include parental "connections" and positive peer influences), and cultural capital— collectively produce K–12 educational outcomes, including high grade point averages, standardized and AP test scores, and SAT scores, that are the primary selection criteria for America's "best" colleges and universities. Thus, the advantages of high class produce the credentials sought by America's elite universities. But there are additional advantages that accrue to class privilege, ranging from the simple ability to *pay* for an elite private college or university education, to the financial ability to take advantage of "early acceptance" programs at such institutions, to elaborate, back-channel "slotting" operations in which highly connected and expert high school and prep counselors work closely with admissions officials to virtually place high SES students at these institutions. Finally, "the increasing concentration of wealth and power among [these select elite institutions] . . . sets them apart from the public colleges and universities in terms of their respective roles in the nurturing of young talent for positions of leadership and lives of intellectual creativity" (Sacks 2003, 10). In short, America's system of higher education is clearly not an "engine of meritocracy" but rather a basic component in a system that reproduces unequal starting points from one generation to the next.

## SUMMARY

Being bright, working hard, and getting more education do help people get ahead. But there is more to it than that. First, the competition for success is structured by an educational system that does not provide equality of opportunity. Second, quite independent of individual ability, the demands of a complex and changing corporate economy condition opportunities and the likelihood for success.

Equality of educational opportunity is a crucial component of the American Dream, but it has never come close to existing in America. Family socioeconomic status and other ascribed characteristics directly and indirectly affect educational attainment. Schools both reflect and re-create existing inequalities in society. Schools reward children of the privileged by certifying and enhancing their social and cultural capital. On the other hand, schools punish children of lower socioeconomic status for their lack of such capital, consigning them to teachers, curricula, tracks, and the self-fulfilling prophecies of low expectations that these produce. The results are that less privileged children are awarded fewer and lower-valued credentials, and inequality is largely reproduced across generations.

The inequalities reproduced across generations are substantial but far from perfect. In part this is because some parents, regardless of class position, are more successful in promoting the futures of their children. And some children, regardless of class position, are more capable than others. As a result, some rich kids fail and some poor kids succeed. These exceptions, however infrequently they do occur, help to sustain at least the outward appearance of meritocracy and the American Dream.

## REFERENCES

Alexander, Karl, Martha Cook, and Edward McDill. 1978. "Curriculum Tracking and Educational Stratification: Some Further Evidence." *American Sociological Review* 43: 47–66.

Aschaffenburg, Karen, and Ineke Mass. 1997. "Cultural and Educational Careers: The Dynamics of Social Reproduction." *American Sociological Review* 62: 573–87.

Becker, Gary S. 1993. *Human Capital: A Theoretical and Empirical Analysis with Special Reference to Education*. New York: Columbia University Press.

Becker, Gary S., and Nigel Tomes. 1986. "Human Capital and the Rise and Fall of Families." *Journal of Labor Economics* 4: S1–S39.

Berg, Ivar. 1971. *Education and Jobs: The Great Training Robbery*. Boston: Beacon.

Bernstein, Basil. 1961. "Social Class and Linguistic Development: A Theory of Social Learning." Pp. 288–314 in *Education, Economy, and Society*, edited by A. H. Halsey, Jean Floud, and C. Arnold Anderson. New York: Free Press.

Blackburn, Robin M., and Michael Mann. 1979. *The Working Class in the Labour Market*. London: Macmillan.

Blau, Peter, and Otis Dudley Duncan. 1967. *The American Occupational Structure*. New York: John Wiley.

Blossfeld, Hans-Peter, and Yossi Shavit. 1993. "Persisting Barriers: Changes in Educational Opportunities in Thirteen Countries." Pp. 1–24 in *Persistent Inequality*, edited by Yossi Shavit and Hans-Peter Blossfeld. Boulder, Colo.: Westview.

Bourdieu, Pierre. 1973. "Cultural Reproduction and Social Reproduction." Pp. 71–112 in *Knowledge, Education, and Cultural Change*, edited by Richard Brown. London: Tavistock.

———. 1984. *Distinction*. Cambridge, Mass.: Harvard University Press.

Bourdieu, Pierre, and Jean-Claude Passeron. 1990. *Reproduction in Education, Society, and Culture*. London: Sage.

Bowles, Samuel, and Herbert Gintis. 1976. *Schooling in Capitalist America*. New York: Basic Books.

———. 2002. "*Schooling in Capitalist America* Revisited." *Sociology of Education* 75: 1–18.

Brint, Steven, and Jerome Karabel. 1989. *The Diverted Dream: Community Colleges and the Promise of Education Opportunity in America, 1900–1980*. New York: Oxford University Press.

Brown, David K. 1995. *Degrees of Control: A Sociology of Educational Expansion and Occupational Credentialism*. New York: Teachers College Press.

———. 2001. "The Social Sources of Educational Credentialism: Status Cultures, Labor Markets, and Organizations." *Sociology of Education* (Extra Issue): 19–34.

Carnegie, Andrew. 1899. "Wealth." *North American Review* 148: 653–64.

Coleman, James S., et al. 1966. *Equality of Educational Opportunity*. Washington, D.C.: U.S. Government Printing Office.

Collins, Randall. 1971. "Functional and Conflict Theories of Educational Stratification." *American Sociological Review* 36: 1002–19.

———. 1979. *The Credential Society*. New York: Academic Press.

Conant, James Bryant. 1938. "The Future of Our Higher Education." *Harper's Magazine* 176 (May): 561–70.

———. 1940. "Education for a Classless Society: The Jeffersonian Tradition." *The Atlantic* 165 (May): 593–602.

Conley, Dalton. 1999. *Being Black, Living in the Red: Race, Wealth, and Social Policy in America*. Berkeley: University of California Press.

Gamoran, Adam, and Robert D. Mare. 1989. "Secondary School Tracking and Educational Inequality: Compensation, Reinforcement, or Neutrality?" *American Journal of Sociology* 94: 1146–83.

Good, Thomas, and Jere Brophy. 1987. *Looking in Classrooms*. New York: Harper & Row.

Heyns, Barbara. 1974. "Social Selection and Stratification within Schools." *American Journal of Sociology* 79: 1434–51.

Hout, Michael, Adrian E. Raftery, and Eleanor O. Bell. 1993. "Making the Grade: Educational Stratification in the United States, 1925–1989." Pp. 25–49 in *Persistent Inequality: Changing Inequality in Thirteen Countries*, edited by Yossi Shavit and Hans-Peter Blossfeld. Boulder, Colo.: Westview.

Isheda, Hisoshi, Walter Muller, and John M. Ridge. 1995. "Class Origin, Class Destination, and Education: A Cross-National Study of Ten Industrial Societies." *American Journal of Sociology* 101: 145–93.

Jencks, Christopher L., et al. 1972. *Inequality: Reassessment of the Effect of Family and Schooling in America*. New York: Harper & Row.

Jencks, Christopher, et al. 1979. *Who Gets Ahead?* New York: Basic Books.

Kozol, Jonathan. 1991. *Savage Inequalities: Children in America's Schools*. New York: HarperPerennial.

Miller, Robert K., Jr., and Stephen J. McNamee, eds. 1998. *Inheritance and Wealth in America*. New York: Plenum.

Rist, Ray C. 1970. "Student Social Class and Teachers' Expectations: The Self-Fulfilling Prophecy in Ghetto Education." *Harvard Educational Review* 40: 411–50.

Rosenthal, Robert, and Lenore Jacobson. 1968. *Pygmalion in the Classroom*. New York: Holt, Rinehart & Winston.

Sacks, Peter. 2003. "Class Rules: The Fiction of Egalitarian Higher Education." *The Chronicle of Higher Education* 49 (July 25): B7–10.

Schultz, Theodore W. 1961. "Investment in Human Capital." *American Economic Review* 51: 1–17.

Sewell, William, and Robert Hauser. 1975. *Education, Occupation, and Earnings: Achievement in the Early Career*. New York: Academic Press.

U.S. Census Bureau. 2002. *Current Population Survey, Detailed Tables PPL-169*. Washington, D.C.: U.S. Government Printing Office.

U.S. Department of Education. 2000. *Digest of Education Statistics, 1999*. Washington, D.C.: National Center for Education Statistics.

———. 2002. *Digest of Education Statistics, 2002*. Washington, D.C.: National Center for Education Statistics.

U.S. News and World Report. 2000. *America's Best Colleges, 2001 Edition*. Washington, D.C.: U.S. News and World Report.

Warren, Elizabeth, and Amelia Warren Tyagi. 2003. *The Two-Income Trap: Why Middle-Class Mothers and Fathers Are Going Broke*. New York: Basic Books.

Warren, John Robert, Robert M. Hauser, and Jennifer T. Sheridan. 2002. "Occupational Stratification across the Life Course: Evidence from the Wisconsin Longitudinal Study." *American Sociological Review* 67: 432–55.

# 6

# Being in the Right Place at the Right Time: The Luck Factor

*I think we consider too much the good luck of the early bird, and not enough the bad luck of the early worm.*

—Franklin Delano Roosevelt

*My aspiration now is to get by luck what I could not get by merit.*

—Mason Cooley, U.S. aphorist (b. 1927)

In thinking about who ends up with what jobs, Americans tend to first think about what economists call the "supply" side. In labor economics, the "supply side" refers to the pool of workers available to fill jobs. The ideology of meritocracy leads Americans to focus on the qualities of individual workers— how smart they are, how qualified they are, how much education they have, and so on. These "human capital" factors, however, represent only half of the equation. The other half, the "demand side," is about the number and types of jobs available. How many jobs are available, how much those jobs pay, and how many people are seeking those jobs are important but often neglected considerations in assessing the impact of merit on economic outcomes. In this chapter we explore the implications of the demand side and being at the right place at the right time.

## FROM FARMER TO FACTORY WORKER TO SALES CLERK

The history of the American labor force can be summarized by three jobs— farmer, factory worker, sales clerk. Figure 6.1 depicts historical changes in

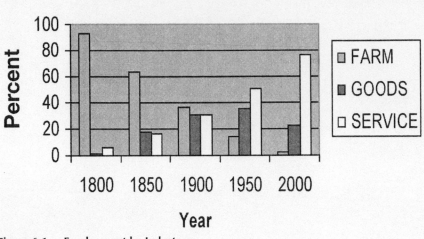

**Figure 6.1.    Employment by Industry**

the American labor force comparing farming, manufacturing, and service occupations. In colonial times, the vast majority of American workers were
farmers. Many worked their own small family farms. Corporations did not
exist. America for the most part was an agrarian and land-based society. With
the beginning of the Industrial Revolution in the mid-nineteenth century,
what the average worker did for a living began to change. Farming became
progressively more mechanized. Herbicides, pesticides, tractors, harvesters,
and other heavy equipment gradually replaced field hands. America could
grow more food with less human labor. By the end of the nineteenth century, urban factories were booming. Displaced farm laborers moved in large
numbers from the rural countryside to urban centers in search of factory
jobs.

More Americans were now factory workers, operating machines that
turned raw goods into finished products. Most were machine operators; some
were skilled craftsmen—electricians, millwrights, tool and die makers, and
the like. Corporations replaced family businesses, and the rate of self-
employment sharply declined. By the middle of the twentieth century, manufacturing had reached its peak. Manufacturing jobs as a proportion of the labor force in the United States, while still significant, began to decline. The rate
of decline accelerated in the latter part of the twentieth century as manufacturing increasingly shifted overseas, where labor was cheaper, less unionized,
and less regulated. At the same time, farming occupations as a proportion of
the total labor force fell off even more precipitously. In the wake of these
changes, the service sector of the economy exploded in growth and now far
outstrips farming and manufacturing as a source of employment. The service

sector includes a mixed bag of occupations ranging from hairstylists to insurance agents, to sales clerks, to computer programmers—all having to do in some way with processing either information or people or both. Instead of being a field hand on the farm or a machine operator in the factory, the typical worker in America is now a sales clerk in a department store.

These changes are significant in terms of how people "experience" intergenerational mobility. Each generation encounters a different array of "slots" to be filled. The changes in the "tasks" that need to be done are not a reflection of individual merit. They are the result of changes in technology and concomitant changes in the division of labor, changes in economic and political policy, and changes in the global economy. Sociologists refer to mobility caused by changes in the division of labor in society as "structural mobility."

For most of the twentieth century, the types of slots available to be filled represented a generalized occupational upgrading. Unskilled farm labor, the backbone of an agrarian economy, was being replaced by factory and office work. Factory work included many "blue-collar" semiskilled and skilled jobs—an upgrading in terms of both earnings and social status. Compared to farming and manufacturing, office work in the service sector was cleaner, less dangerous, less physically demanding, and often conferred higher social status. The general standard of living also rapidly increased. Most of the upward "movement" individuals experienced compared to their parents was the result of these structural changes, not individual merit. The college educated computer programmer whose father was a high school educated factory worker whose father before him was a grade school educated farmer is not necessarily smarter, more motivated, or of higher moral caliber than his father or grandfather. Each faced very different opportunity structures. Fueled by the ideology of meritocracy, however, individuals swept up in these waves of social change are often quick to falsely attribute their rise in social standing to individual merit alone.

Beginning in the early 1970s, the ground shifted. Several trends coalesced to radically alter the American occupational landscape. First, U.S. industrial corporations were, for the first time, beginning to feel the pinch of increasing foreign competition. In the immediate aftermath of World War II, the United States emerged from the conflict as the only industrial nation that had not had its industrial infrastructure damaged or destroyed. Under these conditions, the United States easily dominated global markets. As part of the postwar recovery effort, the United States helped rebuild Germany and Japan. Germany and Japan—among other nations—were now emerging as serious competitors. In 1973, an oil embargo imposed by the Organization of Petroleum Exporting Countries (OPEC) sharply increased production costs, especially detrimental to industries with the least efficient production facilities. The automobile industry in the United States, which had been the backbone of America's postwar industrial might, suffered dramatically from these changes. Japan and Germany, producing smaller, more fuel efficient, and higher quality automobiles, made significant inroads into the American automobile market. Similar scenarios were played out as well in other industries, including steel, textiles, and chemicals—all of which had been part of America's postwar industrial strength.

To compensate for these losses, American industry sought new strategies. In what economists Bennett Harrison and Barry Bluestone (1990) characterize as "the Great U-Turn," American corporations responded to these new competitive pressures through massive corporate "restructuring." Several strategies were pursued simultaneously, including shifting sites of production, encouraging "supply side" government policy, and "downsizing." To reduce costs of production, corporations began shifting production away from the urban industrial centers in the North Central and Northeast parts of the United States to the South and Southwest. As part of the pressure to keep production facilities open or operating in the United States, those that did remain often extracted "concessions" and "give-backs" from workers, further reducing wages and benefits. Corporations aggressively tried to break up existing unions and prevent new ones from forming. These moves reduced costs of production by relocating factory production to states with lower wages, less unionization, and less government regulation. Corporations also aggressively shifted production overseas to take even greater advantage of these savings. As part of "downsizing" campaigns, corporations replaced permanent higher paid workers with "outsourced" contract labor and increased temporary and contingent labor.

At the same time, corporations pressed for changes in government policy. Corporate America found a sympathetic sponsor for these changes in the Reagan administrations, which lowered corporate taxes, deregulated large segments of the economy, and reduced welfare to the poor. Operating in a new climate of relaxed government regulation, big business entered into a frenzy of megamergers, takeovers, and acquisitions. Most mergers resulted in layoffs as combined entities realized savings from increased economies of scale. Billions of dollars were taken out of the economy to finance megamergers. Through mergers and stock manipulations, investors could make money without necessarily increasing production or creating new jobs. When the dust cleared, there were fewer bigger corporations. Wages fell, profits rose, and inequality increased. Economic mobility declined; job instability increased.

Millions of American workers were caught up in the tidal force of these structural changes. Hardest hit were male blue-collar factory workers. Thousands of jobs in the manufacturing sector were lost. In the postwar period, it had been possible for many working-class Americans to realize the American Dream by working in factories with good pay, good benefits, and long-term job stability. With "deindustrialization" and "downsizing," many of these workers were laid off. New jobs were created, but these were mostly in the "soft" low-wage, low-skill, service sector. Legions of working-class men who had poured through the factory gates at the height of the industrial era were now displaced.

Reflecting on her interviews with these workers, economist Paula Rayman put it this way:

> During the early 1980s, many workers in American who thought they had it made in the major industrial corporations of auto, steel, and aircraft found themselves unemployed. . . .They had done everything right: worked hard, done a fair day's work for a fair day's pay. But through no fault of their own, they found themselves cast out of work. And even though they were unemployed because of economic decisions not in their control, they felt personal shame for their failure to hold a job. . . . The personalization of job-loss experiences in the United States is common to many employees from many industries. The Horatio Alger myth is very powerful: the belief that if you rise up, it is due to your own efforts, and if you sink, it is due to your own failures. There is not a powerful story that supports the view that an individual's job history reflects larger situational and organizational forces. In America, the stories are private, based on the individual, not social or based on institutional contexts. (2001, 70, 71)

The American economy has been transformed from auto, steel, and aircraft to hamburgers, day care, and blue-light specials. Table 6.1 shows the Department of Labor's projection of what will be the fastest growing twenty-five jobs in America between 2000 and 2010. This table identifies jobs that are producing the most new slots in the labor force. With a few exceptions such as system analysts, general managers, and college professors, most of the jobs are in the low-wage service sector. Sixty percent of the jobs on the list require only "short-term on-the-job training." Only 20% require a college degree, and only one of those (college professor) requires a graduate degree. The number one fastest growing job in America is "food preparation and serving workers including fast food," emblematic of the new working class. Also included in the list are other low-paid service jobs such as retail sales, cashiers, office clerks, security guards, waiters and waitresses, janitors and cleaners, home health aides, personal and home care aides, and receptionists.

## ALL DRESSED UP AND NOWHERE TO GO

Even if every adult in America were college educated, the "demand" for these slots would remain the same. The only difference is that we would have more college-educated workers filling these slots and higher rates of underemployment in society as a whole. As levels of educational attainment in the population have increased, and as the economy has fallen short of producing jobs that require more education, rates of underemployment have

**Table 6.1.    Occupations with the Highest Projected Growth, 2000–2010**

| Most Significant Occupation | N[a] | %[b] | Education or Training |
| --- | --- | --- | --- |
| Combined food preparation and serving workers, including fast food | 673 | 30 | Short-term on-the-job training |
| Customer service representatives | 631 | 32 | Moderate-term on-the-job training |
| Registered nurses | 561 | 26 | Associate degree |
| Retail salespersons | 510 | 12 | Short-term on-the-job training |
| Computer support specialists | 490 | 97 | Associate degree |
| Cashiers, except gaming | 474 | 14 | Short-term on-the-job training |
| Office clerks, general | 430 | 16 | Short-term on-the-job training |
| Security guards | 391 | 35 | Short-term on-the-job training |
| Computer software engineers, applications | 380 | 100 | Bachelor's degree |
| Waiters and waitresses | 364 | 18 | Short-term on-the-job training |
| General and operations managers | 363 | 15 | Bachelor's degree |
| Truck drivers, heavy and tractor-trailer | 346 | 20 | Moderate-term on-the-job training |
| Nursing aids, orderlies, and attendants | 323 | 24 | Short-term on-the-job training |
| Janitors and cleaners, except maids and housekeeping cleaners | 317 | 13 | Short-term on-the-job training |
| Postsecondary teachers | 315 | 23 | Doctoral degree |
| Teacher assistants | 301 | 24 | Short-term on-the-job training |
| Home health aides | 291 | 47 | Short-term on-the-job training |
| Laborers and freight, stock, and material movers, hand | 289 | 14 | Short-term on-the-job training |
| Computer software engineers, systems softwaree | 284 | 90 | Bachelor's degree |
| Landscaping and groundskeeping workers | 260 | 29 | Short-term on-the-job training |
| Personal and home care aides | 258 | 62 | Short-term on-the-job training |
| Computer systems analysts | 258 | 60 | Bachelor's degree |
| Receptionists and information clerks | 256 | 24 | Short-term on-the-job training |
| Truck drivers, light or delivery services | 215 | 19 | Short-term on-the-job training |
| Packers and packagers, hand | 210 | 19 | Short-term on-the-job training |

[a] Number of jobs in thousands
[b] Percent change
Source: U.S. Department of Labor, *Table 2. Occupations Covered in the 2002–2003 Occupational Outlook Job Growth, 2000-2010.* www.bls.gov/news.release/ooh.t02.htm

increased. In *The Education-Jobs Gap* (1998), sociologist D. W. Livingstone provides the most comprehensive study of this trend. Livingstone identifies five different types of underemployment: the talent–use gap, subemployment, credential underemployment, performance underemployment, and subjective underemployment. The *talent–use gap* refers to the opportunity gap between rich and poor to attain university degrees. Assuming equal levels of potential talent in the population as a whole, those from more wealthy backgrounds are at least twice as likely to complete college degrees. In other words, long before people enter the labor force, potential talent is already wasted through differential access to higher education. *Subemployment* refers to a variety of nonvoluntary substandard conditions of employment such as being unemployed but looking for work, part-time employees who want to work full time, and people working full time at wages below the poverty standard. An estimated 14 to 24% of the U.S. labor force, depending on cyclical variation, falls into this category. *Credential underemployment*, which refers to the condition in which a person's level of formal education exceeds that which is required in the job, affects an estimated 20% of the labor force. This type of underemployment, however, is constantly adjusted as employers raise educational requirements for entry positions often beyond the real skill demands of those positions. A better measure of the overall extent of underemployment in the labor force is *performance underemployment*, which refers to the gap between the skills of the jobholder and the actual skill demands of the job. This type of underemployment affects an estimated 40 to 60% of the currently employed labor force and has been steadily increasing for the past twenty-five years. Finally, Livingstone considers *subjective underemployment,* which refers to workers' perceptions that they hold jobs beneath their ability levels. Livingstone estimates that 20 to 40% of the labor force holds this view.

The implications of these findings are clear. There is no shortage of talent or skill in the labor force. In fact, the situation is exactly the *opposite*. The economy is not producing enough jobs that match the skill and talent available in the labor force.

## THE NON-REVENGE OF THE NERDS

The extent of underemployment is inconsistent with the arguments of the postindustrial society thesis, first advanced by American sociologist Daniel Bell (1976). Observing a shift toward more white-collar employment, Bell theorized that American society had moved beyond industrialization. The emergent "postindustrial" society placed a high premium on formal and technical knowledge. According to this thesis, technical experts would come to dominate America and other advanced societies. Science and technology would be the key to the postindustrial future. In short, the future would belong to the nerds. In some ways, Bell's predictions seem to be realized with the advance of the computer age. The computer became the leading edge of the information society. Computer-related industries, which were populated by young technically competent experts, flourished.

The postindustrial society would presumably create demand for a more highly educated labor force. While it is true that the computer age ushered in a new genre of occupational specialties, it is also true that the bulk of the expansion of new jobs, as we have seen, has actually been very low tech. The assumption of the *need* for a more highly educated labor force outpaced the reality. While computerization created some new jobs with high skill requirements, other jobs have been automated or "deskilled" by computerization. Sales clerks, for instance, no longer need to calculate change. In fast-food chains, entries on cash registers are sometimes made with pictures rather than numbers. Even professional jobs can be deskilled. One example of this professional "deskilling" process is pharmacy, a profession that typically requires five years of undergraduate study. Modern pharmacists rarely mix potions. Most drugs come prepackaged and pre-prepared. Pill counters count out numbers of pills and computer entries check for warnings, side effects, and possible drug interactions. The vast majority of what most pharmacists do is intellectually undemanding and entirely routine.

In a careful study of labor force changes through the 1970s, sociologist Randall Collins (1979) estimated that only 15% of the increase in educational requirements for new jobs could be attributed to the need for a more educated workforce. Most of the rest of the increase in educational requirements could be attributed to credential inflation—requiring higher levels of educational attainment unrelated to the actual skill demand of jobs (see chapter 5). As the labor force became more educated, employers simply increased their educational requirements. The result was an inflationary spiral of educational credentials.

*Not* having a credential (as opposed to the skills required to do a job) can be a nonmerit barrier to mobility. That is, if employers *require* a college degree for jobs that do not actually *need* a college graduate to perform, then *not* having the credential per se can operate against more experienced or skilled candidates. The vast majority of jobs that college graduates hold, in reality, require literacy and not much else. Most of what people need to know—even for jobs that require a college degree—is learned on the job. The formal credentials people hold, as Livingstone states, represent only "the tip of the learning iceberg." Fully 70% of what people need to know to do their jobs is learned informally on the job (1998, 38). As the pace of technological change increases, continuing and on-the-job training become even more important. To this extent, credentials—which are more available to those from more privileged backgrounds—become artificial barriers to true meritocracy. Collins notes that even some of the most technically demanding jobs—physician, engineer, lawyer—could be learned, and historically were, through apprenticeship training. For practical purposes, there is no evidence that would suggest that learning about something by seeing it diagrammed on a blackboard in a classroom is superior to learning the same thing through direct observation and application on the job. Indeed, learning theory suggests that the reverse is probably the case. Colleges have begun to respond to employers' pleas for more practical training by offering more "vocational" majors and embracing more "active" modes of learning, including internships and practica.

One of the problems in matching educational credentials with job demands is the length of training and the changing nature of the job market. The job market is difficult to predict in the long run, and this is a problem for those pursuing jobs that require long periods of formal training. Current "vacancies" and "high demand" may diminish by the time the training period is over. The "market" has ebbs and flows on both the supply and demand side. When demand is high, the market responds by attracting new entrants. Large numbers of new entrants can glut a market, resulting in oversupply—particularly if demand also dries up. In essence, people can be all dressed up with no place to go. One could argue that the truly meritorious would "read" market trends correctly and respond accordingly. The reality, however, is that markets—particularly long-term markets—are highly unpredictable. As rates of change increase, predictability declines. Most job experts agree that the job market is much more fluid now than for prior generations. Over a lifetime, the average worker now makes more job changes both in terms of type and place of employment than her or his predecessors. In short, where any one worker is located in the labor force at any one point in time is at least as much the result of market demands as individual merit.

## BABY BOOMERS AND BABY BUSTERS

The year a person is born matters for one's life chances. Being at the right place at the right time is partly a matter of when people are born and when they enter the labor market. Quite apart from individual ability, how many people are chasing how many and what kind of jobs is of major consequence. The best scenario is one in which a person is part of a small birth cohort and enters the labor force during a period of economic boom; the worst scenario is one in which a person is part of a large cohort entering the labor force during a period of economic retrenchment. The first full-time job after completion of formal education matters, since first jobs set career trajectories. Getting started on a branch higher up the tree in the first place will likely put one higher up from the ground at the end.

The best way to document the effects of cohort differences on mobility chances is to conduct a longitudinal study of different cohorts entering the labor force at different times and following the careers and work histories of individuals in those cohorts over time. A comprehensive analysis of this type, *Divergent Paths: Economic Mobility in the New American Labor Market*

(2001) by Annette Bernhardt, Martina Morris, Mark Handcock, and Mark Scott, has recently been completed. Bernhardt and her associates followed two cohorts of white males. They traced career paths of the first cohort that entered the labor force in the mid-1960s and followed it through the end of the 1970s to the early 1980s. The second cohort entered the labor force in the late 1970s and early 1980s and was followed through the mid-1990s. The systematic comparison of career paths and work histories of these two cohorts provides a means to compare differences in initial job opportunities and opportunities for advancement encountered by these cohorts, net of differences in individual abilities. Comparing cohorts, their key findings are that (1) economic mobility has declined and has become more unequal, (2) job instability has increased, and (3) the low-wage career trap has expanded its grip.

Bernhardt and her associates found that 90% of the most recent cohort of white male workers are doing worse now than their counterparts at corresponding ages twenty years ago. Median wage growth has fallen by 21%, and the distributions of remaining gains have become more unequal. While a small core of the most recent cohort is holding its own, for the most part the net wage decline is a "race to the bottom" (Bernhardt et al. 2001, 174). The growth of income inequality in recent decades is not associated with individuals surging ahead but rather with a few holding on while most have lost ground. The small core of workers holding their own are mostly college graduates. But even here, nearly two-thirds of all college graduates in the more recent cohort fared worse than college graduates in the previous cohort.

Those college graduates in the recent cohort who did do well were not clustered in the high technology areas—as would be predicted by the postindustrial society thesis—but in the "paper tiger" industries of finance, insurance, and real estate. In the recent cohort, those with associate degrees and certificates from vocational, technical, and community colleges barely did better than high school graduates, further calling into question the idea that a gap in technical skills is the driving force behind growing wage inequalities.

Bernhardt and her associates also document a 14% increase in job instability in the recent cohort, regardless of education level. Not only has there been an increase in job instability, but the wage penalties for changing jobs have increased. Those who manage to stay put in stable jobs tend to do better in the long run. Instability early in an individual's work history hurts workers' prospects for future stability: "Wage growth (or lack of it) early in the career can cascade into long-term changes in wage trajectories, so that a little inequality early on is likely to generate greater inequality down the line" (Burnhardt et al. 2001, 109). Part of the reason for the general increase in job instability is the shift to service work, which traditionally pays less, has fewer benefits, higher rates of turnover, and fewer opportunities for advancement. But in the wake of downsizing, restructuring, and mergers, job instability has also increased in the manufacturing sector. The result is the end of an era in which employees could reasonably count on stable employment with a single employer for an entire career.

In terms of the distribution of "slots" to be filled in the labor force, Bernhardt and her associates document an increase in low-wage jobs with little opportunity for advancement:

> The prevalence of low-wage careers has more than doubled, increasing from 12% in the original cohort to 28% in the recent cohort. These are not teenagers taking after school jobs at McDonald's to earn spending money, but rather mature workers chronically cycling through bad jobs over the long run, and we find that they have two things in common. One is that they are increasingly trapped in just a handful of industries, such as retail trade, personal services, entertainment and recreation, and business and repair services. These industries offer few opportunities for wage growth, promotion, and training, making it difficult for workers to escape their grasp. The other is their inability to find stable full-time employment by the time they reach their mid-thirties—indicating a type of job churning that becomes increasingly harmful as workers grow older. (2001, 176)

Many other observers (Blau 1999; Bluestone and Harrison 2000; Fraser 2001; Harrison and Bluestone 1990; Levy 1998; Palley 1998; Perrucci and Wysong 1999; Rayman 2001) have reached similar conclusions. Despite its relatively large size, the baby boomer cohort has done better than the smaller baby buster cohort that followed it. Although there is some disagreement about the causes of the recent job changes, all are in agreement that the ground has shifted and that there are fewer opportunities for good jobs now than for prior generations of workers. Simply put, beyond considerations of individual merit, it matters when you were born and what the labor force looks like when you enter it. But timing is only part of the story; being at the right place also matters.

## THE RUSTBELT AND THE SUNBELT

Throughout the first half of the twentieth century, the South lagged significantly behind other regions of the country. In 1947, for instance, family incomes in the South were 40% less than in other regions (Levy 1998, 127), partially because the South was still industrially underdeveloped. This large gap was also due in part to the long history of racial discrimination that depressed the wages of a high proportion of poor rural blacks that lived there. But wages were also lower for Southern whites compared to whites living in other regions with similar jobs and similar levels of education. Beginning in the 1960s the South began to close the income gap on the rest of the county, and by the early 1990s the gap between the South and other regions had closed to within about 20% (Levy 1998, 136). Economist Frank Levy points to several factors that were responsible for this change—the civil rights movement, which reduced economic discrimination; the extension of the interstate highway system and the development of network television, which helped link the South to other regions; and the spread of air conditioning, making the South more amenable to the "climatically challenged" (Levy 1998, 133). The availability of cheap land, low wages, low taxes, and low levels of unionization also encouraged industrial development in the South. During the same period, deindustrialization of the Northeast and Midwest (the Rustbelt) depressed wages, especially in the manufacturing sectors.

But as regional variation in wages declined, wage differentials between people living in cities and people living in suburbs increased. In 1959, wages in the city trailed wages in the suburbs by only 12%; by 1996 the gap had increased to 27% (Levy 1998, 143–44). Several factors contributed to this increase. The post–World War II era witnessed a surge in suburban development. This exodus was fueled by the relative prosperity of the postwar period combined with government subsidies in the form of highway construction and VA housing loans for returning veterans. More privileged whites, followed by black beneficiaries of the civil rights revolution, fled the inner cities in large numbers. Increasingly, the inner cities were populated by "left-behinds"—people who did not have a viable means to escape—the elderly poor, minority poor, and new ethnic immigrants. Many of the white-collar workers who worked in the urban high-rise offices during the day retreated to suburban bedroom communities at night. With urban manufacturing on the decline, fewer jobs for the unskilled and semiskilled remained. With factories and the middle class leaving inner cities, the tax base of big cities declined, resulting in a deterioration of public services. As urban unemployment and subemployment in the regular economy grew, "work" in the irregular economy—drugs, prostitution, gambling, and so on—also increased. All of these changes focused national attention on inner cities as lightening rods for social problems such as poverty, drugs, and crime.

Apart from the particular job a person does or how good one is at doing it—where one does it makes a difference in how much one is paid. The same job in the South or in inner cities may not pay as well in other regions or in the suburbs. Differences in pay based on place can be illustrated by comparing salaries of public school teachers. Teachers perform the same job, requiring for the most part the same qualifications—a bachelor's degree and a teaching certificate—but rates of teacher pay vary considerably by state. The average public school teacher pay in the 2001–2002 school year in the United States was $44,499 (American Federation of Teachers 2003). However, the range of pay was considerable, from a high of $53,551 in Connecticut to a low of $31,295 in South Dakota (American Federation of Teachers 2003). Even adjusting for cost of living differences among states, substantial pay differentials remain. Defenders of meritocracy might suggest that the really good teachers will gravitate to Connecticut where the pay is higher, and the least meritorious teachers will gravitate to South Dakota where the pay is the lowest. Pay, however, is not the only motivating factor in where people choose to work. Ties to family and community, personal preference, access to information about job openings (social capital), and employer preferences to hire locally are all also clearly factors.

In addition to the community in which the work is performed, the characteristics of the employing organization and the industrial location of the job also matter. Beyond the characteristics of individual workers, pay, benefits, and working conditions vary across employers and industries (Flynn 2003; Tolbert, Horan, and Beck, 1980; Averitt 1968; Weeden 2002). Large, capital intensive, high profit firms with large market shares tend to pay employees the most. Government employment offers less pay but often provides high levels of job security. Level of government (federal, state, county, municipal) also makes a difference, with the federal level generally providing the best packages for employees. The small-business sector, by contrast, generally offers the lowest pay, the least benefits, and the poorest working conditions. A building janitor, for instance, who works in an office building for a major corporation is likely to earn more than a building janitor who works in a county public school building, who, in turn, is likely to earn more than a building janitor who works in a local restaurant. Again, defenders of meritocracy might argue that "the best" and the hardest working janitors will end up working for the major corporations, but there is no evidence to support such a claim. This is because such a claim assumes far more predictability and rationality in how workers are matched with jobs than actually exists. Workers do not systematically work for employing organizations that would pay the most for what they can do. For a variety of reasons, among them that a job was available at a particular place at the particular time someone was seeking it, many people somewhat haphazardly end up working for whom they are working and doing the work they are doing.

Most people who have been in the labor force for any extended period of time, if honest, would acknowledge unanticipated twists and turns along the way that, quite independent of their personal level of merit, resulted in their current location in the labor force. Christopher Jencks et al. (1979, 306–11) identified three sources of wage variation among otherwise indistinguishable workers. First, the business cycle can create market uncertainties, making it impossible for workers to know in advance how many weeks in a year they may end up working in any given job. In this scenario, among similarly skilled workers doing the same kind of work, some might be laid off and others not. Second, large firms often create pay scales for occupational slots, not the people who fill them. A complicated wage structure of a firm is not especially responsive to market changes, so that at any point in time, some individual workers may be paid over the real market rate and some may be paid under the real market rate.

Finally, neither employing organizations nor individual workers have all the information necessary to "optimize" decisions that affect wages. Employing organizations do not always know the minimum they could pay to attract workers with sufficient skill to do the job, and workers do not always know how high a wage they can command. As a result, some employers pay more than necessary and some workers accept less than they could get. As Jencks et al. note, "these suboptimal bargains mean that identical workers do not always earn identical amounts" (1979, 310).

In the end, there is a great deal of what statisticians call "noise" when it comes to accounting for how much people are paid for the work they do. The best models account for only about half of the variance in income attainment and about two-thirds of the variance in occupational attainment. Some of the variance "unexplained" by these models could come from a combination of leaving out factors that matter and from less than perfect measures of the factors that were included. But some of the unexplained or residual variation is also likely due to simple random variation—or, in more everyday language, "luck."

## THE RANDOM WALK HYPOTHESIS

So far in this chapter, our discussion has revolved around education, jobs, and income. We have argued that the "going rate" of return for the jobs that people hold depends, at least in part, on factors that lie outside the control of individual workers themselves. Getting ahead in terms of occupations people hold and the pay they receive involves an element of luck—being at the right place at the right time. There is also an element of luck in the acquisition of great wealth. Indeed, luck may be even more of a factor in wealth attainment than income attainment. The luck factor in wealth acquisition, as we have seen, begins at birth. By an "accident of birth," some are born into great wealth while most are not. Since no one "chooses" their parents, those born into privilege may be thought of as "lucky." But what of "self-made" individuals who acquire great wealth without being born into it? In *Building Wealth* (1999), economist Lester Thurow identifies thirteen "rules" for wealth building. Rule number thirteen states, "Luck is necessary. Talent, drive, and persistence by themselves aren't enough to get wealthy." Elaborating on this rule, Thurow writes:

> although Bill Gates has as much wealth as the bottom 40% of American households, he has no known talents (IQ, business acumen, willingness to take risks) equal to the combined talents of those 110 million people. There are many other individuals just as smart, just as good businessmen, and just as good at everything else who do not have his wealth. Acquiring great wealth is best seen as a

conditional lottery. Luck is necessary. One does have to be in the right place at the right time. . . . Ability is not enough. (1999, 205)

Thurow's point is clear enough; luck matters. Thurow observes that wealth creation comes from taking advantage of "disequilibriums" or shake-ups in market conditions. Change brings about conditions of disequilibrium, and those conditions in turn create new opportunities for the creation of wealth. Thurow identifies three types of disequilibrium—technological, sociological, and developmental. Technological disequilibrium refers to forms of new wealth created through advances in technology (computers) or the development of related products and services surrounding the advance of new technologies (e.g., computer software). Sociological disequilibriums are those that are created by behavioral or social change unrelated to technology. Thurow offers the example of the aging of the American population and how this demographic change creates new economic opportunities in products and services disproportionately consumed by the elderly (e.g., cruise lines, medical and assisted living services). Finally, developmental disequilibrium refers to unequal conditions of development in different countries that create opportunities to introduce products and services available in one place that are not yet available in another place.

To some extent, those who are the most clever or most insightful might be better able to anticipate various market shake-ups. However, "the random walk hypothesis" developed by economists seems to best account for who ends up with the right idea, the right product, or the right service. The argument is simply that striking it rich tends to be like getting struck by lightning—many are walking around but only a few get randomly struck. Large fortunes tend to be made quickly, taking early advantage of market shake-ups. The window for striking it rich is narrow since once it is open others quickly rush in.

## LOTTERY LUCKY

Another way to strike it rich in America is to win a lottery. The odds of getting rich by hitting the lottery, however, are long indeed. Lotteries offer the worst odds of any form of legalized gambling (Gudgeon and Stewart 2001). Lotteries pay back 14 cents on the dollar, compared to 90 cents on typical casino games. The most popular lottery game is the "6/49 Draw." In this game, players pick six numbers from 1 to 49 and hope that they match the winning draw. The odds of winning with each ticket on the "6/49 Draw" are 13,983,816 to 1. At this writing, the largest lump sum payment to a single ticket winner on a government-sponsored lottery was $161.1 million, a considerable sum for most people, but not nearly enough to launch one into the Fortune 400 wealthiest Americans list.

For a handful of very lucky Americans then, winning the lottery can mean the fulfillment of a "rags to riches" American Dream (Kaplan 1978). It is a nonmerit form of rapid mobility but mobility nevertheless. The media hype surrounding this type of mobility encourages the idea that America is a land of opportunity in which anyone at anytime might become instantly wealthy.

Both conservatives and liberals have opposed lotteries. Conservatives sometimes oppose lotteries as a form of vice along with all other forms of gambling; liberals sometimes oppose lotteries because they exploit the poor. The poor are the least able to afford buying tickets and the most vulnerable to the lure of instant wealth. Despite these reservations, lotteries hold great romantic appeal and have become a popular American pastime. In 2000, thirty-seven states and the District of Columbia had lotteries with sales in the $40 billion range (Gudgeon and Stewart 2001). Even multistate lotteries have been developed. As weeks go by without winners, the pots increase in value, which in turn attracts more players. An estimated 75% of Americans have purchased a lottery ticket at least once, and 42% of men and 34% of women buy tickets weekly (Gudgeon and Stewart 2001).

State-sponsored lotteries are only one form of "gaming." Legalized gambling in casinos is available in Las Vegas, Atlantic City, and on some American Indian reservations. Offshore cruise lines whose sole purpose is to provide sites for gambling have flourished. They all market the same product: the hope of instant wealth. Among hopefuls, a few do win big, with great fanfare and excitement. The longer the odds, the larger the purse. The hoopla surrounding the "winners" is part of the marketing strategy to encourage players to play more. But the reality is that most players either lose or, occasionally, win just a little. The odds favor the house, insuring over the long run that the house is ultimately the biggest winner of all. The house edge is the difference between the true odds of winning and the odds that the house actually pays when someone wins. The difference is usually in the neighborhood of 10%, assuring a profit stream for the house in the long run. A toss of the coin, for instance, has a 50-50 even chance of winning. If you bet a dollar to win, the house would pay 90 cents on the dollar for the bet.

Perhaps the largest but least recognized forum for legalized gambling in the United States is the stock market. For all practical purposes, investing in stocks and bonds is equivalent to gambling. The biggest difference between playing the stock market and other forms of gambling is that the odds for winning in the stock market are much better, although the return is usually much less. Odds of "winning" in the stock market can be increased beyond random chance by knowing as much as possible about the companies in which one invests and by being able to predict market changes. Knowing about companies and markets, in part, is a matter of social capital—being in the loop. The more accurate and the more current the information, the better the odds. As recent investment scandals have underscored, these odds can be increased illegally through inside trading. Apart from such schemes, however, there is still an element of investor risk. Indeed, the willingness to "take chances" and "risk" capital is the primary justification for capitalism. If it were possible to predict the future with certainty, then there would be no risk. But as long as the future remains unpredictable, luck is a factor.

But having money to invest in the first place is also a factor, and an important one. Small investments, no matter how good the rate of return, are unlikely to generate great wealth. Like many other aspects of getting ahead in America, it takes money to make money. And the really big money in America, as we have seen, comes not from working for a living but from return on capital investments.

## SUMMARY

Merit hard-liners tend to deny or downplay the role of luck in getting ahead in America. Defenders of meritocracy often claim that "individuals make their own luck," or, sarcastically, "the harder I work, the luckier I become." Despite such claims, the evidence suggests otherwise. In this chapter, we have identified several factors beyond the immediate control of individuals that affect their life chances. While individuals do have some control over how skilled they are, individuals do not have control over what kinds of jobs are available, how many jobs are available, or how many individuals are seeking those jobs. These labor market conditions occur independent of the capacities of discrete individuals—how smart or talented they are, how hard they work, or how motivated they are to get ahead. Most economists agree that labor market conditions have fundamentally shifted since the early 1970s. A combination of circumstances prompted American corporations to sharply reduce manufacturing facilities in the United States, relocate facilities to the Sunbelt and overseas, consolidate through mergers, avoid unionization, "downsize" operations, "outsource" labor, and engage in other sweeping changes that collectively had a dramatic impact on the American labor force.

Although more Americans are getting more education, the economy is not producing enough jobs with good pay, good benefits, security, and opportunities for advancement commensurate with the higher levels of education attained. In essence, many American workers are all dressed up with no place to go. Compared to previous generations of workers entering the labor force, the most recent generation of workers faces fewer opportunities, greater job instability, and a greater chance of being stuck in dead-end jobs.

Beyond occupational success, being at the right place at the right time also matters for acquiring great wealth. Striking it rich—be it through inheritance, entrepreneurial ventures, investments, or hitting the lottery—necessarily involves at least some degree of just plain dumb luck. The simple fact is that there is far more intelligence, talent, ability, and hard work in the population as a whole than there are people who are lucky enough to find themselves in a position to take advantage of it.

## REFERENCES

American Federation of Teachers. 2003. *Rankings and Estimates: Rankings of the States 2001 and Estimates of School Statistics 2002.* Washington, D.C.: American Federation of Teachers.

Averitt, Robert T. 1968. *Dual Economy.* New York: W. W. Norton.

Bell, Daniel. 1976. *The Coming of Post-Industrial Society.* New York: Basic Books.

Bernhardt, Annette, Martina Morris, Mark Handcock, and Mark Scott. 2001. *Divergent Paths: Economic Mobility in the New American Labor Market.* New York: Russell Sage Foundation.

Blau, Joel. 1999. *Illusions of Prosperity: America's Working Families in an Age of Economic Insecurity.* New York: Oxford University Press.

Bluestone, Barry, and Bennett Harrison. 2000. *Growing Prosperity: The Battle for Growth with Equity in the Twenty-First Century.* Boston: Houghton Mifflin.

Collins, Randall. 1979. *The Credential Society: A Historical Sociology of Education and Stratification.* New York: Academic Press.

Flynn, Nicolet. 2003. "The Differential Effect of Labor Market Context on Marginal Employment Outcomes." *Sociological Spectrum* 123, no. 3: 305–30.

Fraser, Jill Anresky. 2001. *White-Collar Sweatshop: The Deteriorations of Work and Its Rewards in Corporate America.* New York: W. W. Norton.

Gudgeon, Chris, and Barbara Stewart. 2001. *Luck of the Draw: True-Life Tales of Lottery Winners and Losers.* Vancouver: Arsenal Pulp Press.

Harrison, Bennett, and Barry Bluestone. 1990. *The Great U Turn: Corporate Restructuring and the Polarizing of America.* New York: Basic Books.

Jencks, Christopher, et al. 1979. *Who Gets Ahead? The Determinants of Economic Success in America.* New York: Basic Books.

Kaplan, Roy. 1978. *Lottery Winners: How They Won and How Winning Changed Their Lives.* New York: HarperCollins.

Levy, Frank. 1998. *The New Dollars and Dreams: American Incomes and Economic Change.* New York: Russell Sage Foundation

Livingstone, D. W. 1998. *The Education-Jobs Gap: Underemployment or Economic Democracy.* Boulder, Colo.: Westview.

Palley, Thomas. 1998. *Plenty of Nothing: The Downsizing of the American Dream and the Case for Structural Keynesianism.* Princeton, N.J.: Princeton University Press.

Perrucci, Robert, and Earl Wysong. 1999. *The New Class Society.* Lanham, Md.: Rowman & Littlefield.

Rayman, Paula. 2001. *Beyond the Bottom Line: The Search for Dignity at Work.* New York: Palgrave.

Thurow, Lester C. 1999. *Building Wealth: The New Rules for Individuals, Companies and Nations in a Knowledge-Based Economy.* New York: HarperCollins.

Tolbert, Charles, Partick Horan, and E. M. Beck. 1980. "The Structure of Economic Segmentation: A Dual Economy Approach." *American Journal of Sociology* 85: 1095–16.

U.S. Census Bureau. 1975. *Historical Statistics of the United States: Colonial Times to 1970*. Washington, D.C.: U.S. Government Printing Office.

————. 2001. *Statistical Abstract of the United States: 2001. Table No. 596. Employment by Industry, 1980–2000*. Washington, D.C.: U.S. Government Printing Office.

U.S. Department of Labor. 2001. *Table 2. Occupations Covered in the 2002–2003 Occupational Outlook Job Growth, 2000–2010*. www.bls.gov/news.release/00h.t02.htm [accessed December 2003].

Weeden, Kim. 2002. "Why Do Some Occupations Pay More than Others? Social Closure and Earnings Inequality in the United States." *American Journal of Sociology* 108: 55–101.

# 7

# I Did It My Way:
# Self-Employment and Mobility

*I ate it up, and spit it out. I faced it all and I stood tall, and did it my way.*

—Lyrics from the song, "My Way," written by Paul Anka, as performed by
Frank Sinatra (1969)

An important part of the American Dream is the opportunity to strike out on your own, be your own boss, own a business, and be master of your own fate. Self-employment, in many ways, epitomizes the American Dream. Being self-employed exemplifies independence, initiative, self-reliance, rugged individualism—virtues held in high regard in American society. The entrepreneur who builds a business from scratch and turns it into a success is an American icon. Celebrated examples abound—Andrew Carnegie (Carnegie Steel), Henry Ford (Ford Motor Company), Thomas Edison (General Electric), and, more recently, Ray Kroc (McDonalds), Sam Walton (Wal-Mart), and Bill Gates (Microsoft).

The image of the rugged individualist fit well with conditions in early American society. Estimates are that in colonial America over 80% of the labor force was self-employed (Phillips 1958, 2). Most were farmers who owned their small family farms. Others were craftsmen, shopkeepers, and artisans. A few were fee-for-service professionals such as lawyers and physicians. Even the most prosperous of businesses employed relatively few workers, at least by modern standards. Among the small segment that was not self-employed, the largest contingent was slaves and indentured servants.

Wealth and property were primarily tied to the land, and the land was vast and only sparsely inhabited. After independence, the federal government acquired vast tracks of land on its western frontier. The government had acquired

so much land that it was willing to give tracts of it away to white settlers who
would stake a claim. For at least white settlers, America was literally the *land*
of opportunity. The idea of rugged pioneers setting out against all the odds to
stake their own claim and conquer the West became a deep and abiding image
in the American psyche.

Self-employment also fit well with the principles of free market capitalism.
Economic self-interest, individual ownership, and unbridled competition
would be the cornerstones of the new economy. Self-employment resonated
with the experience of the new nation. Americans were on their way to "doing it my way."

Since those early days, however, economic conditions have changed dramatically. Self-employment has sharply declined to only about 7% of the total labor force (U.S. Census Bureau 2002). Large corporations now dominate
the American economic landscape. Despite these colossal shifts in the economy, many Americans continue to cling to the romantic image of the lone in-
ventor and the individual entrepreneur as the backbone of the American
economy. In this chapter, we chronicle these changes and discuss the impact
of them for the prospect of meritocracy.

## MOM AND POP, WHERE ART THOU? THE DECLINE
## OF SELF-EMPLOYMENT

Estimating historical rates of self-employment can be tricky business (Aronson 1991, 137–42; Wright 1997, 142–45). Despite problems of comparability,
counting, and classification, the overall historical pattern is clear. No matter
how you calculate them, rates of self-employment in America have sharply
declined (Aronson 1991; Phillips 1958, 1962; Mishel et al. 2003; Wright 1997).
Self-employment as a percent of the total labor force has plummeted from an
estimated 80% in 1800 (Phillips 1958, 2) to 34% in 1900 (Wright 1997, 124) to
7% in 2000 (U.S. Census Bureau,2002).

Early declines in self-employment were mainly the result of the Industrial
Revolution and the mechanization of agriculture, which displaced many small
family farms. At the same time, opportunities for wage employment increased
in the growing industrial sector. Although the decline of self-employment was
most rapid in agriculture, self-employment also declined in the nonagricul-
tural sector as well. Smoke stack factories replaced handmade craft shops. Su-
permarkets and chain convenience stores replaced "mom and pop" groceries
and dry goods stores. Giant suburban malls with corporate chain outlets replaced the "mom and pop" shops and specialty stores. Chain motels and ho-
tels replaced "mom and pop" roadside inns. Fast-food and franchise restaurants replaced "mom and pop" diners. HMOs and joint specialty practices
replaced the "hang out a shingle" solo family doctor. While remnants of tra-

ditional local independent businesses remain, each of these arenas of the economy has become increasingly bureaucratized, moving gradually away from sole proprietorships to partnerships to larger corporate establishments.

The U.S. Department of Labor (2002b) reports that for the year 2000, the occupations with the most self-employed workers included farmers and ranchers (1,251,000); supervisors of retail sales workers (801,000); child care workers (470,000); carpenters (344,000); hairdressers, hairstylists, and cosmetologists (309,000); real estate agents (235,000); painters, construction, and maintenance workers (228,000); booking, accounting, and auditing clerks (200,000); lawyers (193,000); and retail salespersons (170,000). Significantly, between 2000 and 2010, farmers and ranchers, who in 2000 accounted for one in ten of all self-employed workers in the United States, are expected to have by far the largest loss of employment of any single occupation in the U.S. labor force (U.S. Department of Labor 2002a).

Even the current small percentage of self-employed counted in the regular labor force may be inflated, at least in terms of how self-employment has been traditionally conceived. For instance, individuals who own franchises licensed through major corporations strongly identify as self-employed (Bills 1998). Franchises operate in such diverse areas as motels, restaurants, convenience stores, clothing outlets, and even funeral homes. From 1967 to 2000, the percentage of sales made by all franchise outlets increased from 10 to nearly 50% (Domhoff 2002, 38). Although franchisees may be owners or part owners of establishments, they are not entrepreneurs in the traditional sense. They do not create new business concepts, nor do they develop new products. They often rely on the franchisor to provide training, financing, and marketing. Most franchisees are contractually bound to follow standardized procedures and operations established by the franchisor. Franchisees are therefore neither fully independent owners nor fully dependent wage employees. Instead, they represent a kind of in-between status that sociologist David Bills (1998) has identified as "dependent self-employment."

Another "dependent" type of self-employment includes those who are self-employed but have only one client. Such enterprises may be spin-offs of parent businesses that are established separately for tax purposes. Instead of representing true entrepreneurial activity, such employment may be a new way for employers to hire outsourced workers under arrangements of homework, freelancing, or subcontracting (Wright 1997, 140). Large construction firms, for instance, frequently subcontract trade work to individuals or small companies, often for less pay and benefits than the firm would pay its own full-time employees. Although individual craft workers or owners of the subcontracting companies may be "self-employed," they are often largely or wholly dependent on a single client, reducing their leverage and true autonomy.

Professionals in group practices may also identify themselves as self-employed or declare themselves self-employed for tax purposes, but they are not sole practitioners in the classical sense. There are clear advantages for professionals who work in these settings, such as taking turns being "on call" for the practice, having colleagues immediately available to consult, and sharing expensive equipment and overhead costs. But increasingly their work and conditions of employment are subject to control by others.

While these arrangements may inflate reported rates of self-employment, other forms of self-employment that go unreported have the opposite effect. Those who work "under the table" or "off the books" in what economists refer to as the "irregular economy" confound the estimates (Dallago 1990; Greenfield 1993; Schlosser 2003). Individuals who work in the irregular economy may be self-employed or work for someone else. Much of the economic activity that occurs in this sector is illegal. Forms of work in this sector are varied, ranging from housewives watching other people's children in their homes for undeclared pay; to undocumented immigrants working in sweatshops; to persons directly involved in illegal activities such as theft, fencing, drug dealing, gambling, prostitution, loan sharking, or smuggling. The full extent of these activities is unknown.

In many ways, the irregular economy is a bastion of unadulterated free enterprise. The irregular economy is, in effect, unregulated and untaxed, and it creates opportunities for ambitious, risk-taking entrepreneurs. For some, the irregular economy has long been one of the few sources of employment or mobility in economically depressed areas (Fusfeld 1973). Although employment in the irregular economy may, for some, be a vehicle of upward mobility, and in some cases a pathway to eventual employment in the regular economy, it is not generally considered a legitimate part of the "American Dream."

## BETWIXT AND BETWEEN: THE CLASS POSITION
## OF THE SELF-EMPLOYED

The class position of self-employed workers is at best ambiguous. Karl Marx initially distinguished two main social classes in capitalist societies—those who own the means of producing wealth (bourgeoisie) and those who sell their labor to others (proletariat). The bourgeoisie, however, include several subcategories (Wright 1977). One group of bourgeoisie, *rentier capitalists*, own businesses and hire the labor of others but do not, themselves, work for an income. Another group of bourgeoisie, *entrepreneurial capitalists*, both work in the businesses they own and hire the labor of others. *Petty bourgeoisie*, on the other hand, own their own businesses and work in them but do not hire the labor of others.

Petty bourgeoisie and entrepreneurial capitalists occupy what sociologist Erik Olin Wright refers to as "contradictory" locations within the class structure. That is, in some ways these groups share characteristics with capitalists, and in some ways they share characteristics with wage laborers. Like other capitalists, the petty bourgeoisie own their own businesses, but unlike other capitalists, the petty bourgeoisie do not hire or control the labor of others. Entrepreneurial capitalists and the petty bourgeoisie share with the proletariat the characteristics of working for an income. But unlike the proletariat, the work of entrepreneurial capitalists and the petty bourgeoisie is not supervised or controlled by others.

In later stages of industrial development, these class divisions become even more blurred. Some sociologists, for instance, make a distinction between the "old middle class" and the "new middle class" (Mills 1951). The "old middle class" consisted mostly of entrepreneurial capitalists and the petty bourgeoisie, that is, small businessmen, family farmers, and solo fee-for-service professionals. The "old middle class" was considered generally respectable, mostly well-to-do, and fiercely independent. However, in later stages of industrialization, a "new middle class" of managers, administrators, and technicians emerged. The "new middle class" was brought about with the advent of the "managerial revolution" and the "separation of ownership from control" (Berle and Means 1932). In the early part of the twentieth century, more and more owners withdrew from day-to-day control of their businesses and began to hire managers to run them. As businesses became larger and more complex, layers of bureaucracy were added, and the ranks of management grew. Remnants of the "old middle class" remain, but it is outnumbered and overshadowed by the ascendance of the "new middle class."

## CHARACTERISTICS OF THE SELF-EMPLOYED

Compared to the wage labor force, self-employed workers tend to be older, white, and male. Self-employed workers are older by an average of about ten years (Aronson 1991, 6). Older workers are more likely than younger workers to have both the work experience and the accumulated capital required to start new businesses. Also, in some cases older workers may opt for self-employment as an alternative to retirement or as a way to control the amount and pace of work as physical stamina declines.

Self-employed workers are twice as likely to be male as female, although the *rate of growth* of self-employment among women is higher (Aronson 1991, 5; Arum 1997; McCrary 1998). The disproportionate growth of self-employment among women is associated with several factors. First, rates of self-employment tend to be higher in the growing service sector of the economy where women have historically been overrepresented. Although some of the increase of female self-employment has occurred in the high-wage professional part of the service sector (e.g., physicians and lawyers), most of the increase has occurred in the low-wage nonprofessional part of the sector (e.g., child care workers, hairdressers) (McCrary 1998). Second, some women may select self-employment because it affords them greater scheduling flexibility in combining the demands of work and family. Finally, some women may start new businesses to circumvent the glass ceiling effects often encountered in wage employment.

Although self-employment is often seen as a vehicle of upward social mobility for ethnic minorities, whites have higher rates of self-employment than do ethnic minorities (Aronson 1991, 8–10). Whites are three times more likely to be self-employed than blacks. Some of this difference may be attributed to reluctance among white customers to patronize black-owned businesses and whites' assumptions that black-owned businesses produce inferior products or services (Feagin and Sikes 1994). Blacks, who have less wealth than whites, also have less capital to start businesses and have more difficulty securing business loans. Finally, blacks have encountered difficulty in locating their businesses in "white" areas. For similar reasons, the rate of self-employment for whites is also about twice the rate for Hispanic Americans. Asians, with cultural norms that encourage the pooling of familial capital among extended kin networks, are the only minority group whose rate of self-employment approaches that of whites.

Some studies suggest that the self-employed tend to have different individual or psychological characteristics than do wage-workers (cf. Thornton 1999 for a systematic review). These studies suggest, for instance, that need for achievement, internal locus of control, risk taking, and independence are associated with the likelihood of self-employment. Other studies suggest that self-employment disproportionately attracts workers with low productivity who might otherwise have difficulty finding suitable employment in the wage sector. Such studies, however, are plagued by methodological problems, especially related to separating cause and effect (e.g., do individual characteristics lead to self-employment, or does self-employment create such characteristics in individuals?). Regardless of the direction of causality, the idea that individual characteristics alone account for self-employment or entrepreneurship has largely been abandoned in favor of more multidimensional models that take into consideration the influence of organizational, market, and environmental influences (Thornton 1999).

At least some self-employment, for instance, occurs not as a matter of individual choice or personal preference but as the result of unemployment (e.g., a downsized white-collar executive who freelances as a self-employed "consultant"), subemployment (the laid off factory worker who works as a self-employed "handyman"), or outsourced employment (a former wage employee who contracts with an employer to perform the same services as a contract laborer, often for less pay and no benefits) (Wright 1997, 139–42). In addition, some employment in the "irregular" economy is probably nonvoluntary as well. Most studies indicate that increases in the availability of wage employment reduce the level of activity in the irregular economy, suggesting that at least a portion of this form of self-employment is nonvoluntary.

The income of self-employed workers is difficult to assess. According to the U.S. Census Bureau (2003), in 2001 the mean (mathematical average) annual earnings of self-employed workers was $46,523 compared to the mean of $35,034 for all workers. Mathematical averages, however, are sensitive to extreme scores; that is, a few high values can skew the overall average. In cases where distributions are highly skewed, median scores (that divide the population into two equal halves) are generally understood to be better measures of central tendency. Using median scores, the annual income difference between self-employed workers ($26,923) and all workers ($26,002) is essentially reduced to parity. The greater difference between the mean and median earnings of self-employed compared to the mean and median of all workers reflects the more highly skewed distribution of earnings among self-employed workers. This is to be expected for owners of small businesses, some of which are highly profitable. A few do very well (driving up mathematical averages), but many more struggle (lowering the median).

Assessing the real income of self-employed workers is further complicated because self-employed workers, in an attempt to reduce tax liability, are more likely to underreport income than are wage workers (Aronson 1991). Or, as in the case of the illegal irregular segment of the economy, self-employment earnings may be disguised or not reported at all. What is more, self-employed workers who own their own businesses tend to work longer hours than wage laborers, which effectively reduces the hourly rate of return among the self-employed. In addition, income alone does not tell the whole story, since self-employed workers must fund their own retirement, medical insurance, and vacation time, the effective value of which far exceeds the $921 median advantage in self-employed earnings. The recent inflationary surge in the costs of private medical insurance and the lack of pooled risks for self-employed persons have especially eroded effective wage benefits for the self-employed.

Another characteristic of self-employment is that it is high risk—especially for those striking out alone to start a new business. Rates of business survival for new business starts are notoriously low. According to a recent U.S. Small Business Administration study, data from the U.S. Census Bureau's Business Information Tracking Series show that the rate of closure for new business starts is 44% after two years, 51.4% after four years, and 61.5% after six years. Further, data from the U.S. Census Bureau's Characteristics of Business Owners survey estimated that about two-thirds of owners of firms that closed identified their firms as unsuccessful at closure (Headd 2002). Another study found that after the first two or three years, 50 to 60% of those who venture into self-employment return to wage employment, become unemployed, or drop out of the labor force (Evans and Leighton 1989).

This is nothing new; self-employment and new business starts have always been high risk. But the presence of large corporations makes such ventures even more risky. Small businesses that take on established corporations for market share are at a distinct disadvantage. Small business starts that have the best chance of success are those that find new, localized, or unique market niches. Even then, such establishments run the risk of being swallowed up by larger concerns seeking entry into niche markets, especially if these niches yield high returns and offer opportunities for national or global expansion. We now turn our attention to the flip side of declining self-employment—the growth of corporate production and employment.

## SWIMMING WITH THE SHARKS: THE ASCENT OF THE MODERN CORPORATION

At the time of the American Revolution, corporations did not exist. In colonial America, a handful of joint stock companies such as the East India Company, the Massachusetts Bay Company, and the Hudson Bay Company were chartered by the British Crown to reap the bounty of the New World (Derber 1998). With the establishment of American independence, a few establishments were granted corporate charters by states and sometimes the federal government to provide specific public services such as roads, bridges, colleges, or canals. In exchange for these expressly public services, such private entities were granted powers normally delegated to governments, such as the power to collect tolls.

At first, corporate charters were granted only under strictly delimited conditions. In addition to requiring that corporations explicitly serve the public interest, corporate charters were granted for limited time periods and restricted the amount of assets corporations could accumulate (Derber 1998, 122). These restrictions were consistent with the distrust that early legislators had of any large organizations, including corporate entities (Perrow 2002, 33–35). Individual states, however, competed with one another for corporate revenue by offering increasingly lenient statutes for incorporation. One small state, Delaware, host to a particular large and important corporation, the Du Pont Company, ultimately offered the most lenient statutes for incorporation and became the darling of large corporations everywhere. Roughly half of today's Fortune 500 companies, regardless of where they conduct business, are incorporated in the state of Delaware. With most government restrictions lifted, the modern corporate form emerged (Derber 1998; Miller 1977; Perrow 2002; Roy 1997). Corporations now account for 89% of all business revenue, while partnerships account for only 6% and proprietorships only 5% (Caplow et al. 2000, 246).

Crucial to the establishment of the modern corporation was a series of legal decisions that redefined the essence of the corporation. These decisions allowed corporations to operate for private gain without explicitly serving the public interest, established the principle of limited liability, and extended the legal rights of individuals to corporations. The elimination of the requirement for public service enabled an unrestricted profit motive. Under the principle of limited liability, investors in corporations would risk only the amount of money invested in the corporations. Investors would not be "liable" for whatever other debts the corporation acquired. Especially critical to these court rulings was the extension of the legal rights of individuals to corporations. These rulings allowed the pooling of enormous amounts of capital from multiple investors in single companies, a phenomenon that has been described as the "socializing of capital" (Roy 1997).

When ratified in 1787, the Constitution of the United States did not contain the word "corporation," nor does it today. It is understandable that its framers, otherwise concerned about concentrations of power not directly accountable to the public, overlooked corporations since the corporate-like entities of the day were neither numerous nor powerful. As corporations became more numerous and powerful, constitutional issues related to corporations arose. Since the Constitution recognizes only two legal entities—the government and the individual—the courts in essence had to decide which of these applied to corporations. In a series of key U.S. Supreme Court decisions in the early 1800s, corporations were interpreted legally as individuals under the provisions of the Constitution. As such, corporations were extended the legal rights of individuals, especially with regard to the Fourteenth Amendment, which provides for "equal protection" under the law.

Among the rights granted to corporations was the right to buy and sell property. With the legal ability to buy and sell property like individuals, corporations ferociously bought and sold each other. The history of corporations in America is the history of the big fish eating the little fish and eventually the big fish eating each other. Most major markets in the United States became dominated by a few big fish. The 1880s and 1890s marked an era of rapid consolidation. Through trade associations, pools, trusts, cartels, and other organizational devices, turn-of-the-century capitalists managed to consolidate economic power to an alarming degree. Widespread consolidation led to artificially inflated prices, which provoked organized efforts to reinstate more competitive conditions. Political agitation from farmers and small businessmen, who were caught in the grip of railroad combinations, prompted the establishment of the Interstate Commerce Commission in 1887, the government's first major attempt to regulate trade, and the Sherman Anti-Trust Act of 1890, the government's first organized effort to control monopolies. With monopolies illegal, the major "smokestack" industries in the United States that made America an industrial giant—autos, steel, chemicals, and oil—became dominated by a few large corporations and settled into their current oligopolistic structure. (The rule of thumb in defining an oligopoly is an industry in which the leading four companies have at least 60% market share.) The American automobile industry is one example. In the early part of the twentieth century when automobiles were first introduced, scores of companies entered the new market. Gradually, the bigger fish ate the smaller ones, and then the big fish ate each other, so that by the early 1960s the industry had consolidated into the current "Big Three": General Motors, Ford, and Chrysler. As the bigger companies gobbled up the smaller ones, the bigger companies retained the trade names of the product lines, giving the appearance of more competition than actually existed. General Motors, for instance, consists of several divisions, most of which were formerly stand-alone companies, such as Cadillac, Oldsmobile, Buick, Chevrolet, and Pontiac. In the aftermath of the formation of the international Oil Producing and Exporting Countries (OPEC) oil cartel, the "Big Three" U.S. auto manufacturers began to experience a sharp rise in competition from foreign auto producers (especially Japanese and German companies), which offered smaller and more fuel efficient cars. In the 1990s the "Big Three" began consolidating with their foreign competitors as Chrysler merged with Mercedes and became Daimler Chrysler (including Dodge and Jeep divisions); Ford (including Lincoln, Mercury) acquired major interests in Volvo, Mazda, Jaguar, Austin Martin, and Land Rover; and General Motors added Saab and Fiat to its product lines.

In a frenzy of megamergers accelerating in recent decades, the largest corporations have become even larger. The mergers of AOL with Time Warner ($162 billion), Mobil with Exxon ($77 billion), Citicorp with Travelers ($72 billion), Bank America with Nations Bank ($62 billion), Amoco with BP ($54 billion), and McDonald Douglas with Boeing ($25 billion) are just a few of the largest. In 1961, the 100 largest U.S. industrial firms had 22% of the total assets of all nonfinancial corporations; by 2000 they had almost one-third (Phillips 2002, 148).

Not only have the large corporations merged with one another within industry groups, they also have merged with one another across industry groups in the form of corporate conglomerates. A particularly prominent example is the Altria Company (formerly the Philip Morris Company), which in the aftermath of several high-profile lawsuits changed its name in 2002. Originally a tobacco company, Philip Morris acquired the General Foods Corporation, Kraft Foods, and a controlling interest in the Miller Beer Company. Each of these companies, in turn, has numerous product names and labels, often acquired through prior buyouts. It is difficult now for American shoppers to walk out of a supermarket without at least one of several Altria products in their grocery carts, including Oscar Mayer Meats, Kraft Cheese, Claussen Pickles, Maxwell House Coffee, Chips Ahoy Cookies, Planters Nuts, Tang, Jell-O puddings, Miracle Whip, Cool Whip, Kool-Aid, Tombstone, Jack's, or DiGiorno Frozen Pizzas, Bull's Eye Barbecue Sauce, Grey Poupon

Mustard, Minute Rice, Light and Lively Yogurt, Philadelphia Cream Cheese, Miller Beer (or a variety of other Miller-owned labels), Philip Morris cigarettes (or a variety of other Philip Morris–owned labels), and many others.

With name changes and acquisition of new product lines, the average consumer simply cannot keep up with who owns what. In classical economics, the consumer is seen as "king" and every purchase is seen as a "vote" in the economic marketplace. If customers are dissatisfied with the products or policies of any particular company, they are free to take their business elsewhere (including using boycott as an organized form of protest). However, if choices are limited or nonexistent or if the consumer does not know what the choices represent (who owns what), then this form of restraint on the marketplace is vastly compromised.

The largest corporation in America is now the Wal-Mart Corporation, the major retailer in the United States and emblematic of the postindustrial shift from goods production to retail and service industries. As measured by both total annual revenues ($219 billion) and total number of employees (1.3 million) ("Fortune 500 Largest U.S. Corporations" 2002, F-1, F-31). Wal-Mart "Super Stores" and Wal-Mart "Sams" discount retail warehouses are a long way away from the "mom and pop" grocery stores of the 1950s.

Despite the expansion of the size and power of corporate goliaths, small business is often heralded as the backbone of the American economy. Small businesses are thought to be responsible for most new employment growth as well as most innovation in the economy. Business establishments with less than twenty employees account for 85% of all business establishments but only 24% of all employment. At the other end of the continuum, business establishments with over 500 employees account for only two-tenths of 1% of all business establishments but 21% of total employment (U.S. Census Bureau 2002, Table 713). Even these numbers exaggerate the independence of the small business sector. Business establishments are defined as single physical locations where business is conducted, but these also include branch offices and franchise sites for larger corporations. In addition, many smaller establishments are tied to the larger firms as suppliers or retailers of products and services provided by the megacorporations. Larger corporations often create "vertical networks" of smaller contractor firms under their control while at the same time downsizing their own labor forces (Harrison 1994, 47).

Not only are small businesses not dominant in the economy as a whole; they are also not the major source of product innovation. In 1901, 80% of U.S. patents were issued to individuals. By 1999, 80% of patents were issued to corporations (Caplow et al. 2000, 258). While some new technologies may originate with individuals and small businesses, most do not have the capital or resources for research and development, to set up large-scale production facilities, or to market new technologies. As a result, larger established corporations often buy out small-time players. Buying out promising new technologies from individuals and smaller companies is often a way for large corporations to stay technologically competitive without heavily investing in expensive basic research programs that may not yield tangible results. Other major sources of technological innovation occur outside the private sector altogether through government- and university-sponsored research (Nader 2000, 57–67).

All of this is far removed from the self-employed entrepreneur. The ascendance of large-scale corporations affects self-employment in several ways. First, large corporations create barriers of entry for small businesses, especially sole proprietorships. That is, small businesses do not have the capital nor can they generate the volume of business to challenge large businesses operating in similar markets. Second, compared to employment in large corporations, employment in the small business sector is generally less stable, does not pay as well, and generally does not provide as good benefits. Third, the ascendance of large corporations has no doubt reduced opportunities for rapid social mobility. When sole proprietors had no corporations to compete against, it was more possible for individual entrepreneurs to establish new market niches and grow their businesses rapidly. Rags to riches scenarios, while never common, are now even less common. The decline of self-employment and the dominance of large bureaucratic corporations changes mobility in another way. Starting a new business requires different individual characteristics than maintaining an established one. The "entrepreneurial personality"—bold, visionary, risk taking, ruggedly individualistic—while well suited for launching new business ventures, is not well suited for running large bureaucratic organizations. Once you are already ahead, the idea is to stay ahead, and the best way to do that is to play it safe.

Bureaucracies generally reward compliance, not defiance. In bureaucratic settings, one does not typically advance by being the defiant, rugged, and fiercely independent individualist of American folklore, but rather by going along to get along, being a team player, following rules and procedures, and slowly climbing the bureaucratic ladder one step at a time.

Clearly, some individual entrepreneurs who strike out on their own manage to defy the odds and do very well. Those who succeed do not necessarily work harder than those who fail, nor are they necessarily more inherently capable or meritorious. Having sufficient start-up capital to launch new enterprises (it takes money to make money) and coming along at the right time in the right place with the right idea (random walk hypothesis) do, however, have a great deal to do with entrepreneurial success. In rare circumstances, such individuals may take advantage of temporary market imbalances and launch new enterprises that start out small but evolve into corporate giants. One such enterprise is the Microsoft Corporation, cofounded by Bill Gates and Paul Allen.

## BILL GATES

Bill Gates, the richest person in the world with an estimated net worth of $43 billion started his own company, Microsoft, with cofounder Paul Allen, the third richest person in the world with a net worth of $22 billion (*Forbes* 2003). Gates is often portrayed as a paragon of entrepreneurial virtue, who through talent and hard work became the richest person in the world. Although listed by *Forbes* as "self-made," Bill Gates's story is not one of rags to riches but more accurately one of modest riches to staggering riches. William H. Gates III was born in 1955 in Seattle to a privileged family. Using a common upper-class serial designation, his parents refer to him simply as "Trey." Bill (Trey) Gates's mother, Mary Gates, is a socialite from a wealthy upper-class family. Her father and grandfather were both wealthy bankers. Bill Gates's father, William H. Gates Jr., is a prominent attorney. Bill Gates's father, while very successful in his own right, is from a modest background and was the first in his family to attend college. Bill Gates's parents met at the University of Washington, where his mother was an undergraduate and his father a law student.

Bill Gates benefited from many of the cumulative advantages of inheritance identified in chapter 3. An especially critical part of the story is the expensive, exclusive, all boys, private prep school, Lakeside, that Bill Gates attended beginning at age eleven. Lakeside was Seattle's most elite school and known for its academic excellence. As one biographer put it:

> Lakeside was a crucible that would fire his creative genius. . . . It was here that the proper mix of ingredients needed to forge Gates' inner fire came together: energy, intelligence, intensity, competitiveness, obsessiveness, drive, desire, business acumen, entrepreneurship and luck. (Wallace and Erickson 1992, 18)

Without the experience at Lakeside, Gates's individual traits alone would probably not have resulted in his spectacular success in the world of computing software. When Gates enrolled at Lakeside in the late 1960s, the combination grade school and high school had what many universities did not have at that time—a computer lab. Bill Gates, who was especially proficient at mathematics, was captivated by the lab and spent most of his spare time there. Among the other privileged students frequenting the Lakeside computer lab was Paul Allen, who became Gates's friend and cofounder of Microsoft.

After graduating from Lakeside, Bill Gates went on to Harvard University, not an uncommon destination for someone with his abilities and social class background. While Gates was still a student at Harvard, Gates and Allen read an article about a new personal computer, the Altair, which was being made in Albuquerque, New Mexico. Until then, most computers were large, expensive mainframes used by the military, corporations, and universities. The vision of Ed Roberts, the founder of Micro Instrumentation and Telemetry Systems (MITS) and the manufacturer of the Altair, was to build affordable, desktop computers for individual use. Gates and Allen contacted the company and offered to write software for the Altair. They secured the contract, and Allen became a full-time software director at MITS. With help from Gates's attorney father, Gates and Allen entered into a licensing agreement with MITS for their software program. Gates and Allen had formed a separate company that they named Microsoft ("micro" for small personal computers and "soft" for software).

From there, Gates and Allen secured license contracts for their software with other companies just entering the field as well, including the National Cash Register Company, General Electric, Radio Shack, Texas Instruments, Commodore, Apple, and Intel (Wallace and Erickson 1992, 134). Microsoft expanded rapidly, adding additional programmers, and the money was beginning to pour in. Allen quit MITS to work full-time at Microsoft and Gates dropped out of Harvard to do the same. Although Microsoft was doing very well with its licensing contracts with these companies, the big prize was IBM. IBM was coming out with a new line of personal computers and needed an operating system to run on a 16-bit Intel chip. Such a system had been developed by Tim Paterson at Seattle Computer Products. Paterson called his operating system "Quick and Dirty Operating System" (QDOS for short). The rest of the story is legend. Paterson leased his system to Microsoft which, unbeknownst to him, was negotiating with IBM for its software contract. Gates and Allen ultimately bought the rights to Paterson's QDOS for a sum of $50,000 (Wallace and Erickson 1992, 202). Gates and Allen modified the program and leased it to IBM under the label Microsoft DOS. Instead of selling the program outright, Microsoft secured a royalty on DOS with every computer IBM sold, catapulting Microsoft and its young owners into computing history.

Securing the contract with IBM was pivotal to Microsoft's success. Although Microsoft was a growing company with an expanding track record, there was no guarantee that it would end up with the IBM contract. One of the interesting circumstances surrounding the IBM deal was that Bill Gates's socialite mother, Mary, was an acquaintance of John Opel, then CEO of IBM. Mary Gates and John Opel served together on the National Board of the United Way of America. Whether this particular connection had anything to do with Microsoft and her then twenty-four-year-old son getting the IBM contract is unknown, but it does serve to underscore Gates's upper-class background.

With the IBM contract secure, Microsoft went on to become the industry leader in computing software. In the early days of Microsoft, Bill Gates frequently expressed the desire for Microsoft programs to become "the industry standard" (Wallace and Erickson 1992). With MS-DOS and Windows, Gates had largely achieved that goal, so much so that beginning in the early

1990s, Microsoft became a U.S. Justice Department target for antitrust litigation. Ironically, the once-upstart Microsoft Company was now accused of squelching its own would-be competitors. Although the case remains unresolved, the decisions to date seem to favor Microsoft. Partly as the result of the extended antitrust suits, the value of Microsoft stock declined in the 1990s but has recovered despite current market conditions. Thus, despite the antitrust litigation and the recent stock market "corrections," Bill Gates remains the richest person in the world.

The Bill Gates story serves to illustrate the presence of many factors that occasionally coalesce to bring about great entrepreneurial success. Bill Gates exhibits many of the personal characteristics often associated with great entrepreneurs—intensity, intellect, vision, determination, brashness, as well as business savvy. But such individual traits alone do not create entrepreneurial success. Gates was poised to take advantage of these traits through inheritance of privilege (especially the Lakeside experience) and luck (being at the right place at the right time). In other words, we do not know how many potential Bill Gateses are out there—with similar individual abilities and character traits, who are just as capable, but whose life circumstances did not position them to take advantage of their capabilities.

## SUMMARY

Americans embrace the ideal of the self-made person. It is quintessentially American to "go your own way" and "do your own thing." In economic life, this ideal is best exemplified by self-employment. Since colonial times, however, the proportion of self-employed in the total American labor force has steadily declined. Despite the mystique of self-employment, the reality for many who are self-employed is often less than glamorous. Compared to their wage-worker counterparts, the self-employed tend to work longer hours, often for effectively lower earnings. Some are forced into reluctant self-employment when their jobs as employees disappear. And while a few overcome the odds and do very well, striking out on one's own to start a new business is a high-risk pursuit.

The rapid historical decline in self-employment corresponds to the ascendance of large corporations in the American economy. The collective assets and associated economies of scale of the corporate behemoths tend to undercut competition from smaller companies and discourage new entrants. Despite the reality of an economy dominated by increasingly large corporations, many Americans cling to the imagery of the go-it-alone entrepreneurial spirit as the backbone of the American economy. Such language, however, no longer accurately describes the circumstances of the vast majority of a labor force that now works for somebody else.

# REFERENCES

Aronson, Robert L. 1991. *Self Employment: A Labor Market Perspective*. New York: ILR Press.

Arum, Richard. 1997. "Trends in Male and Female Self Employment: Growth in a New Middle Class or Increasing Marginalization of the Labor Force?" Pp. 209–38 in *Research in Stratification and Mobility*, Volume 15, edited by Michael Wallace. Greenwich, Conn.: JAI Press.

Berle, Adolf A., and Gardiner C. Means. 1932. *The Modern Corporation and Private Property*. New York: Macmillan.

Bills, David B. 1998. "A Community of Interests: Understanding the Relationships between Franchisees and Franchisors." Pp. 351–69 in *Research in Stratification and Mobility*, Volume 16, edited by Kevin T. Leicht. Greenwich, Conn.: JAI Press.

Caplow, Theodore, Louis Hicks, and Ben J. Wattenberg. 2000. *The First Measured Century: An Illustrated Guide to Trends in America, 1900–2000*. Washington, D.C.: AEI Press.

Currie, Elliott, and Jerome H. Skolnick. 1997. *America's Problems: Social Issues and Public Policy*. 3rd ed. New York: Longman.

Dallago, Bruno. 1990. *The Irregular Economy: The "Underground Economy" and the "Black" Labour Market*. Hants, U.K.: Dartmouth Publishing.

Derber, Charles. 1998. *Corporation Nation: How Corporations Are Taking Over Our Lives and What We Can Do about It*. New York: St. Martin's Griffin.

Domhoff, G. William. 2002. *Who Rules America? Power and Politics*. New York: McGraw-Hill.

Evans, David G., and Linda Leighton. 1989. "Some Empirical Aspects of Entrepreneurship." *American Economic Review* 79 (June): 519–35.

Feagin, Joe R., and Melvin P. Sikes. 1994. *Living with Racism*. Boston: Beacon Press.

*Forbes*. 2003. "The Forbes 400." 172, no. 7 (October 6): special issue.

"Fortune 500 Largest U.S. Corporations." 2002. *Fortune* (April 15): F1–F31.

Fusfeld, Daniel. 1973. *The Basic Economics of the Urban Racial Crisis*. New York: Holt Rinehart & Winston.

Greenfield, Harry I. 1993. *Invisible, Outlawed, and Untaxed: America's Underground Economy*. Westport, Conn.: Praeger.

Harrison, Bennett. 1994. *Lean and Mean: The Changing Landscape of Corporate Power in the Age of Flexibility*. New York: Guilford Press.

Headd, Brian. 2002. "Redefining Business Success: Distinguishing between Closure and Failure." *Small Business Economics* 21: 51–61.

Leonard, Madeleine. 1998. *Invisible Work, Invisible Workers: The Informal Economy in Europe and the U.S.* New York: St. Martin's Press.

McCrary, Michael. 1998. "Same Song, Different Verse: Processes of Race-Sex Stratification and Self-Employment." Pp. 319–50 in *Research in Social Stratification and Mobility*, Volume 16, edited by Kevin T. Leicht. Greenwich, Conn.: JAI Press.

Miller, Arthur Selwyn. 1977. *The Modern Corporate State: Private Governments and the American Constitution*. Westport, Conn.: Greenwood Press.

Mills, C. Wright. 1951. *White Collar: The American Middle Class*. New York: Oxford University Press.

Mishel, Lawrence, Jared Bernstein, and John Schmitt. 2003. *The State of Working America, 2002–2003*. Ithaca, N.Y.: Cornell University Press.

Nader, Ralph. 2000. *Cutting Corporate Welfare*. New York: Seven Stories Press.

Perrow, Charles. 2002. *Organizing America: Wealth, Power, and the Origins of Corporate Capitalism*. Princeton, N.J.: Princeton University Press.

Phillips, Joseph D. 1958. *Little Business in the American Economy*. Urbana: University of Illinois Press.

———. 1962. *The Self Employed in the United States*. Urbana: University of Illinois Press.

Phillips, Kevin. 2002. *Wealth and Democracy: The Dangerous Politics of American Prosperity*. New York: Broadway Books.

Roy, William. 1997. *Socializing Capital: The Rise of the Large Industrial Corporation in America*. Princeton, N.J.: Princeton University Press.

Schlosser, Eric. 2003. *Reefer Madness: Sex, Drugs, and Cheap Labor in the American Black Market*. Boston: Houghton Mifflin.

Thornton, Patricia. 1999. "The Sociology of Entrepreneurship." Pp. 19–46 in *Annual Review of Sociology*, Volume 25, edited by Karen S. Cook and John Hagan. Palo Alto, Calif.: Annual Reviews.

U.S. Census Bureau. 2002. Table 713, "Establishments, Employees, and Payroll by Employment Size Class: 1990–2000." In *U.S. Statistical Abstract*. Washington, D.C.: U.S. Government Printing Office.

———. 2003. Table P-52, "Class of Worker of Longest Job—Workers (Both Sexes Combined) by Median and Mean Earnings: 1974–2001." In *Historic Income Tables*. Washington, D.C.: U.S. Government Printing Office.

U.S. Department of Labor. 2002a. "Occupations Losing the Most Jobs, 2000–2010." *Monthly Labor Review* (January 4).

———. 2002b. "Self Employed in 2000." *Monthly Labor Review* (January 28).

U.S. Small Business Association. 2002. *Small Business by the Numbers*. Washington, D.C.: U.S. Government Printing Office.

Wallace, James, and Jim Erickson. 1992. *Hard Drive: Bill Gates and the Making of the Microsoft Empire*. New York: John Wiley.

Wright, Erik Olin. 1997. *Class Counts: Comparative Studies in Class Analysis*. New York: Cambridge University Press.

# 8

---

# An Unlevel Playing Field:
# Racism and Sexism

*I have a dream that my four little children will one day live in a nation where they will not be judged by the color of their skin but by the content of their character.*

—Martin Luther King Jr., address at Lincoln Memorial during
March on Washington, August 29, 1963

*It is better for a woman to compete impersonally in society, as men do, than to compete for dominance in her own home with her husband, compete with her neighbors for empty status, and so smother her son that he cannot compete at all.*

—Betty Friedan, *The Feminine Mystique* (1963)

According to the ideal of the American Dream, America is a land in which merit is the sole basis of vast and almost limitless opportunity. Discrimination, however, invalidates the American Dream. Discrimination not only interferes with merit, it is the antithesis of merit. Discrimination allows some, who are not necessarily meritorious, to get ahead of others. In this way, discrimination creates a terrible irony—the very discrimination that invalidates the American Dream for many Americans creates conditions that appear to validate it for others and enables them to embrace it so fervently. By excluding entire segments of the American population from equal access to opportunity, discrimination reduces competition and increases the chances of members of some groups getting ahead on what they often presume to be exclusively their own merit.

# DISCRIMINATION: INDIVIDUAL AND INSTITUTIONALIZED

We may define discrimination as a set of exclusionary practices by which individuals and groups use their power, privilege, and prestige to define criteria of eligibility for opportunity in terms of a set of characteristics (usually their own and often ascribed) and to then exclude those who lack those characteristics. Thus, discriminatory behaviors, actions, and practices involve the exercise of power and are exclusionary. Individuals can and do discriminate, but the most consequential discrimination occurs at the group, organizational, community, and institutional levels. This latter form, sometimes called *institutional discrimination*, includes actions, practices, and policies embedded in the organization of society that have negative impacts on individuals and groups that have socially specified characteristics. These actions and practices are not episodic or sporadic; rather they are practices and policies that groups, organizations, communities, and institutions engage in on a routine, everyday basis. Such exclusionary practices and policies may not have been designed to harm and are not necessarily conscious or intentional. In fact, intent to harm is typically vigorously denied, and elaborate ideologies that legitimate such practices are either in place or constructed post hoc to deny such charges. Intentional or not, the effects or consequences are what is important. For example, bail policies that consider only the employed to be eligible for bail clearly discriminate against minorities that have higher rates of unemployment than whites. Similarly, collective decisions to decommodify K–12 schooling but not higher education discriminate against minorities because they tend to have lower incomes and wealth than the dominant group. Finally, policies used for the determination of mortgage loan eligibility and setting mortgage interest rates that use economic criteria such as net assets, credit history, mortgage experience, and the like discriminate against minorities on a number of counts.

Most important for our analysis is the fact that discrimination involves unequal treatment of individuals and groups on the basis of characteristics that have little if any relation to what could conventionally be considered to be individual merit. Further, discrimination can easily become self-perpetuating. Over time, individuals and groups affected by discrimination become as unequal as they have been treated. By depriving access to opportunities, discrimination often leads to lack of qualification for them. The involuntarily ascribed and negatively evaluated categorical status that emerges from discrimination not only takes precedence over any achieved status, it reduces the probability of such achievement, thereby lowering all life chances. Put another way, discrimination makes it more difficult for the objects of discrimination to develop merit *and* reduces the likelihood that merit will be recognized and rewarded.

# RACIAL AND ETHNIC DISCRIMINATION IN AMERICA

The long history of deliberate discrimination against racial and ethnic groups in America belies the American ideology of individual freedom and equality of opportunity. From the near-genocide of Native Americans and the banishment of survivors to reservations, to importation and enslavement of Africans, to subsequent Jim Crow legislation that legalized racial segregation and unequal opportunity in the South, to exclusionary acts and discriminatory immigration quotas, to land displacement of Mexican Americans, to the internment of Japanese Americans during World War II, to current forms of residential, occupational, and educational discrimination against various minorities, the American experience has for many been more of an American *Nightmare* than an American *Dream*.

While most Americans acknowledge historical forms of discrimination, many insist that discrimination against racial and ethnic minorities is a thing of the past. Many assert that we have moved beyond this sordid past and that this is, in itself, a testimony to the American Dream. Indeed, great strides to reduce discrimination have been made. Since World War II, the position of the federal and state governments has gradually changed from requiring, supporting, or tacitly accepting discriminatory practices to one of formally and actively opposing discrimination. These changes began in the late 1930s and culminated with the passage of the Civil Rights Acts of 1957, 1960, 1964, 1965, and 1968. For example, court rulings, legislation, and executive orders were designed to desegregate the military, end educational segregation and discrimination, protect voting rights, and require federal contractors to comply with nondiscrimination policies. The banning of overt discrimination and segregation in privately owned businesses came later in the form of legislation against employment and housing discrimination. Finally at the local level, numerous antidiscrimination ordinances and laws have been passed. Thus, by the late 1960s the clear position of American law was against discrimination. This represents a near total reversal of the situation twenty-five to thirty years earlier, when the position of American law had been somewhere between tolerating and requiring such discrimination.

Unfortunately, these legal changes have not eliminated discrimination. Discrimination in America is down but not out. Since most forms of discrimination are now illegal, today's discrimination is either more subtle or elaborately cloaked and thus more difficult to detect. To put it another way, discrimination has been driven underground. Scratching just below the surface, however, reveals a diminished but continued pattern of political, occupational, educational, housing, and consumer discrimination.

## Discrimination in the Political and Legal Systems

Until the mid-1950s, the American political and legal systems enforced and even required discrimination against minorities. Today, government at all levels, at least formally, has taken an antidiscrimination position, yet problem areas remain. Past discrimination by government policy has led to minority disadvantage, and current government inaction and unwillingness to undo the effects of past discrimination perpetuate minority disadvantage.

Several sources of evidence verify this pattern. The higher a person's socioeconomic status, for instance, the greater the availability and amount of government services and benefits (Kerbo 2000, 41–44). Thus, many patterns of government spending differentially harm minorities simply because large proportions remain poor. In federal spending for various programs that provide money or services for individuals (such as health care), benefits provided to minorities and the poor are much smaller than imagined. America remains the only industrialized nation in the world without a national health care program, and subsidies to public transportation systems have been neglected. What is more, discrimination continues in legal and educational institutions that are largely funded and controlled by governments.

It is becoming increasingly clear that the welfare reforms of the late 1990s are not doing much to help the minority poor. Public preoccupation with the welfare system and its purported benefits to the minority poor diverts attention from the *wealthfare* system—a purposefully hidden but larger and more lucrative system that benefits the privileged. Essentially, wealthfare is revenue forgone through a variety of tax breaks and subsidies for which only the privileged qualify (Phillips 2003; Domhoff 2002; Beeghley 2000; Turner and Starnes 1976).

Government policies designed to slow inflation tend to harm the poor and minorities, and government policies designed to reduce unemployment don't really help minorities. Wage and labor law, including the low minimum wage and probusiness and antiunion policy, continue to harm the interests of workers in general and minority workers in particular. The geographical patterns of federal spending are such that large urban areas (high proportion minority) pay more to the federal government in taxes than they get back.

With respect to foreign policy, in the post–World War II era, the U.S. government permitted trade and formed allied relationships with openly racist regimes such as South Africa. Continued worldwide military "actions" and interventions drain government resources away from programs that would benefit minorities and the poor. Historically, such warfare has led to differentially higher minority casualty rates. Minorities are overrepresented in the military, partially because of lack of job opportunities in the civilian economy.

Discrimination continues in voting and other forms of political participation, including office holding. Minorities are underrepresented in major elected and appointed offices at the state and federal levels. The more powerful the office, the greater the minority underrepresentation. Hacker (1995) and Cose (1995) have pointed out that whites remain unwilling to vote for blacks and other minorities, and that minorities who appear to be "angry," who "have an agenda," or who are merely liberal, are simply eliminated by the candidate screening processes of both major parties. The voting power of minorities has been exaggerated. Historically, voting and political participation have been directly correlated with socioeconomic status. Minority overrepresentation among the less privileged partially explains the lower political participation of minorities. Thus, political power of blacks and other minorities is limited by their numbers, geographical concentrations and residential segregation, overrepresentation among the less privileged, and continuing individual and institutional discrimination.

Abundant research documents a continuing pattern of racial discrimination throughout the American legal system. From the definition of crime itself, to decisions concerning severity of penalties for behavior defined as criminal, to the various stages of the criminal justice process, to the lack of protection of the rights of law-abiding minority citizens, there is evidence of discrimination against racial minorities. Crime in America is highly racialized. The focus is violent street crime. Hate crime and corporate crime, including employee and white-collar crime, get much less attention.

Discrimination is well documented at each step in the criminal justice process, from police scrutiny and detection of crime to severity of sentencing (Walker, Spohn, and DeLone 2003; Farley 2000; Kennedy 1997). If one's criminal activity is not detected, then one is not arrested. Most would agree that the detection of crime is a good thing. But police stereotypes and negative expectations about blacks lead to elevated police scrutiny and racial profiling, which in turn lead to racial discrimination in crime detection. Varying degrees of racial discrimination have been documented in all of the following: police decisions to follow up on observations of possible violations, to apprehend, and to arrest suspects; decisions whether to prosecute, to refer a case to the court system, and if so, to what type of court; the setting and administration of bail for the accused; decision of the judge, judicial panel, or jury whether the accused is guilty or innocent (conviction decisions); and decisions regarding the nature and severity of penalties for crimes (sentencing decisions). Minorities receive longer and more severe sentences (controlling for criminal record and severity of crime).

Discrimination based on the race of the victim is also well documented. At any given step of the criminal justice process, the bias may be large, small, or even nonexistent, but enough bias exists in enough places at each step so that, even though the effect at any one step may be small, the cumulative effect over the entire course of the criminal justice process can be substantial (Walker, Spohn, and DeLone 2003; Farley 2000). At the point of arrest, the population of accused is quite racially mixed, but the proportion of racial minorities rises substantially as one moves through the criminal justice process to the endpoint of the imprisoned population. The consequences of the criminal label can be severe. Former convicts (and sometimes those merely arrested but not convicted) often face reduced employment and credit opportunities. Denial of legitimate opportunities can increase chances of recidivism and entrapment in a vicious circle.

Blacks and other minorities have long complained of various forms of inadequate police protection—from inadequate patrol of their neighborhoods to inadequate response to calls for assistance. Minorities have also complained, sometimes bitterly, of police brutality, of lack of respect shown them by police, and of the inability of police to distinguish law-abiding minorities from minority criminals. Again, while complaints have at times been exaggerated for political purposes, it is clear that minorities experience more police violence and receive less respect from police than apologists for the police can explain away. Finally, there is abundant evidence that the historic failure of the American court system to protect the legal rights of minorities continues. For example, the courts have failed to protect minorities against police brutality and other abuses by the state. Further, because civil courts make no presumption of the right to an attorney, racial minorities have less ability to make use of civil courts to protect or pursue their economic interests. We conclude that as custodians of the American Dream, the political and legal systems have constructed and are administering an unfair game.

## Income and Occupational Discrimination

Overwhelming evidence demonstrates that income and employment discrimination based on race in America lingers and is pervasive (Feagin and McKinney 2003; Bonilla-Silva 2003; Farley 2000; Feagin and Feagin 1999; Cose 1995; Feagin and Sikes 1994). In 2001 the average family income of blacks was only 62% that of whites, and the corresponding figure for Hispanics was only 64% (Mishel et al. 2003, 41). Some of these differences reflect the current effects of past discrimination, including unequal access to educational attainment. But current discrimination also continues to contribute to these huge income deficits.

Discrimination has been found in recruitment, hiring, promotion, layoff, and discharge practices. It may take the form of selective placement of job advertisements, the use of word-of-mouth and informal recruitment networks, or recruitment limited to local areas. Exclusive union referral systems exclude nonunion workers and permit nepotism. Discrimination has also been found in screening practices, where it may take the forms of discriminatory hiring standards and procedures. Credentials requirements, including educational and physical requirements, can be discriminatory when, for instance, such requirements are irrelevant to the demands of a particular job. Nonvalidated credentials—those that cannot be demonstrated to measure what they purport to measure or cannot be demonstrated to be necessary for satisfactory job performance—continue to be used to the disadvantage of minorities and women. Employment interviews may be used to screen out candidates who have unwanted characteristics unrelated to merit. Presumptions of inferiority and use of negative stereotypes that lead to constant scrutiny and overly close supervision are discriminatory. Promotion practices that give high consideration to subjective evaluations and recommendations of supervisors can be discriminatory. Various forms of tracking can be discriminatory. Segregative tracking into "ghettos"—dead-end jobs in departments or units with short mobility ladders, as well as organizational rules that do not permit movement out of such units—can be discriminatory. Assignments to "fast-track" jobs are often based on nonmerit criteria. Discriminatory informal workplace relations can create a "hostile workplace environment." Selective mentoring, sponsorship, and exclusion from "old boy" networks can be discriminatory.

Beyond these forms of discrimination, basic characteristics of the American industrial structure produce differentiated occupational opportunities that are allocated in discriminatory ways. As discussed in chapter 5, wages and benefits received for doing essentially the same job vary by the type of organization, industry, and region in which the job is performed. Large, capital-intensive, high-profit firms with large market shares in the "core" economic sector pay employees the most. Small, labor-intensive, low-profit businesses with small market shares in the "periphery" sector pay employees the least. Being a janitor at the NBC office building in New York, for instance, pays better and has better benefits than doing essentially the same job in a textile mill in Thomasville, North Carolina.

Research shows that minorities and women are underrepresented in core employment, and when they do obtain employment in the core, they are paid less than white males. Research also reveals that a set of individual characteristics that could be taken as measures of "merit" actually explain little of the core–periphery differences in wages and little of the race and gender differences in wages found *within* the industrial sector. Finally, research suggests that individual characteristics that could be taken as measures of "merit" are more highly rewarded in the core than in the periphery. In short, controlling for what people do for a living, rewards for "merit" are contingent upon characteristics of the employing organization, race, and gender.

## Affirmative Action

Affirmative action—for white males only—has been in place throughout most of American history. What is currently referred to as affirmative action came into being because existing antidiscrimination legislation did not effectively combat continuing race and sex discrimination. Affirmative action grew out of civil rights laws, presidential executive orders, court cases, federal implementation efforts, and human resource practices voluntarily implemented by employers. Affirmative action involves proactive employment practices whose object is to prevent discrimination. It refers to a complex set of actions, policies, and procedures designed to combat ongoing job discrimination in the workplace and to equalize employment opportunity. Thus, like antidiscrimination laws, the goal of affirmative action is to make equal opportunity a reality for members of groups that have commonly been the object of discrimination. Unlike antidiscrimination laws, which provide remedies to which workers can appeal after they have suffered discrimination, affirmative action policies aim to keep discrimination from occurring.

Affirmative action in employment was one of the most highly politicized social reforms of the latter half of the twentieth century. While the large majority of white Americans oppose affirmative action, few understand what affirmative action in employment actually entails. Affirmative action has been demonized by its opponents, who characterize it as "reverse discrimination"—the use of unfair quotas that require the hiring of unqualified minorities over more qualified whites. They cry that it is "un-American" and violates the American Dream, which requires that individual merit be the only legitimate consideration in hiring and promotion. They claim that affirmative action is antimeritocratic, amounts to reverse discrimination, and has led to the hiring and promotion of thousands of minorities (blacks) over more qualified white males.

Research findings suggest otherwise. The truth is that employment discrimination—affirmative action for white males—continues, largely unacknowledged by its beneficiaries, and seemingly American as apple pie. Discrimination against minorities and women in employment continues and remains a far larger problem than employment discrimination against white males. Affirmative action programs exist only because of such discrimination. Their clear purpose is to extend to members of previously excluded groups opportunities for full and equal participation in the American Dream. Actually, few white males have been denied jobs or promotions, and fewer still have been fired, because of affirmative action programs (Reskin 1998, 71–74).

Affirmative action programs have, in fact, expanded employment opportunity to minorities and women, but for a variety of reasons, they have been less successful than commonly assumed. Employers in the United States who are required to engage in affirmative action include state and federal agencies and private employers holding large contracts with the U.S. government or firms that have been ordered by courts to engage in affirmative action to remedy egregious violations of antidiscrimination law. Actually, relatively few employers are required by the federal government to practice affirmative action. More than half of American firms do not engage in affirmative action. Of all the types of affirmative action programs, voluntary programs of private firms are the most common, but they tend to be the weakest. Finally, affirmative action programs have been successfully misrepresented by their opponents; opposition to them remains widespread and may be found even among minorities and women. In sum, although affirmative action has expanded employment opportunities for minorities and women, it has not been a silver bullet. For many, employment discrimination still hinders pursuit of the American Dream.

## Discrimination in Educational Systems

Chapter 5 is devoted to a discussion of the relationships between education and the American Dream. Basically, the American education system is viewed as the means though which the American Dream can be achieved. Accordingly, education is a crucial mechanism of meritocracy because it is a system within which information, training, and skills can be attained and credentials for their attainment awarded, based solely on objectively measurable and demonstrated mastery, which presumably directly reflects individual merit and indirectly reflects intelligence, ability, and other desirable individual qualities. Thus the education system is seen as a means to produce, measure, and certify merit. Discrimination in educational systems, however, erodes the very foundation of the American Dream because it invalidates this basic assumption of meritocracy.

Throughout American history, access to education has varied by class, race, and gender. In colonial times, education was reserved for privileged white males. Since then, the history of American education has been one of increasing access to education for previously excluded groups. While access has been expanded, discrimination continues.

One form of educational discrimination is continuing segregation of schools by race and socioeconomic status. Although *Brown v. Topeka Kansas Board of Education* (1954) signaled the end of blatant de jure segregation, de facto segregation continues, and America's public schools remain highly segregated. For example, in 1988, almost one-third of black students attended schools that were 90% or more black, and in 1992, almost three-quarters of Hispanic students attended schools that were 50% or more minority (Farley 2000, 378). Within school districts, segregation exists not only among schools but also within individual schools. What is more, today much of the segregation that exists is *between* school districts and is due to largely minority cities surrounded by white suburbs. Finally, official segregation figures underestimate the actual amount of segregation because calculations are typically based only on public school data. Private schools, except for some inclusive Catholic schools in large cities in the northeast, are overwhelmingly white.

Although expenditures per pupil do not, in themselves, explain much of the racial variation in academic achievement (Coleman et al. 1966), such expenditures tend to be lower in schools that have large minority enrollments. This is partially because school revenues come from local property taxes, which tend to produce less revenue in the racially segregated areas in which the schools that minorities attend are located. Schools with high minority enrollments are more likely to be older or run down; have inadequate facilities, programs, and technology; be overcrowded; have larger classes; have less experienced and qualified teachers; have student bodies that are disproportionately lower in socioeconomic status; and have a host of other characteristics that hinder academic achievement.

Racial segregation is not the only form of discrimination in education. Minorities may be excluded or reduced to stereotypes in curricula, texts, and other teaching materials. Blacks (and other minorities) need to see real, complete, and unbiased images of themselves. Teachers and administrators may discriminate against minority students in a variety of ways. For example, teacher expectations can be discriminatory. Low teacher expectations of minorities create self-fulfilling prophecies and lower achievement.

Tracking or ability grouping is almost universal in secondary schools. In situations in which track placement is based on valid measures of ability and performance, tracking seems to have a positive effect on achievement. However, some studies have revealed that ability, aptitude, performance, and other individual "merit" factors explain less than 40% of the variance in track placement. The discriminatory placement of minorities in low tracks, regardless of ability, creates self-fulfilling prophecies by lowering aspirations and achievement. In short, tracking based on factors other than valid measures of ability and achievement remains a problem.

Another problem has been an inability to recruit and keep minority teachers. Blacks and other minorities are underrepresented in the teaching profession and in positions of authority within education. As we move from elementary school to secondary school to higher education, the underrepresentation increases. Thus, blacks and other minority students have few role models and must learn in an authority structure and culture that is largely white.

Modest and half-hearted efforts to reduce various forms of educational discrimination have produced mixed results, and many have been less effective than hoped. Busing is a good example. Busing simply cannot achieve racial integration in large central city school districts that are predominantly minority because of more than a half-century of white suburbanization. What is more, courts have ruled that cross-district (city–suburb) busing cannot be required unless there is compelling evidence that the districts were created with the intent to discriminate. Even districts that have relatively small proportions of minorities may not effectively integrate schools because of residential segregation and white opposition to busing that produces "white flight." Those bused tend to be disproportionately minority children, which to some seems to be another form of discrimination. Under some conditions, busing may actually increase "white flight," possibly exacerbating the problem of school segregation. Finally, busing may lead to desegregation but not integration. That is, minorities who are bused are not accepted and instead become isolated and marginalized in their new schools.

Despite the considerable success of efforts to increase access of women and minorities to higher education, continuing economic discrimination and K–12 educational discrimination have limited access of lower SES and thus minority students to higher education. Affirmative action programs put in place in the 1960s and 1970s were part of an effort to increase minority enrollments. From the outset, such programs faced strong opposition, and by the mid-1990s a large-scale dismantling of such programs had occurred. Thus, by the end of 1998, consideration of race in higher education admissions for purposes of having a diverse student body had become illegal in Texas, Louisiana, Mississippi, California, and Washington (Farley 2000, 506). The recent Supreme Court decision based on the University of Michigan's program seems to reaffirm the principle of affirmative action in admissions for the purpose of achieving diversity as a legitimate and compelling interest of the institution but prohibits quotas or other categorical means to achieve it. While this may signal a reversal of the previously described trend, we believe that it is too soon to tell.

According to the American Dream, there is a strong correlation between educational achievement and occupational success; doing well in school is seen as the ticket for a good job. But educational discrimination against minorities reduces their chances for academic achievement, and occupational discrimination reduces their chances for occupational success. Even if minorities manage to transcend educational discrimination and become academically successful, research consistently shows that minorities receive much lower income and occupational returns on equivalent amounts of educational attainment than do whites.

## Discrimination and Segregation in Housing

A major component of the American Dream is home ownership, and it is easy to understand why. Equity in a home is the major form of wealth for the large majority of Americans. A home is a nest egg that can be sold for a handsome tax-exempt profit in one's later years or be bequeathed to the next generation. One's home and the neighborhood in which it is located are a material representation of one's achievements and social class. Finally, homes have a psychological value. One's home is a safe haven, a place of refuge from the realities of the harshly competitive and increasingly graceless world in which we live.

According to the American Dream, home ownership is equally open to all, limited only by ability to pay. We are all equally free to live where we want, as long as we can afford it. In fact, a sizable proportion of Americans do *not* own homes because they cannot afford to own one. Home ownership and socio-economic status are positively related; most of the privileged are homeowners, while most of the poor are not. This is reflected in highly unequal rates of home ownership by race. In 2001, the rate of home ownership for whites was 71%, but the corresponding figures for blacks and Hispanics were 48% and 47% respectively (Mishel et al. 2003, 292). Yet the issue is not simply owning or not owning a home. Inequalities in home ownership are much greater if one considers the *value* of homes. For example, an upper-middle-class and a working-class family may both own homes. However, the home of the former may be worth from a few hundred thousand dollars to over one million dol-lars, while the home of the latter may be worth less than one hundred thou-sand dollars. What is more, many of the privileged own second "vacation" homes that sit empty most of the year or are rented to pay a mortgage and build equity for the owner. Many of the poor, on the other hand, settle for housing that is not only inadequate, it is worth less than the second homes of many of the privileged. The differences in both rates of home ownership and the value of homes owned further contribute to the staggering wealth differ-ences by race. For instance, whereas blacks on average earn about 65% of what whites do, blacks have only 12% of the net worth (assets minus liabili-ties) of whites (Mishel et al. 2003, 283).

Even if families can afford to own homes at various income levels, they may not be able to live anywhere they choose. The findings of social science research clearly show that freedom of housing choice is a myth. There con-tinues to be considerable racial and ethnic segregation of housing. The sim-plest and most commonly reported measure of such segregation is the index of dissimilarity. Ranging from 0 (no segregation) to 1.00 (complete segrega-tion), it indicates the proportion of one group that would have to move to a different census tract to reproduce the residential pattern of the other group. In 1980, there were 220 metropolitan areas (of the 330 total) with 3% or 20,000 or more blacks. The average index of black/white residential segre-gation for these 220 metropolitan areas declined from .73 in 1980 to .66 in 1990 to .64 in 2000 (Iceland, Weinberg, and Steinmetz 2002, 60). Although this represents a clear reduction, 64% of blacks (or whites) would have to move to a different census tract to reproduce the residential pattern of the other group. This is considered to be substantial segregation.

What causes such massive segregation? The most widely accepted expla-nation is economic. Blacks as a group have lower socioeconomic status than whites and are therefore seen as unable to afford to live in the same areas as whites. But using a technique called *indirect standardization*, we can pre-cisely estimate the number of blacks and whites that one would expect to live in each neighborhood of a city based on the neighborhood's income distribution. From these estimates it is possible to compute what the segregation index for a city would be if income differences between blacks and whites were the only reason for housing segregation. Several studies conducted in different cities from 1960 to 1990 reveal that only 20 to 25% of black–white residential segregation is explained by economic factors. Thus, actual black–white racial residential segregation is 4 to 6.3 times greater than that expected based on income differences.

Another proposed explanation is that blacks (and other minorities) simply prefer to live in all-black neighborhoods. But several surveys of black and white housing preferences have shown that blacks prefer to live in integrated neighborhoods. Obviously, blacks aren't getting what they prefer.

What then is the explanation? The same surveys reveal that most whites prefer to live in white neighborhoods or minimally integrated (one or two black families) neighborhoods. Thus, white preferences are crucial. Once a neighborhood becomes minimally integrated, it becomes more attractive to blacks but less attractive to whites. More blacks move in, but whites move out, and fewer move in to take their places. The result can be rapid "racial turnover" or resegregation. Coupled with white housing preferences, institutionalized housing discrimination has maintained high levels of racial residential segregation.

Discrimination in the sale and rental of housing became illegal with the Civil Rights Act of 1968 and subsequent fair housing laws. But federal enforcement of fair housing legislation has been weak, and housing discrimination continues in a variety of forms. It is estimated that there are more than two million cases of housing discrimination every year, and about 60% of black home seekers face discriminatory treatment (Feagin and Sikes 1994, 269). Some whites simply refuse to sell to minorities with little need to fear being punished. In the past, supported by the FHA, the real estate industry practiced blatant forms of housing discrimination. Today, more subtle and covert forms of housing discrimination, including racial steering, continue. Studies have also revealed that although it is illegal, banks, mortgage companies, and insurance companies discriminate, as indicated by black–white differences in loan approval rates, mortgage interest rates, and insurance rates that cannot be accounted for by black–white differences in income and other relevant characteristics. The federal government, through weak enforcement of fair housing laws, as well as Federal Housing Administration and the Department of Housing and Urban Development practices, continues to be implicated in housing discrimination. Finally, local governments continue to use exclusionary or "snob" zoning and control of the location of publicly subsidized housing to discriminate and perpetuate racial segregation of housing.

The impacts of housing discrimination are severe. Minorities, especially African and Mexican Americans, are not permitted to live where they can afford, pay more and get less for their housing dollar, and are underrepresented as homeowners at every income level. They are thus disproportionately denied a major means of wealth accumulation, and this jeopardizes their ability to transmit wealth to their children. Housing discrimination differentially excludes minorities from the intangible status recognition of living in prestigious neighborhoods. It forces minorities to live in neighborhoods with fewer resources, services, and amenities; poorer schools; and higher rates of poverty than whites of similar socioeconomic status. Stores in poor and minority areas tend to have poorer selection, lower quality, and higher prices (Caplovitz 1967). Further, *residential* segregation contributes to *school* segregation that requires busing for integration. Denial of quality education and neighborhoods to working- and middle-class blacks leads to an inability to transmit class position to their children (Massey 1990). Further, the residential segregation of groups with high proportions in poverty leads to concentrated poverty and the additional problems it creates (Massey and Denton 1989; Wilson 1987). Residential segregation often limits its victims to areas of declining job opportunities. Finally, the racial residential segregation produced by housing discrimination isolates and marginalizes people, denying them full and equal participation in American society. In short, this egregious form of discrimination most certainly violates the American Dream.

## A WORD ON THE INTERCONNECTEDNESS OF INSTITUTIONALIZED DISCRIMINATION

Despite angry protests to the contrary, institutionalized political, legal, educational, and economic (job, housing, and consumer) discrimination are facts of life in America, providing advantages for some and excluding others for reasons that have nothing to do with merit. Institutional discrimination leads to mutually reinforcing disadvantages because all forms tend to have important negative side effects. For example, discrimination in the political system reduces the power and influence of its victims, which in turn reduces access to all forms of economic opportunity. Educational discrimination is so damaging because it reduces chances of getting a good job and all the things that depend on the income from a good job, like wealth accumulation, housing, and quality education for one's children. In itself, job discrimination can be psychologically damaging, but it also leads to reduced earnings, which limits housing opportunity and educational opportunity for one's children. Housing discrimination, in turn, may reduce access to areas in which good jobs, good schools, and shopping are located. Discrimination by the police and criminal justice system increases chances for criminal victimization as well as for arrest and conviction, which lower subsequent employment opportunity.

## GENDER DISCRIMINATION

Women experience all the forms of employment discrimination discussed above for racial and ethnic minorities, as well as several that are unique to women. Despite more than thirty years of feminism; increased educational achievement and labor force participation; and continuing social, economic, and cultural change, the power structure of the United States remains heavily male dominated. In both the public and private sectors, nearly all of the positions at the top, such as corporate officers, members of boards of directors, and high elected officials, are held by males. Men continue to dominate socially, politically, and economically. In short, gender—a factor that has no demonstrable independent effect on individual merit—conditions access to opportunity, and women have been denied full participation in the American Dream. Indeed, women's subordinate status is visible in practically every aspect of American life.

### The Pink-Collar Ghetto

Historically and cross-culturally, the degree of male dominance in society is directly related to the kind and extent of female participation in economic production. That is, the more women participate in economic production and the more equally women participate in economic production, the less the degree of male dominance. Since the 1960s, female labor force participation has steadily increased. Today, about three-fifths of all adult women are employed. The fastest increase in working women has been among those with school-aged children. About three-quarters of mothers with children aged six to thirteen are employed, and almost two-thirds of mothers with children under age six are employed.

Although the level of female participation in the labor force is now almost equivalent to that of men, women are not equally spread out within the labor force. More than any other group, women are confined to certain occupations, which produces gender occupational segregation. Collectively, the jobs in which women are highly concentrated—such as secretary, elementary school teacher, day care worker, nurse, dental hygienist, and so on—represent what has come to be called the *pink-collar ghetto*. Bureau of Labor Statistics researchers have compiled a segregation index to estimate the percentage of women who would have to change their jobs to make the distribution of men and women in each occupation within the labor force mirror the relative percentage of each sex in the adult working population. A recent BLS study showed that 54% of women workers would need to switch jobs to create a labor force without gender segregation. While there has been a steady decline in occupational segregation, there is still a substantial amount of sex-based occupational segregation in the labor force. Moreover, the

movement of men and women into and out of job categories has been un-
even. Women, for instance, have been rapidly moving into some traditionally male-dominated professions, especially as lawyers, doctors, professors,
veterinarians, and pharmacists. Men, however, have not been moving as
quickly into traditionally female dominated professions such as social work,
nursing, and elementary school teaching. Likewise, there is very little movement of women into traditionally male-dominated blue-collar trades.

Some jobs in which women are concentrated, such as nursing and teaching, pay moderately well and carry moderate prestige. Nevertheless, they are
far lower in pay and prestige than "men's jobs" that require equivalent levels
of skill and training. These jobs also tend to be "order-taker" rather than
"order-giver" positions and are often located in direct relation to an occupationally defined chain of command: nurses take orders from doctors, secretaries take orders from bosses, and so on. Often these are "dead-end" jobs because promotion opportunities are either limited or nonexistent; that is, they
have short mobility ladders with few rungs available for advancement. A
nurse, for instance, may aspire to be "head nurse," but there are not many
rungs on the advancement ladder beyond that. Even if one is an especially
skilled and competent nurse, the head nurse on the floor may also be competent, forty years old, and going nowhere. Many pink-collar jobs are disproportionately located in the low-wage service sector of the economy. The jobs
themselves are insecure, and those who hold them face higher than average
risks of irregular employment, involuntary part-time work, and layoff or firing. These jobs typically carry limited fringe benefits, and some require shift
work. Pink-collar jobs and the industries in which they are located are typically not unionized, and therefore workers do not benefit from protections
won by the collective power of unions. Change has occurred in a few of the
female-dominated professions such as social work, teaching, and nursing,
which formed more powerful occupational associations. But most pink-collar
jobs are in the low-wage service sector of the economy, which is grossly un-
represented by either unions or professional associations. Finally, pink-collar
jobs are often extensions of traditional domestic female sex roles—nurses and
nurses' aides taking care of the sick and the elderly, teachers and day care
workers taking care of children, and so on. These nurturing tasks are critical
to any civilized society, but as paid labor they are grossly underappreciated,
undervalued, and underrewarded.

## The Gender Pay Gap

In 2001, the median hourly wage of female workers was 78% of the median hourly wage of male workers, whereas in 1979 it was only 63% (Mishel
et al. 2003, 172). However, the rate at which the male–female wage gap has
declined has slowed in the last decade and most of the wage gap reduction

is due to the falling wages of men rather than increasing wages of women. Despite the closing of the gap, women on average still earn 25% less than men. Differences in the occupational distributions of men and women—occupational segregation of women into "women's jobs," which are lower paying—explains some of this disparity. However, women still earn less than men in almost every field, even those dominated by women. Women earn less than men even when race and education are held constant; that is, college-educated women working full time make less than comparably educated men. A detailed analysis of the gender wage gap, considering schooling, employment history, time with current employer, and medical leave of absence, found that all these factors can explain less than 42% of the wage differences between men and women (Wellington 1994; Tomaskovic-Devy 1993). The remaining differences were largely attributable to discrimination.

Efforts to eliminate employment discrimination against women have not been successful. The Federal Equal Pay Act of 1963, which mandates equal pay for equal work, applies to a relatively small proportion of female workers: those who perform the same job as male workers for the same employer. Although these women's wages have increased as a result of the Equal Pay Act, as we noted above, many women remain segregated in a small set of occupations in which few or no men work. The 1964 Civil Rights Act and its enforcement arm, the Equal Employment Opportunity Commission, address cases of sex discrimination. But neither this nor subsequent federal legislation has removed all employment discrimination against women.

Since men and women tend to do different kinds of work, the call for "equal pay for equal work" did not fully address pay equity issues for · women. During the 1980s, pay equity or *comparable worth* was proposed as a means to address the tendency for the paid work that women perform in the labor force to be undervalued. Comparable worth calls for equal pay for different types of work that are judged to be comparable in value by measuring such factors as employee knowledge, skills, effort, responsibility, and working conditions. In terms of the actual skills needed to do the job, for instance, the female office secretary might score higher than the male truck driver working in the same firm who earns more. Except for some local initiatives mostly in government employment, comparable worth programs have not been widely implemented.

Although such proposals make sense from an equity and merit standpoint, one of the problems in implementing them is that people do not ordinarily get paid on the basis of "merit" in the first place. According to market principles, people get paid on the basis of whatever the market will bear, which may not be directly affected by the demands of the job, the qualifications of employees, or the contribution of employees to employing organizations or to society as a whole.

## The Glass Ceiling

The phrase "glass ceiling," another form of employment discrimination, refers to discriminatory policies that limit the upward mobility of qualified women and minorities, keeping them out of top management positions. As previously noted, many of the jobs in which women are concentrated have short mobility ladders. Secretaries rarely become bosses. Even though many secretaries *could* do the work of their bosses—and indeed many times they *are* doing the work of the bosses—they do not get the credit, the salary, or the opportunity to move up—regardless of their level of competence. The glass ceiling operates so that although all applicants may be welcomed by a firm at entry levels, when it comes to powerful managerial and executive positions, there are limits—generally unstated—on the number of women and nonwhites welcomed or even tolerated. Women may be doing better in getting top management positions than minorities, but they still lag well behind men. Constituting only 29% of the workforce, white men hold 95% of all senior management positions. One 1998 study showed that only 10.6% of the seats on the boards of directors of the Fortune 500 companies were held by women, and about one out of six companies had no women board members (Catalyst 1998; Blau 1998).

Part of this overall differential is due to lag effects of women's more recent entry into the professions in particular and to the labor force in general. It often takes twenty or thirty years in a company or a profession to ascend to the highest levels of management. Even though women now are graduating from law schools at rates comparable to men, for instance, few women occupy judgeships and senior partnerships in major law firms, in part because few women graduated from law schools twenty or thirty years ago and those who did were often subjected to much more severe discrimination than occurs now, derailing their prospects for advancement. Net of these lag effects, however, discrimination continues. Even among younger cohorts, research shows that women do not ascend as often or as quickly as men.

## Old Boy Networks

Regardless of where women are located in the labor force (e.g., doctor or secretary), women as a group face unique nonmerit impediments that make it more difficult to compete evenly with men. One of those impediments is lack of sponsorship—one form of social capital. Since the most powerful and influential positions are usually held by men, women are at a critical disadvantage. Mentor–protégé relationships are crucial for advancement, especially in the professions. After all, it is the senior partners in the law firm, the full professors in the department, and the top management in the corporation who have the most experience and the most knowledge to impart to aspiring protégés. Mentors take their protégés under their wings, show them the ropes, and when the time comes, go to bat for them.

Women are less likely to receive these benefits: they receive far less informal support, inclusion in networks, mentoring, and sponsorship than do men. Men seem to be less willing to mentor and sponsor women than other men, partially because climates of sexual tension or appearances of sexual harassment may make cross-gender mentorship and sponsorship seem dangerous or uncomfortable for both men and women. In the business world for example, women have been denied equal access to male-dominated "inner sanctums": many deals are cut on the golf course, on the racquetball court, over drinks at the men's club, "at the game," or at sites not fully open to women.

Women who do occupy higher ranks and who could serve as mentors to other women generally have more limited resources than their male counterparts. They are more likely to be relative newcomers themselves and may be quite busy surviving and succeeding on their own in the absence of support from men. Finally, some women distance themselves from other women as a means of consolidating their own positions in male-dominated upper echelons. Like Ellis Cose's "king shits"—highly successful blacks who have convinced themselves that they made it on their own, who do very little to assist other blacks, and who sometimes even subvert other blacks to maintain their vanity and status monopoly—these "queen bee" women operate on a false consciousness that convinces them that their sisters "can make it on their own, just like I did."

### Family versus Career

Women experience a greater degree of perceived role conflict between family and career than men do. Role conflict occurs when the expectations and requirements associated with one position that an individual occupies interfere with or are in conflict with those of another position. Although males can act as homemakers and caretakers for children, women have customarily performed these roles. Men are far less likely to feel that they must make an either/or choice (homemaker-caretaker versus paid employment) or to attempt to "burn a candle at both ends." Research, for instance, shows that even though fertility has declined *and* having children no longer keeps most women out of the labor force *and* it is illegal to discriminate on the basis of marital or family status, some employers still assume that women are temporary workers in the labor force whose careers will be derailed by childbirth. As a result, such employers may be reluctant to hire women in the first place and, if they hire them, invest less in their training and career development. This precludes eligibility for lop level positions and forces women into a career trajectory with lower chances for advancement.

Related to the issue of child care is the issue of reproductive freedom. A rapid decline in fertility has coincided with the increased participation of women in the labor force. As women have fewer children, they are freer to participate in the labor force. And as women participate in the labor force, they choose to have fewer children. By increasing control over their reproductive lives, women are more able to compete as equals in the public domains from which they had previously been excluded. In concrete terms, reproductive freedom means freedom to pursue educational and occupational goals, unconstrained by unplanned or unwanted pregnancy. In more abstract terms, it means freedom to construct and pursue a dream of one's own making.

Another type of role conflict for women has sometimes been referred to as the *fear of success syndrome*. This is a misnomer because women do not fear success. Instead, some women are understandably leery of being stigmatized for exhibiting behaviors associated with a formula for success defined in male terms. The formula for success for the successful business*man*, for instance, includes being assertive and aggressive. Business talk often mimics athletic or military jargon—"beating the enemy at their own game," "hitting a home run," "coming on board," and the like. Men who exhibit these behaviors and orientations are perceived as "self-starters" and "go-getters" and on the fast track to success. Women, however, who exhibit these same behaviors are labeled as "pushy," "bitchy," or "cold." Such double standards and stigmatizing labels are clearly discriminatory against women.

## The Second Shift

Beyond child care, women spend more time than males providing other forms of household labor. Women do more housework and spend more time on child care than men, whether it is on a workday or when off work. Although the differences are narrowing, women perform about two-thirds of all housework. The husbands of working women typically spend no more time on housework than do husbands of full-time homemakers. What is more, men tend to take little initiative, only doing housework when asked, doing less of the planning, and assigning themselves the "easier," less-demanding tasks. Women are much more involved than men in the invisible mental labor associated with taking care of children and planning for their activities. Also, women disproportionately care for aging parents. Finally, women do the bulk of the "emotional work" that sustains relationships—between husband and wife, between parents and children, and between the immediate and extended families and friends (Hochschild 1989, 1990). For instance, women typically make the phone calls, send birthday and anniversary cards, buy and send gifts, plan special family events, and the like.

Sociologist Arlie Hochschild (1989, 1990) has used the term *second shift* to describe this double burden—work outside the home followed by child care and housework—that many women face and that few men share equitably. She noted, for instance, that women spend fifteen fewer hours in leisure activities *each week* than do their husbands. In a year, that amounts to an extra month of twenty-four-hour days.

These extra duties off the job may affect performance on the job. Despite the image of the "24/7" woman who can do it all and have it all, the reality is that any one person has only a finite amount of time, energy, and attention available. Women are at a collective nonmerit disadvantage in the labor force competing with men who do not have these additional burdens. Young professionals, especially, work long hours and are often called upon for additional work duties on short notice. It is the fast-track professional on the make who "goes the extra mile" who gets the promotion—not the one who has to rush home immediately after work to take care of the kids, is chronically sleep deprived, or is unavailable to fly off to London over the weekend to seal a deal. In this way, unequal household division of labor creates severe handicaps for women who bear these responsibilities and a distinct nonmerit advantage for men who do not.

### Sexual Harassment

Prior to women's recent surge into the labor force, men and women mostly operated in separate social worlds—the home was women's domain and the workplace was men's domain. As women have entered the labor force in larger numbers and as they have become less concentrated in a limited number of jobs, nonfamily related men and women more often are working in the same social space. This, along with heightened sensitivity to the issue, has increased the incidence as well as awareness of sexual harassment in the workplace. Sexual harassment is another nonmerit impediment that women face in the labor force in far greater proportion than men. Social scientists know that opposite sex social interaction is different than same sex social interaction. Opposite sex interaction is more sexually charged, often resulting in an element of flirtation that is missing in same sex interaction. Most of this casually flirtatious behavior is innocent enough and falls outside the realm of sexual harassment. The line is crossed when flirtatious behavior becomes unwanted and unwelcome sexual advances that interfere with a person's ability to perform a job and enjoy its benefits. Sexual harassment may include everything from blatant demands for sex to more subtle pressures regarding sexual activity, to a panoply of behaviors that create a hostile workplace environment. Depending on how sexual harassment is defined, as many as one-quarter to one-third of all working women report having been sexually harassed in the workplace—an alarming rate of victimization.

In the 1986 decision in *Meritor Savings Bank v. Vinson*, the Supreme Court declared that sexual harassment is a form of discrimination and therefore violates Title VII of the 1964 Civil Rights Act. Since then, the courts have typically used thirty-one pages of guidelines from the Equal Employment Opportunity Commission to protect employees from conduct considered illegal under that act. Nevertheless, sexual harassment has continued in the military, and numerous women have filed suits against government agencies, private sector companies, and universities. Not only is sexual harassment an indicator of the continuing dominance of men in the workplace; it is a form of discrimination that jeopardizes women's chances for occupational success and impinges upon their pursuit of the American Dream.

## Political Activity and Office Holding

Women constitute 53% of the voting population and about half of the labor force but only a small percentage of those holding high government positions. The number of women in Congress increased from 10 (out of 435 members) in 1969 to 56 in 1999, and the number of women in the Senate increased from 1 (out of 100) in 1969 to 9 in 1999 (Center for the American Woman and Politics 1999). What is more, the number of women in state legislatures in 1999 (1,605) was more than five-and-one-third times larger than it was in 1969 (301), but in 1999 only three states had a woman governor. Since women have secured voting rights, they have not been able to use their political power to win a proportional share of elected offices. For decades, women's representation in national, state, and local elected offices has remained abysmally low.

The low number of women officeholders has not been due to women's inactivity in politics. About the same proportion of eligible women and men vote in presidential elections, and women have worked actively in both political parties. The League of Women Voters, for example, founded in 1920, performs valuable functions in educating the electorate. Nevertheless, perhaps women's most visible role in politics until recently has been as unpaid campaign workers for male candidates.

Institutional sexism has been a serious barrier to women interested in holding office. Most political careers evolve out of training, experience, and leadership in law or business—areas from which women have been largely excluded until the last few decades. Politics has been a male bastion for many generations—men have controlled the major political parties and have resisted placing women in positions of organizational power or as candidates for high office. Male politicians long viewed females as outsiders whose way of life and feminine values were not only irrelevant to important political issues but made it difficult for women to even fully understand such issues. Both men and women tended to prefer and place more confidence in male leaders. Finally, women do not form a voting bloc because they are not residentially segregated and are distributed across the socioeconomic spectrum. Thus, women have been courted for their votes but not as candidates for office. It seems that women were good enough to serve as "support personnel"—as unpaid campaign laborers and fund-raisers for men—but not as officeholders.

Thus, while women's political office holding is increasing, they remain severely underrepresented in major elected and appointed offices at the state and federal levels; the more powerful the office, the greater the underrepresentation. Even today, female candidates still have to overcome the prejudices of both men and women regarding women's fitness for leadership, and if elected they often encounter prejudice, discrimination, and abuse. In short, gender inequality continues in the political system. The continued denial of full and equal political participation also denies women equal access to the American Dream.

## MULTIPLE JEOPARDY: CLASS, RACE, AND GENDER

The form and meaning of gender inequality varies among different social classes. Upper-class women, while leading a privileged lifestyle, have nevertheless been subordinate to upper-class men. Upper-class women are freed from the burdens of housework (performed by domestics and servants) and, to some extent, child care (performed by nannies and boarding schools). While upper-class men occupy command positions in business and politics outside the home, upper-class women have traditionally been involved in "volunteer work"—supporting the arts and charities in the community (Ostrander 1984; Daniels 1988). Younger upper-class women, however, are beginning to play more active roles in business and the professions. Compared to other women, upper-class women have greater access to resources (often their own inheritances) to pursue these options.

Among middle-class women, the industrial era brought about a housewife role. The expectation was that the husband would be the breadwinner, while the wife would remain at home, raising the children and taking care of the house. Until a few decades ago, this was the experience of most women in middle-income families. In the 1960s and 1970s, economic necessity and feminism led them to enter the labor force in record numbers, and they began to seek professional careers that had been male dominated.

For many working-class and minority women, however, the housewife role never became the norm. These women never had the option of leaving the paid labor force to become housewives because economic necessity required that they work for pay even at a time when most women did not.

Women from the lowest social classes face the greatest obstacles. Since World War II, increasing proportions of the poor in America have been women—many of them divorced or never-married mothers. One out of every two families headed by women now lives in poverty. Poor women share many social characteristics with poor men: low educational attainment, lack of market-relevant skills, and residence in economically deteriorating areas. The burden of supporting a family is difficult for single mothers not only because of low wages but also because of lack of child support from the fathers. For example, of the 4.9 million American women scheduled to receive child support payments from their former husbands in 1991, only three-quarters actually received *any* money, and of those, most received only small amounts.

Displaced homemakers, women whose primary occupation had been homemaking but who could not find full-time employment after being divorced, separated, or widowed, are, like single mothers, four times as likely to live in poverty as other households in the United States. In short, the *feminization of poverty* is an outcome of various forms of discrimination against women. Such discrimination has most certainly denied women equal access to the American Dream.

Finally, the historical oppression of women as well as minorities has created multiple jeopardy for poor minority women (Weber 2001). Constituting over 15% of the total population, African American and Hispanic women are overrepresented among the poor and remain a highly marginalized segment of American society. For minority women, sexual harassment and violence, racial and gender discrimination in hiring and pay, and the general low pay and powerlessness of women in service jobs and other working-class occupations have been significant problems. In recent years, minority women have increasingly been working in nonhousehold service occupations. In terms of most criteria, these are the worst jobs of the pink-collar ghetto. When a white non-Hispanic woman works at a low-wage job, it is likely that she is either supporting only herself or is combining her income with her husband's income to support a family. Black and Latina women, however, are both more likely to work in low-wage service occupations *and* more likely to be the sole source of support for a family.

## SUMMARY

Discrimination against racial and ethnic minorities has created a playing field that is anything but level. For many Native Americans, African Americans, Mexican Americans, Asian Americans, and recent immigrants, various forms of institutional discrimination make it more appropriate to speak not of an American *Dream* but of an American *Nightmare*. Moreover, discrimination, while on the decline, is not just a relic of the past. It continues into the present, albeit in less blatant forms. Even if the weight of continued discrimination were somehow miraculously lifted today, the inertial force of past discrimination would continue to reach into the present. By creating unequal starting points in the race to get ahead, centuries of discrimination continue to affect life chances in the present.

As a group, women have been subjected to forms of discrimination similar to those faced by racial and ethnic minorities. Because of gender inequalities produced by discrimination, men have better jobs, higher pay, more political power, greater life satisfaction, and more leisure time than women. Economic production is critical in understanding the kind and extent of gender inequality in society. In this regard, women have increased their participation in the labor force but remain concentrated in the low-wage, pink-collar sector of the labor force.

Despite these impediments, women are in a relatively better position with respect to men than are people of color. The reason for this is *class*. Upper- and middle-class women, in particular, are better poised to take advantage of new opportunities as they do become available. This is because larger proportions of racial and ethnic minorities start at or near the end of the line. Thus, even when new opportunities do become available, "catching up" means having more distance to make up. Those who face multiple jeopardy, that is, those who are subjected to discrimination along multiple axes of class, race, and gender, have the most to overcome.

## REFERENCES

Beeghley, Leonard. 2000. *The Structure of Social Stratification in the United States*. Boston: Allyn and Bacon.

Blau, Francine D. 1998. "Trends in the Well-Being of American Women, 1970–1995." *Journal of Economic Literature* 36 (March): 112–65.

Bonilla-Silva, Eduardo. 2003. *Racism without Racists: Color-Blind Racism and the Persistence of Racial Inequality in the United States*. Lanham, Md.: Rowman & Littlefield.

Caplovitz, David. 1967. *The Poor Pay More: Consumer Practices of Low-Income Families*. New York: Free Press of Glencoe.

Catalyst. 1998. *Women in Corporate Leadership: Progress and Prospects*. New York: Catalyst.

Center for the American Woman and Politics (CAWP). 1999. *Women in Elective Office*. New Brunswick, N.J.: CAWP.

Coleman, James S., et al. 1966. *Equality of Educational Opportunity*. Washington, D.C.: U.S. Office of Education.

Conley, Dalton. 1999. *Being Black, Living in the Red: Race, Wealth, and Social Policy in America*. Berkeley: University of California Press.

Cose, Ellis. 1995. *The Rage of a Privileged Class*. New York: HarperCollins.

Daniels, Arlene Kaplan. 1988. *Invisible Careers: Women Civic Leaders from the Volunteer World*. Chicago: University of Chicago Press.

Domhoff, G. William. 2002. *Who Rules America? Power and Politics*. 4th ed. Boston: McGraw-Hill.

Farley, John E. 1995. *Majority-Minority Relations*. 3rd ed. Upper Saddle River, N.J.: Prentice Hall.

———. 2000. *Majority-Minority Relations*. 4th ed. Upper Saddle River, N.J.: Prentice Hall.

Feagin, Joe R., and Clairece Booher Feagin. 1978. *Discrimination American Style.* Upper Saddle River, N.J.: Prentice Hall.
———. 1999. *Racial and Ethnic Relations.* Upper Saddle River, N.J.: Simon & Schuster.
Feagin, Joe R., and Karyn D. McKinney. 2003. *The Many Costs of Racism.* Lanham, Md.: Rowman & Littlefield.
Feagin, Joe R., and Melvin P. Sikes. 1994. *Living with Racism: The Black Middle-Class Experience.* Boston: Beacon.
Hacker, Andrew. 1995. *Two Nations: Black and White, Separate, Hostile, Unequal.* New York: Ballantine.
Hochschild, Arlie. 1989. *The Second Shift: Working Parents and the Revolution at Home.* New York: Viking.
———. 1990. "The Second Shift: Employed Women Are Putting in Another Day of Work at Home." *Utne Reader* 38 (March–April): 66–73.
Iceland, John, Daniel H. Weinberg, and Erika Steinmetz. 2002. *Racial and Ethnic Residential Segregation in the United States: 1980–2000.* U.S. Census Bureau, Series CENSR-3. Washington, D.C.: U.S. Government Printing Office.
Kennedy, Randall. 1997. *Race, Crime, and the Law.* New York: Vintage Books.
Kerbo, Harold R. 2000. *Social Stratification and Inequality: Class Conflict in Historical, Comparative, and Global Perspective.* New York: McGraw-Hill.
Massey, Douglas S. 1990. "American Apartheid: Segregation and the Making of the Underclass." *American Journal of Sociology* 96: 239–57.
Massey, Douglas S., and Nancy A. Denton. 1989. "Hypersegregation in the U.S. Metropolitan Areas: Black and Hispanic Segregation along Five Dimensions." *Demograhy* 26: 373–91.
Mishel, Lawrence, Jared Bernstein, and Heather Boushey. 2003. *The State of Working America: 2002/2003.* Ithaca, N.Y.: Cornell University Press.
Ostrander, Susan A. 1984. *Women of the Upper Class.* Philadelphia: Temple University Press.
Phillips, Kevin. 2003. *Wealth and Democracy: A Political History of the American Rich.* New York: Random House.
Reskin, Barbara F. 1998. *The Realities of Affirmative Action in Employment.* Washington, D.C.: American Sociological Association.
Schaeffer, Richard T. 2000. *Racial and Ethnic Groups.* Upper Saddle River, N.J.: Prentice Hall.
Tomaskovic-Devy, Donald. 1993. "The Gender and Race Composition of Jobs and the Male/Female, White/Black Pay Gaps." *Social Forces* 72: 45–76.
Turner, Jonathan H., and Charles E. Starnes, 1976. *Inequality: Privilege and Poverty in America.* Pacific Palisades, Calif.: Goodyear Publishing.
Walker, Samuel, Cassia Spohn, and Miriam DeLone. 2003. *The Color of Justice: Race, Ethnicity, and Crime in America.* Belmont, Calif.: Wadsworth/Thomson Learning.
Weber, Lynn. 2001. *Understanding Race, Class, Gender and Sexuality: A Conceptual Framework.* Boston: McGraw-Hill.
Wellington, Alison. 1994. "Accounting for the Male/Female Wage Gap among Whites: 1976 and 1985." *American Sociological Review* 59: 839–48.
Wilson, William Julius. 1987. *The Truly Disadvantaged: The Inner City, the Underclass, and Public Policy.* Chicago: University of Chicago Press.

# 9

# Discrimination by Any Other Name: Other Isms

*Superstition, bigotry and prejudice, ghosts though they are, cling tena-ciously to life; they are shades armed with tooth and claw. They must be grappled with unceasingly, for it is a fateful part of human destiny that it is condemned to wage perpetual war against ghosts. A shade is not easily taken by the throat and destroyed.*

—Victor Hugo (1802–1885) from *Les Misérables* (1862)

When we discuss discrimination and its victims, we are not talking about a few people. More than half of the population is female, at least a third of the population is minority, and a sizable proportion is both. Although race and gender discrimination are its most prevalent forms, ranking first and second in number of charges filed with the Equal Employment Opportunity Commission from 1992 to 2002 (U.S. EEOC 2003), they are not the only forms of discrimination. Other less visible forms of discrimination continue to operate in much the same way to deny equal opportunity to their victims.

In this chapter we summarize evidence that shows that discrimination against gays and lesbians, the elderly, the disabled, the less attractive, and to a lesser extent, religious and regional minorities is quite real and damaging. All of these forms of discrimination hinder peoples' ability to get ahead in America on the basis of their individual merit, thereby preventing their full and equal participation in the American Dream.

## DON'T ASK, DON'T TELL: DISCRIMINATION
## AGAINST GAYS AND LESBIANS

Today, *homophobia* and *heterosexism*, individual and institutionalized prejudice and discrimination against gays and lesbians, is present in every facet of
life—the family, organized religion, the workplace, official policies, and the
mass media. While there are anecdotal accounts of public recognition of homosexuality throughout American history, it was not until the 1920s and 1930s
that it became visible. Before then, most gays and lesbians, apparently fearing
hostility and discrimination, hid their sexual orientation from public view, remaining "in the closet." Whatever fears they may have had were justified; as homosexuality became more visible, efforts to suppress it grew and became institutionalized. As recently as 1960, no cities or states protected the rights of gays
and lesbians, sodomy was outlawed in every state, and no openly gay or lesbian individuals held elected office. Well into the 1960s, discrimination against
gays and lesbians was common and legal. Psychiatrists thought homosexuality
was a disease and efforts were made to prevent, control, and "correct" it.

The gay and lesbian rights movement emerged in the 1960s to fight discrimination on the basis of sexual orientation. However, despite their efforts,
in 1986 the Supreme Court ruled in *Bowers v. Hardwick* that the Constitution
does not protect homosexual relations between consenting adults, even in
the privacy of their own homes. Today federal law still discriminates against
gay men and lesbians, most notably by banning them from military service.
President Clinton's attempt in 1993 to end this discriminatory policy was met
with severe opposition in Congress and among some segments of the general population. In the end, the discriminatory law was retained, modified by
the "don't ask, don't tell" compromise. Although military recruits no longer
have to state their sexual orientation, and the military is not supposed to in-
quire about it, current policy still permits investigations and dismissals of military personnel if evidence is found that they have engaged in homosexual
acts. Ironically, according to a 2000 report, more gay and lesbian troops have
been discharged from the military since this policy was put into place than
were under the old, supposedly harsher rules (Schaefer 2004, 471).

Another form of discrimination against gay and lesbian couples is the
withholding of legal recognition of their relationships. Legal recognition of
what have come to be called *domestic partnerships* provides numerous benefits and protections for gay and lesbian couples with respect to inheritance,
parenting, pensions, taxation, housing, immigration, workplace fringe benefits, and health care. Several dozen cities now recognize domestic partnerships. But in anticipation that some states might allow gay and lesbian couples to legally marry, Congress enacted the Defense of Marriage Act in 1996,
which denies federal recognition of same-sex marriages. The measure was
very popular with the public.

The gay liberation movement has been publicly active in efforts to gain rights and access for gays and lesbians, and its activism has contributed to a decline in negative *attitudes* toward homosexuality. Using General Social Survey data from 1973 to 1998, Loftus (2001, 778) found that the American public clearly makes a distinction between whether homosexuality is morally wrong and whether homosexuals should be allowed certain civil rights. Americans' attitudes regarding the *morality* of homosexuality became more liberal, but the majority of Americans in all years viewed homosexuality as "always wrong" (56% in 1998). Over the same twenty-five-year period, self-reported willingness to restrict the civil liberties of homosexuals declined steadily. Recent polls, however, indicate that a sizable plurality of Americans still do not agree that gays and lesbians should be protected from discrimination by law.

We should not assign undue weight to the results of any *attitude* surveys, because regardless of what such surveys may seem to tell us, gays and lesbians tell us that they still face discrimination in most areas of life including employment. For instance, there is especially strong resistance to hiring those known to be gay or lesbian in certain occupations, such as teaching and the clergy. Open avoidance, stereotyping, name-calling, physical threats, and assaults against gays and lesbians remain commonplace, and antigay hate crimes, including physical attacks, appear to have increased during the 1990s. Prejudices against gays and lesbians remain so strong that laws protecting them from discrimination have been repealed by popular referendum in some states, counties, and cities. In fact, of the literally hundreds of cities in America, only around fifty have passed local ordinances forbidding discrimination on the basis of sexual orientation. And despite recent court decisions that protect sex between consenting gays and lesbians, it seems that in many circles, homophobia remains a respectable form of bigotry.

The "causes" of sexual orientation are still unknown, although most evidence points strongly toward inherited biological predispositions. The weight of the evidence strongly suggests that while any sexual behavior is a choice, homosexual orientation—sexual attraction to people of the same sex—is *not* a choice. It is something that people more or less gradually discover about themselves. In short, rather than choosing to be gay or lesbian, it appears that gays and lesbians gradually discover their sexual orientation. And with that discovery, others quickly follow: They have become objects of prejudice and discrimination on the basis of an identity they did not choose, and the discrimination and exclusions they face severely jeopardize their access to opportunity and pursuit of the American Dream.

Finally, it has become clear that the *transgendered*, a term applied to individuals whose gender identity does not "match" their sexual identity in conventional ways, face much of the same stereotyping, hostility, discrimination, and outright exclusion as gays and lesbians.

# WHERE THE HANDICAPPED GET PARKED:
## DISCRIMINATION AGAINST THE DISABLED

Americans with disabilities have long been the victims of prejudice and stereotypes and the objects of various forms of discrimination, which have denied them equal opportunity to pursue the American Dream. Disabilities may result from congenital defects, injury, or disease and include a wide range of impairments and limitations (Thomason et al. 1998).

In 1997, 19.7% of the population had some level of disability and 12.3% had a severe disability (McNeil 2001). The most common causes of disability are arthritis, back or spine problems, and heart trouble. About 13% of all employed people have disabilities, and about 3% have severe disabilities. All told, about twenty million Americans are limited in the kind or amount of work they can do. The proportion of people with disabilities continues to increase. Because of advances in medicine, many people who once would have died from an accident or illness now survive. As more people live longer, they are more likely to experience diseases that have disabling consequences (Albrecht 1992). Disabilities are found in all segments of the population, but racial and ethnic minorities are disproportionately more likely to experience them *and* have less access to assistance.

Individuals with disabilities are the victims of prejudice, stereotypes, and discrimination, including various forms of employment discrimination. Employers have been reluctant to hire people with disabilities even when the disabilities do not keep them from doing the job. Only about 29% of working age persons with a disability in the United States are employed, compared to 79% of the nondisabled, and African Americans and Hispanics with disabilities are even more likely to be jobless. Baldwin and Johnson (1998) found that after controlling for differences in productivity, there are large wage differentials between disabled and nondisabled persons that constitute evidence of labor market discrimination. They also note a number of misconceptions. For example, contrary to the stereotype of the disabled person as someone forced into a wheelchair due to a traumatic accident or birth defect, most disabled persons suffer from musculoskeletal or cardiovascular conditions caused by chronic degenerative processes. Further, the onset of disability typically occurs in middle age, so that most disabled persons were not subject to discrimination upon their initial entry into the labor market.

In addition to employment discrimination, design characteristics of public buildings and transportation facilities have made it difficult for people with disabilities to gain access to education, work, shopping, and entertainment, even when their disabilities do not impair their actual ability to study, work, shop, or enjoy entertainment facilities.

Stigmas attached to many forms of disability have become the basis of stereotypes and discriminatory treatment. For example, individuals with *physical* disabilities must deal with those who assume that they have *mental* limitations as well. People with disabilities are often viewed in unidimensional terms as *disabled* people, so that the single characteristic of their disability comes to define their identity. For example, they are seen only as blind, rather than as complex human beings with individual strengths and weaknesses whose blindness is but one aspect of their lives. The media have contributed to the stereotyping of people with disabilities, often treating them with a mixture of pity and fear. For example, some nationwide charity telethons have unwittingly contributed to negative images of the disabled as being childlike, dependent, and nonproductive. In literature and film, evil characters with disabilities—Captain Hook, Dr. Strangelove, and Freddy Krueger—sometimes imply that disability is a punishment for evil. Efforts to discourage drunk driving or to encourage safety in the workplace have used images of people with disabilities to frighten people into "safe" behavior. In short, the stigmas attached to disability and discrimination imposed on persons with disabilities are widely institutionalized and often become a greater handicap than the disability itself.

World War II, the Korean War, and the Vietnam War produced thousands of disabled veterans. Increases in the number of disabled Americans have produced a growing effort to ensure people with disabilities the same rights as enjoyed by others. By the early 1970s, a strong social movement for disability rights had emerged in the United States, and legislation and labor–management contracts have forbidden discrimination on the basis of disabilities not related to job performance. Discrimination against the disabled was forbidden by the Rehabilitation Act of 1973, but only for federal employment and private employers with federal contracts. In 1992, the Americans with Disabilities Act (ADA) went into effect and greatly extended these protections. This law broadens protections for people with disabilities against discrimination, requires that employers accommodate them, and requires public facilities to be accessible. Among the specific provisions is a ban on discrimination against people with physical and mental disabilities in hiring and promotion. This ban applies to all employers with more than twenty-five employees and allows people to directly sue the organizations that discriminate. It also outlaws tests that have the effect of screening out job applicants with disabilities unless it can be shown that the tests relate to a worker's ability to perform the job. In addition to strengthening the ban on discrimination, ADA requires that workplaces and public accommodations be made accessible to people with disabilities. Restaurants, colleges and universities, transportation systems, theaters, retail stores, and government offices are among the kinds of public facilities that must now be accessible. Finally, employers are required to make "reasonable accommodations" for employees with disabilities. The word *reasonable*, however, is subject to various, often self-serving, interpretations. Many with disabilities have interpreted this and other provisions to mean that they are to be fully *integrated*. Many employers, on the other hand, have operated on much narrower interpretations.

It is difficult to quantify gains that those with disabilities may have made because of this legislation. From the time the EEOC began enforcing ADA in July 1992, formal complaints of violations have fluctuated from a low of 15,274 (1993) to a high of 19,798 (1995) and have averaged over 17,000 per year (U.S. Equal Employment Opportunity Commission 2003). The most common causes of complaint have been discharges of employees, failure to make reasonable accommodation as required by the ADA, and harassment. While these figures suggest considerable discrimination, studies also reveal that people with disabilities feel empowered and perceive increased access to employment opportunities.

The ADA and similar legislation, as well as the results of opinion polls, suggest increasing public support for equal rights for the disabled. However, Lee and Thompson (1998) conclude that relatively few individuals have successfully challenged employer decisions under the ADA, and that it is unlikely that employers have increased their recruitment and hiring of individuals with disabilities. They also note that federal courts have interpreted the definition of "disability" narrowly so that many persons with impairments are excluded, and that interpretations of other key provisions have similarly limited the application of the ADA. It is doubtful then, that ADA and similar legislation has been successful in bringing about true equality of opportunity for those with disabilities. In effect, millions of Americans are denied "equal access" to the American Dream.

## OLD DOGS AND NEW TRICKS: AGE DISCRIMINATION

Older Americans are the victims of stereotypes, prejudice, and various forms of discrimination that jeopardize their chances to fulfill important parts of the American Dream. While older Americans constitute a significant segment of the population (about 12% over sixty-five in 2001), one does not become the object of age discrimination until one grows old. In short, one does not suffer a *lifetime* of age discrimination, and many who die young never face age discrimination at all. However, everyone *hopes* to grow old, and those who do eventually face age discrimination. Further, the population is aging—an increasing proportion of the population is composed of older people—and therefore more people suffer age discrimination. Finally, since people are now living longer, they are the objects of age discrimination for more years and a larger proportion of their lives.

According to the American Dream, after a lifetime of employment one has earned the right to a comfortable and secure retirement. Pensions, savings, Social Security, and other programs to which one has contributed during the working years are now "paid back," so that one may live the remainder of one's life as a financially secure and respected member of one's community. If one's resources prove to be inadequate, society will provide any needed assistance.

It is clear, however, that the American Dream is not fulfilled for many because of various forms of discrimination. Negative stereotypes of old age are strongly entrenched in our youth-oriented society. In 1968, Robert Butler, the founding director of the National Institute on Aging, coined the term *ageism* to refer to prejudice and discrimination against the elderly. Ageism reflects a deep uneasiness among young and middle-aged people about growing old. For many, old age symbolizes disease and death, and seeing the elderly serves as a reminder that they too may someday become old and infirm. By contrast, American culture glorifies youth, identifying it with beauty, the future, and all that is good. According to Levin (1988), the young are viewed as active, powerful, healthy, attractive, energetic, involved, and intelligent. The elderly, by contrast, are seen as inactive, sickly, slow, ugly, unreliable, lazy, socially isolated, and dull. Aging leads to loss of basic social roles that provide power, privilege, and social integration. Older people no longer produce or reproduce, and if they do remain employed, they are often resented for their salaries or for "holding on" to a job that could go to a younger person.

There is considerable evidence of institutionalized age discrimination in America. For example, the American Association of Retired Persons (AARP) conducted an experiment in 1993 that confirmed that older people often face discrimination when applying for jobs, and Matloff (1998) found rampant age discrimination in the computer software industry, which supposedly is plagued by chronic labor shortages. Age discrimination has been increasingly evident in the disproportionate firing of older employees during layoffs; older employees in long-term jobs lose work at a higher rate than younger counterparts. Further, the number of age discrimination complaints received by the Equal Employment Opportunity Commission increases when layoffs increase.

Age discrimination has led to legislation as well as court rulings against it. For example, the Federal Age Discrimination in Employment Act of 1968 was passed to protect workers aged forty and older from being fired because of their age and replaced with younger workers who presumably could be paid less. The Older Workers Benefit Protection Act of 1990 requires companies to provide workers with age-specific data about who is targeted and who remains on the job after layoffs or early retirement buyouts. According to the EEOC, since 1992, age discrimination complaints have ranked third (behind race and sex discrimination). While they fell during the 1990s, they have turned upward recently, and this increase has been greater than for all other forms of discrimination (U.S. Equal Employment Opportunity Commission 2003).

Age discrimination has led to protective and advocacy efforts by groups who are the objects of such discrimination. Although the American Association of Retired Persons (AARP), founded in 1958, is the most well known of such organizations, there are numerous others, including the Gray Panthers and OWL (Older Women's League).

Conflict along generational lines has emerged: Younger segments of the population have come to fear and resent what they perceive to be the growing power of AARP and older Americans in general. For example, younger people have become increasingly unhappy about paying Social Security taxes and underwriting the Medicare program, especially since they worry that they themselves will never receive benefits from these fiscally insecure programs. They believe that what the elderly "get" comes at their expense. Americans for Generational Equity (AGE), established in 1984, reflects this position and has argued that the poor and the young suffer because society misappropriates too much funding for older people.

There can really be little doubt that ageism is pervasive in America. Partly because of negative stereotypes and discrimination, no one wants to "look old," and a vast and complex multibillion-dollar "anti-aging industry" has grown to exploit this aspect of ageism. Billions are spent annually on hair coloration and replacement, cosmetics, plastic surgery, exercise and fitness programs, diets, drugs, herbs, and other potions, as Americans attempt to mask evidence of aging and delay its effects.

We argue that discrimination in the workplace against those who are merely older is increasingly common, and that many if not most Americans who live long enough will face some form of age discrimination. Ironically, for many of those fortunate enough to grow old, ageism can jeopardize their chances to fulfill the final major component of the American Dream.


## GETTING STUNG BY THE WASP: RELIGIOUS DISCRIMINATION

One might argue that an important component of the American Dream is freedom of religious belief and practice. However, even during colonial times, instances of religious intolerance and discrimination were not uncommon. Throughout the eighteenth, nineteenth, and early twentieth centuries, religious minorities—Catholics, Jews, and Mormons, for example—were victims of severe discrimination, persecution, and even violence.

Catholics were not welcomed to America (Cullen 2001). By the mid-seventeenth century, all the colonies had passed laws designed to thwart Catholic immigration, most of them denying Catholics citizenship, voting rights, and office-holding rights. Large-scale Catholic immigration began in the 1830s, and as it increased throughout the remainder of the century, anti-Catholic hostility grew. American Catholics became the objects of severe discrimination, including vicious pamphlets and books, hostile political party platforms, Know-Nothing and Ku Klux Klan demonstrations and violence, and American Protective Association activities. Catholic beliefs and practices were misrepresented and stereotyped. Harsh attempts at religious assimilation in the public schools as well as discrimination in higher education were factors that led to the development of Catholic schools and universities. Catholics faced job and housing discrimination, as well as various other forms of social exclusion.

Jews who migrated to America encountered many of the same problems as Catholics, often victimized by the same nativist groups. Overt anti-Semitism, stereotyping, and various forms of discrimination and exclusion continued well into the twentieth century. Even today there is some evidence that Jews face a glass ceiling similar to that experienced by women, and Jews are often excluded from or at least not welcomed to the most exclusive clubs, resorts, boarding schools, and residential areas.

Members of the Church of Jesus Christ of Latter-Day Saints (Mormons) were another persecuted religious minority. The westward movement of Mormons from New York to Utah involved violence and a series of expulsions from several states, including Ohio, Missouri, and Illinois. Joseph Smith, founder of the faith, was lynched by a mob that broke into a jail to get him. In some circles, Mormons are still stereotyped as polygamists, racists, and sexists, whose beliefs and practices are not "truly Christian."

It is sometimes difficult to distinguish discrimination based on religious identity from discrimination based on ethnicity because of the considerable overlap of religion and ethnicity. However, it should be clear that Mormons are not an ethnic group. Those who converted to Mormonism included immigrants from several European nations, especially England and the Scandinavian countries. Similarly, Catholics have never represented a single ethnic group, but include Germans, Irish, Italians, and other Europeans, who while enormously different in national and cultural backgrounds, all shared one important characteristic in the eyes of the Protestant majority—they were Catholics. There is much merit to the argument that Jews are not really a religious group but are best considered an ethnic group. Jews migrated from several different regions and nations of Europe. But to dominant group Christians, it mattered little that a Jew might be a German, or a Pole, or a Ukrainian—what mattered was that Jews were not Christians.

Even a cursory reading of American history clearly reveals that full religious freedom has been granted only to Christians, and then only to those within the mainstream of Protestant (and later Catholic) belief and practice. Historically, Americans who have practiced nondominant religions, including sectarians and cultists of all stripes, have been the victims of hostility, discrimination, and exclusion that have denied them equal opportunity to pursue the American Dream.

Even today, severe competition, intolerance, and hostility among various religious groups surfaces sporadically. For example, recently Southern Baptists held their annual convention in Salt Lake City, the world center of the Mormon Church, and proselytized there to give the Mormons "a taste of their own medicine." In interviews with the media, Baptist leaders publicly "doubted" that Mormons are, in fact, Christians. More recently, anti-Muslim stereotypes and hostility surfaced following the terrorist acts of September 11, 2001, and Islam has been stereotyped as a fundamentally flawed and intolerant faith that sanctions violence against "infidels" and women.

Notwithstanding these and similar occurrences, we argue that religious pluralism, the privatization of religion, and other aspects of continuing secularization have largely eliminated *institutionalized* forms of religious discrimination in America. Individual-level religious bigotry, however, continues to deny full participation in the American Dream to the unchurched and those of nondominant faiths. For example, Pentecostal and Holiness groups, Jehovah's Witnesses, Seventh Day Adventists, and other nondominant Christian groups, as well as non-Christian groups including Muslims, Hindus, and Rastafarians, continue to suffer hostility, discrimination, and exclusion at the hands of individual religious bigots. Finally, the truly *antireligious* and merely *nonreligious* have witnessed enough of the bigotry of the righteous to simply keep their beliefs to themselves.

In America, the extent of religious freedom has been exaggerated. Religious freedom has been an ideal, but until relatively recently, the realities have been quite different. During the latter half of the twentieth century, religious tolerance appeared to be growing, and even groups that were formerly vilified and persecuted are now within the American mainstream. Compared to other forms of discrimination today, religious discrimination appears to be a relatively minor problem. Indeed, in 2002 there were more than eleven times as many race discrimination charges and ten times as many sex discrimination charges filed with the EEOC. However, since 1992 the number of charges of religious discrimination filed has increased each year. In fact, the number of such charges filed in 2002 was almost double that in 1992 (U.S. Equal Employment Opportunity Commission 2003).

## YOU TALK FUNNY: REGIONALISM AND THE YANKEE ADVANTAGE

The United States has been characterized by regional subcultures that are based in large part on isolation and historical differences among regions in timing and patterns of economic development that in turn led to political-economic conflict and social and cultural differences. Strong subcultures developed in the eastern region of the United States, especially in areas that remained relatively isolated for long periods of time. For example, individuals from New England and the Northeast more generally came to be identified as Yankees, while those from the vast southeastern region came to be known as Southerners.

Regional consciousness and identification are largely ascribed nonmerit characteristics that have, until recently, affected access to opportunity in America. Discrimination based on regional grievances and stereotypes led to advantages for some but disadvantages for others. The "Yankee advantage" refers to the differentially greater opportunities historically available to Northerners, based at least partially on regional differences in structures of occupational opportunity and positive dominant group self-stereotypes of "Yankees" as industrious, hardworking, reliable, intelligent, and practical people. On the other hand, prejudices and negative stereotypes have put Southerners at a disadvantage. Variously stereotyped by Northerners as lazy, slow-talking, dull-witted, inbreeding, redneck racists, Southerners have suffered from presumptions of inferiority and varying degrees of discrimination and exclusion. This minority status, in turn, created a somewhat defensive "reactive consciousness" that is absent from Northern and other regionalisms. For these reasons, of all the "regionalisms," Southern regionalism is arguably the strongest and most persistent.

John Shelton Reed is a sociologist and the foremost authority on Southern regionalism. In *Southerners*, he argued that "it should be clear that regional groups are social and psychological facts. They exist in people's minds and serve to order individuals' perceptions of others" (1983, 95). He found that a good many Southerners hold stereotypes of Northerners as well as their own group. He concluded, however, that "compared to other animosities, sectional ill will is apparently at a fairly low level. Although considerable fractions of our sample agreed with each of the statements that we used to measure prejudice against non-Southerners. . . . [I]t would be wrong to say that sectional prejudice is substantial or widespread" (1983, 99). And although Reed found that sizable proportions of Southerners expressed "social distance" from non-Southerners, as indicated by preferences for Southerners over non-Southerners in most social relationships (dating, marriage, friendships, coworkers, bosses), he argued that these have only minor implications for actual behavior. "Southerners in the South seldom translate them into discriminatory behavior toward non-Southerners" (1983, 104). Reed thus concluded that while Southern regionalism had persisted into the 1980s, even then it did not form the basis for discriminatory treatment of non-Southerners.

Since Southern regionalism is its most pronounced form, if Reed is correct, we should not exaggerate regionalism as a nationally significant source of discrimination in contemporary America. Nevertheless, it must be recognized that historically, regionalism operated as a nonmerit factor that conditioned the allocation of opportunity. As individuals pursued the American Dream, regional identity could be an asset or a liability. Continued industrialization, mass education, and vastly expanded contact technologies of communication and transportation have produced considerable geographical mobility, as well as national job markets and a national media and culture that have severely eroded regional subcultures and identities. Institutional-level discrimination based on regional identity has all but disappeared, and individual-level regionalist bigotry continues to decline to the point that it has become relatively inconsequential—perhaps found only among those of lower socioeconomic status who are not in a position to do much harm. Compared to other forms of discrimination, its effects are small and difficult to measure.

## SURVIVAL OF THE PRETTIEST: THE ADVANTAGES OF ATTRACTIVENESS

Physical attractiveness is another nonmerit factor that affects getting ahead in America. *Lookism*—discrimination against the unattractive—creates a structure of unequal opportunity, providing unearned advantages to the attractive and disadvantages to the unattractive. While it is often claimed that "beauty is in the eye of the beholder"—that the assessment of attractiveness is a highly subjective matter—in fact there are high levels of agreement about attractiveness that are largely unaffected by the "beholder's" sex, age, or socioeconomic status. There is even substantial cross-cultural agreement.

We don't have the space to present a detailed definition of physical attractiveness, but a growing body of research reveals that for both men and women, attractiveness is rooted in manifestations of physical health (smooth, taut, flawless skin, thick shiny hair) and fertility. It also includes facial and body symmetry and proportionality, tallness, and slenderness. Additional components of attractiveness are sex-specific. For example, overall youthful appearance, including ample well-formed breasts and buttocks, an "hourglass" figure (0.7–0.8 waist-hip ratio) and evidence of nulliparous status are components of female attractiveness. Components for male attractiveness include evidence of physical dominance including size and strength, as well as evidence of social dominance including power and privilege.

"Good looks" for both men and women provide decided advantages in almost every aspect of life. In *Survival of the Prettiest*, Nancy Etcoff concludes, "Beauty is howlingly unfair. It is a genetic given. And physical appearance tells us little about a person's intelligence, kindness, pluck, sense of humor, or steadfastness, although we think it does" (1999, 242). It is claimed that "beauty is only skin deep" and that "pretty is as pretty does." Americans seem to know that the link between beauty and goodness is spurious, yet attractive people tend to be the beneficiaries of positive stereotypes and unearned opportunities. Beautiful is good, and the good get all sorts of advantages.

Unattractive people, on the other hand, receive no such benefits, but are instead victimized by negative stereotypes and discrimination. After all, while beauty may be only "skin deep," we are told "ugly goes to the bone," and fat people are often assumed to be lazy, lacking in self-control, and greedy.

Etcoff argues that

> preferential treatment of beautiful people is extremely easy to demonstrate, as is discrimination against the unattractive. From infancy to adulthood, beautiful people are treated preferentially and viewed more positively. This is true for men as well as women. Beautiful people find sexual partners more easily; and beautiful individuals are more likely to find leniency in the court and elicit cooperation from strangers. Beauty conveys modest but real social and economic advantages and, equally important, ugliness leads to major social disadvantages and discrimination. (1999, 25)

She reviewed a large body of research and cataloged the numerous advantages of attractiveness. Lookism affects us all from an early age: Parents respond more affectionately to physically attractive newborns. Attractive school children differentially benefit from positive teacher expectations. People are more likely to help attractive individuals, and this holds even if they don't like them. People are less likely to ask good-looking people for help. Efforts to please good-looking people with no expectation of immediate reward or reciprocity are clear evidence of unearned rewards of beauty that are not unlike being born into the nobility or inheriting wealth. Etcoff also reports research showing that good-looking people are given more "personal space" than unattractive people and are more likely to win arguments and persuade others of their opinions. People divulge secrets to them and disclose personal information. "Basically people want to please the good-looking person, making conciliatory gestures, letting themselves be persuaded . . . and backing off from them, literally, as they walk down the street" (Etcoff 1999, 47).

Attractive people are expected to be better at everything, and such expectations at school and work can be self-fulfilling. Despite the "dumb blonde" stereotype, people presume that attractive people of both sexes are more, not less, intelligent than unattractive people. Better looking women are more likely to marry than unattractive women, and the former tend to "marry up"—marry men with more education and income than they have. The better one looks, the better looking one's partner is likely to be, and having a good-looking partner increases men's status. Good-looking people are more likely to get away with anything from shoplifting to cheating on exams to committing serious crimes.

Etcoff reports research findings that good looks are an advantage in the boardroom. "Although it does not approach racism or sexism in magnitude, lookism appears to be a form of discrimination in the workplace. . . . Good-looking men are more likely to get hired, at a higher salary, and to be promoted faster than unattractive men" (1999, 83). The evidence for women is less clear. Some studies show that good-looking women fare better than plainer women. Other studies reveal that whether or not good looks are an advantage depends on the kind of job; especially attractive women are more likely to become victims of the "glass ceiling" (see chapter 8). One thing is certain—it pays to look at least *average*. Homely women are truly disadvantaged economically—they are less likely to get hired or to earn competitive salaries at work. They are less likely to marry, and if they do marry they are less likely to marry a man with resources. Attractiveness contributes to educational and occupational success and compensates for their lack, especially for women, who, as we noted, can "marry up." While research findings suggest that such advantages tend to be small to moderate, they are advantages nonetheless. In this connection, Etcoff notes there is some evidence that the penalty for ugliness might be even greater than the reward for beauty.

The rhetoric of proponents of the American Dream is that the advantages that accrue to the attractive are legitimate because they are *achieved*. That is, meritocracy applies to considerations of beauty because it is argued that beauty is attainable through hard work and effort. Every woman can be beautiful if she wants to be; there are no homely women, only careless or lazy women. But just what is the specific form of merit that produces beauty? In short, *how* does one "achieve" attractiveness? A vast and complex billion-dollar beauty industry (cosmetics, plastic surgery, diets, drugs, vitamins, herbs, potions, creams, ointments, food supplements, physical fitness and exercise, and fashion) supposedly provides the level playing field—equal opportunity to achieve beauty through hard work and effort. But the "opportunities" offered by the beauty industry are not equal. Natural variation in beauty creates different starting points, and "working hard" or "really wanting" to be pretty usually takes money, sometimes lots of it. In short, the drop-dead beauty doesn't have to work very hard, and the woman who is rich but ugly won't be ugly for long—she has the resources needed for major repair and reconstruction work.

To sum things up, one can hardly doubt the considerable advantages that attractiveness provides in pursuit of the American Dream. What is more, there is no level playing field since attractiveness as well as opportunities to "earn" it are distributed unequally. It is good to be pretty or handsome; it is not good to be homely. No sane person, offered a chance to be more attractive, would turn it down. While attractiveness does not guarantee happiness any more than money does, having either is good, and having either helps get the other.

## SUMMARY

Although race and sex discrimination are the most visible and damaging forms of discrimination in America, other forms of discrimination also interfere with the pursuit of the American Dream. Although heterosexism, ageism, discrimination against the disabled, religious intolerance, regionalism, and lookism may not victimize as many Americans as sex and race discrimination, it would be difficult to convince its victims that their effects are any less real. Discrimination by any other name is still discrimination.

## REFERENCES

Albrecht, Gary L. 1992. *The Disability Business: Political Economy of Rehabilitation in America.* Beverly Hills, Calif.: Sage.

Baldwin, Marjorie L., and William G. Johnson. 1998. "Dispelling the Myths about Work Disability." Chap. 2 in *New Approaches to Disability in the Workplace,* edited by Terry Thomason, John F. Burton, and Douglas E. Hyatt. Madison: University of Wisconsin, Industrial Relations Research Association.

Cullen, Jim. 2001. *Restless in the Promised Land: Catholics and the American Dream.* Chicago: Sheed and Ward.

Etcoff, Nancy. 1999. *Survival of the Prettiest: The Science of Beauty.* New York: Doubleday.

Lee, Barbara A., and Roger J. Thompson. 1998. "Reducing the Consequences of Disability: Policies to Reduce Discrimination against Disabled Workers." Chap. 6 in *New Approaches to Disability in the Workplace,* edited by Terry Thomason, John F. Burton, and Douglas E. Hyatt. Madison: University of Wisconsin, Industrial Relations Research Association.

Levin, William C. 1988. "Age Stereotyping: College Student Evaluations." *Research on Aging* 10 (March): 134–48.

Loftus, Jeni. 2001. "America's Liberalization in Attitudes toward Homosexuality, 1973 to 1998." *American Sociological Review* 66, no. 5: 762–82.

Matloff, Norman. 1998. "Now Hiring! If You're Young." *New York Times* (January 26): A21.

McNeil, Jack. 2001. *Americans with Disabilities: Household Economic Studies.* U.S. Bureau of Census, Current Population Reports, P70-73. Washington, D.C.: U.S. Government Printing Office.

Parrillo, Vincent N. 2000. *Strangers to These Shores: Race and Ethnic Relations in the United States.* Needham Heights, Mass.: Allyn and Bacon.

Reed, John Shelton. 1983. *Southerners: The Social Psychology of Sectionalism.* Chapel Hill: University of North Carolina Press.

Schaefer, Richard T. 2004. *Racial and Ethnic Groups.* 9th ed. Upper Saddle River, N.J.: Pearson/Prentice Hall.

Thomason, Terry, John F. Burton Jr., and Douglas E. Hyatt. 1998. "Disability and the Workplace." Chap. 1 in *New Approaches to Disability in the Workplace,* edited by Terry Thomason, John F. Burton, and Douglas E. Hyatt. Madison: University of Wisconsin, Industrial Relations Research Association.

U.S. Equal Employment Opportunity Commission. 2003. *Charge Statistics FY 1992 through FY 2002.* www.eeoc.gov/stats/charges.html [December 13, 2003].

# 10

# Running in Place:
# The Long Wage Recession

*All animals are equal but some animals are more equal than others.*

—George Orwell (1903–1950), *Animal Farm* (1945)

This book has challenged widely held assertions about meritocracy in America. According to the American ideology of meritocracy, individuals get out of the system what they put into it. The system is seen as fair because everyone is assumed to have an equal or at least adequate chance to get ahead. Getting ahead is ostensibly based on merit—on being made of the right stuff. Being made of the right stuff means being talented, working hard, having the right attitude, and playing by the rules. Anyone who is made of the right stuff can seemingly overcome any obstacle or adversity and achieve success. In America, the land of opportunity, the sky is presumed to be the limit—you can go as far as your *individual* talents and abilities can take you.

But merit is only part of the story. We have not suggested that merit itself is a myth or that merit has no effect on who ends up with what. What we have suggested is that, despite the pervasive rhetoric of meritocracy in America, the reality is that merit is only one factor among many that collectively influence who ends up with what. Nonmerit factors are also at work. These nonmerit factors not only coexist with merit, blunting its effects; they also act to *suppress* merit, preventing individuals from realizing their full potential based on merit alone.

Chief among the nonmerit factors is inheritance, broadly defined as the effect of where one starts on where one finishes in the race to get ahead. If we had a true merit system, everyone would start at the same place. The reality, however, is that the race to get and stay ahead is more like a relay race in which we inherit our starting positions from our parents. The passing of the baton between generations profoundly influences life outcomes. Indeed, the most important factor in getting and staying ahead in America is where one starts in the first place. Most parents wish to maximize the futures of their children by providing them with every possible advantage. To the extent that parents are successful in transferring these advantages to their children, life outcomes of children are determined by inheritance and not merit.

Social capital (whom you know) and cultural capital (what you need to know to fit into the group) are also nonmerit factors that effect life outcomes. These factors, in turn, are related to inheritance. It helps to have friends in high places, and the higher up one starts in life the greater the probability that one will travel in high-powered social circles. One must also have the cultural wherewithal to be fully accepted within these high-powered social circles. Those who are born into these circles have a nonmerit cultural advantage over those not born into these circles, who have the difficult task of learning the ways of life of the group from the outside in.

We have shown that education is both a merit and nonmerit factor. Education is widely perceived as the preeminent merit filter, sifting and sorting on the basis of demonstrated individual achievements. Although individuals "earn" diplomas, certificates, and degrees based on demonstrated individual competencies, the nurturing of individual potential and opportunities to earn these credentials are unequally distributed. Parental social class markedly affects the amount and quality of education children are likely to acquire.

We have also shown that luck plays a part in where people end up in the system. Being in the right time and the right place matters. It matters not just for lucky lottery winners but for others as well. Factors such as the year one was born, the number and types of jobs available, where one lives, where one works, and the ups and downs of economic cycles profoundly factor into individual life chances—above and beyond individual merit or lack of it. The imperfections and ultimate uncertainty of both the stock market and the labor market add an undeniable element of luck into the mix of who "wins" and who "loses."

In many ways, the greatest expression of the ideals of rugged individualism, meritocracy, and the American Dream is starting your own business and becoming your own boss. We have seen, however, that rates of self-employment in the United States have fallen sharply. The dominance of increasingly large corporations and national chains has severely compromised the entrepreneurial path to upward mobility.

Finally, we have reviewed the avalanche of evidence demonstrating the continuing effects of discrimination on life chances. Discrimination is not only a nonmerit factor; it is the antithesis of merit. In a pure merit system, the only thing that would matter would be the ability to do the job—irrespective of any non-performance-related criteria. To the extent that nonperformance criteria affect life outcomes, meritocracy does not exist. At the beginning of the twenty-first century, discrimination is clearly on the decline and certainly less blatant than during earlier periods, especially the first half of the twentieth century. Although less visible and subtler, its remaining, contemporary forms remain damaging. The "underground" nature of modern forms of discrimination makes them especially damaging because it has enabled the emergence of an aggressive and popular denial of its persistence and continuing damaging effects. In addition to race and sex discrimination, we have shown how ageism, heterosexism, religious bigotry, "lookism," and other forms of discrimination create differential access to opportunity and rewards that is quite independent of individual merit.

Americans desperately want to believe in the ultimate fairness of the system and its ability to deliver on its promises. To a great extent, this is the basis of the strength and durability of meritocratic notions and the American Dream. Opinion polls consistently show that Americans continue to embrace the American Dream. But as they strive to achieve it, they have found that it has become more difficult to simply keep up and make ends meet. Instead of "getting ahead," Americans find themselves working harder just to stay in place, and despite their best efforts, many Americans find themselves "falling behind"—worse off than they were earlier in their lives or compared to their parents at similar points in their lives.

## INDIVIDUAL COPING STRATEGIES

Over the past several decades, there has been growing economic inequality in America. Until the recent economic slowdown, those who live off investments have done very well. Many wage earners, on the other hand, have experienced flat or declining wages in what amounts to a long wage recession extending as far back as the 1970s. During this period, rates of upward mobility have slowed. In response to growing economic pressures and the lack of opportunity, Americans have resorted to a variety of strategies to try to make ends meet or at least maintain a lifestyle to which they have become accustomed. Among these strategies are multiple family wage earners, working longer hours, and borrowing more.

### Multiple Wage Earners

In 1950, 28% of the civilian labor force was female (U.S. Census Bureau 1953); by 2000 that percentage had soared to 60% (U.S. Census Bureau 2002). There are many reasons for the dramatic increase in female labor force participation, including declining fertility, increasing divorce rates, growth of the service sector in which women have been historically overrepresented, increasing levels of educational attainment among women, and the changing role of women in society. Another generally acknowledged factor is that women work for the same reason men do—to make ends meet. As prices have increased and wages remain stagnant, more women have been drawn into the labor force to help make ends meet.

Besides a sharp rise in female-headed households, there has also been a sharp increase in dual income families. Among all family types, adult female-headed households increased from 11% of the total in 1967 to 17% of the total in 2000 (Mishel et al. 2003, 49). Between 1951 and 1997, the percentage of married couple families with wives in the paid labor force almost tripled, from 22.9% to 61.7% (U.S. Census Bureau 1998, 27). The rate of increase in dual income families has slowed in recent years, suggesting that these trends are approaching a "ceiling" of the share of working wives. That is, except in cases of bigamy, married men have only one wife who can enter the labor force. The next line of defense would presumably be children, especially adult children working part-time while going to school. There is increasing evidence that this too is occurring as a larger proportion of college students work while going to college and take longer to graduate (U.S. Department of Education 2002).

## Working More Hours

Americans at all economic levels are working more. The U.S. Census Bureau reports that in 2000, 31% of workers age sixteen and over worked more than forty hours a week, including 8% who worked sixty hours or more a week. Between 1979 and 2000, the average number of weeks worked by married couple families with children, head of household ages twenty-five to fifty-four, rose from 3,331 hours a year to 3,719 hours a year (Mishel et al. 2003, 99), with the sharpest rates of increase occurring in more recent years and among middle- and low-income families. The increase in the number of hours worked corresponds to the flat or declining hourly wage income over the same period. This suggests that many families are working more hours to offset losses in hourly wages or as a means to increase purchasing power in the absence of increases in wages. Working more outside the home comes at a cost. Additional work-related costs such as transportation, child care, and clothing reduce net gains in discretionary income. Additional work hours also come at the cost of lost leisure hours and lost hours available for household maintenance and time with children. As with women working outside the home, increasing number of hours worked per wage earner has upper limits.

## Greater Debt

Another strategy to make up for shortfalls in income is to go into debt (Schor 1998; Sullivan et al. 2000; Warren and Warren Tyagi 2003). During the long period of wage recession, Americans carried record levels of debt. Household debt as a percentage of income rose from 20% of personal income at the end of World War II in 1947 to 109% in 2001 (Mishel et al. 2003, 295). Much of this debt was in the form of high interest credit cards. Between 1968 and 2000, credit card debt (adjusted for inflation) increased from less than $10 billion to more than $600 billion (Warren and Warren Tyagi 2003, 130). Mounting debt, especially at high interest rates, ultimately leads to personal bankruptcy, which is also increasing. Between 1979 and 1997, personal bankruptcy filings increased by more than 400% (Sullivan et al. 2000, 3). In 2001, about 7 out of every 1,000 adults declared personal bankruptcy, a rate over three times as high as in 1980 (Mishel et al. 2003, 302). Job loss, divorce, or medical problems can trigger a free fall of debt. For American families with children, these three factors combined account for 87% of the reasons for filing bankruptcy (Warren and Warren Tyagi 2003, 81). Even in the absence of such tragic events, debt and bankruptcy are on the increase as costs have risen while wages and salaries of ordinary Americans remain generally stagnant. In a desperate attempt to maintain at least the outward appearances of being "middle class" and to secure their children's futures, many American families are becoming mired in debt. Overextended in debt and without a safety net of savings, life in the middle class has become increasingly precarious.

In short, in response to the increasing wage, income, and wealth inequalities of the past twenty years, Americans have developed numerous strategies in attempts to achieve the American Dream: increasing reliance on multiple wage earners, working longer hours, moonlighting, and increasing levels of credit card spending and debt. Each, however, has its upper limits, which are quickly being realized: There are usually only two spouses who can work, any one person can work only so many hours a week, and a spiral of borrowing and spending can ultimately result in bankruptcy.

## WHAT CAN BE DONE?

These individual coping strategies are responses to societal-level imperatives, but will not, in themselves, change social institutions, larger organizational forms, or the ways that resources are distributed. In short, they will not change America's social class system, and they will not make America more equal, more meritocratic, or more fair. Changes of this magnitude would require reductions in socially structured inequality, especially inequalities of wealth and power. How could such change be effected? There are several policy options, all of which ultimately depend on the will of those in charge. Policy is determined as the outcome of competing visions regarding what kind of society people think we *ought* to have. However, if the goal is to reduce levels of economic inequality and make the system operate more like a meritocracy, then several options could be considered.

## Affirm Affirmative Action

Discrimination remains a major source of nonmerit inequality. For America to extend true equality of opportunity to all, discrimination would have to be eliminated or at least significantly reduced. Several specific reform strategies could be pursued to this end. Antidiscrimination laws could be strengthened and more effectively enforced. Additional resources could be made available for individuals to pursue complaints. Punishments for demonstrated acts of discrimination could be made more certain and consequential. Beyond mere passive nondiscrimination, more proactive measures designed to reduce the effects of past discrimination and prevent future discrimination could be more aggressively pursued. Such proactive measures generally fall under the label of what has become known as *affirmative action*.

Like antidiscrimination laws, the goal of affirmative action policies is to make equal opportunity a reality for members of groups that have historically been the objects of discrimination. Unlike antidiscrimination laws, which provide remedies to which individuals can appeal after they have suffered discrimination, affirmative action policies aim to keep discrimination from occurring. Affirmative action can prevent discrimination by replacing practices that are discriminatory—either by intent or default—with practices that safeguard against discrimination. Rather than a single policy that involves the same procedures, affirmative action is a complex set of policies and practices including admission standards for schools and universities, guidelines for hiring practices, and procedures for the granting of government contracts. Each has is own characteristics and complex history (Reskin 1998).

The reach of mandated affirmative action programs is limited and has actually shrunk with the dismantling of many affirmative action programs in higher education. The most common type of affirmative action in employment is various human resources policies that have been voluntarily adopted by employers. Ironically, these are the weakest type of affirmative action and cover less than half the U.S. labor force. Not surprisingly, opponents of affirmative action have criticized affirmative action in terms of its most rare type—those employing quotas. Opponents of affirmative action argue that such programs constitute "reverse discrimination." Affirmative action has been characterized as a set of highly discriminatory policies and practices that require the use of quotas in hiring, promotion, and admission decisions, which result in the selection of unqualified racial minorities over qualified white males. In this view, the irony of affirmative action is its use of discriminatory practices to fight discrimination.

Proponents of affirmative action, however, point out that relatively few employers are required by the federal government to practice affirmative action. Private sector firms that do not hold large federal contracts and have not been sued for violating federal antidiscrimination laws have no obligation to practice affirmative action. Work organizations and educational institutions that practice affirmative action voluntarily are subject to federal antidiscrimination laws that bar reverse discrimination. Hence, they may not use quotas. In fact, quotas have only rarely been used, and the few instances of their use have been the result of court orders to engage in affirmative action to remedy egregious violations of the law. In 2003, in an important test case involving admission procedures in use at the University of Michigan, the U.S. Supreme Court reasserted the ban against quotas but condoned the use of race as a factor in admission decisions that may be used, not in any across-the-board fashion but in conjunction with other factors, to pursue a legitimate institutional goal of diversity of access.

Another general criticism, however, is that affirmative action has been largely unsuccessful. More specifically, critics argue that affirmative action has only benefited middle-class and more privileged minorities, leaving the growing urban underclass untouched. Affirmative action benefits middle-class minorities rather than minority members of the underclass because the former are the ones who are more likely to be qualified (educationally and occupationally) to take advantage of opportunities opened by affirmative action. As a group women have benefited more than racial minorities for the same reason: a larger proportion of women than racial minorities are middle class and in a position to take advantage of opportunities opened by affirmative action. Apparently then, the criticism that affirmative action benefits unqualified minorities is not valid.

While affirmative action may have benefited women more than racial minorities, and the relatively more advantaged from both groups, evidence of benefits is substantial. Affirmative action in higher education has led to increased admission, enrollment, and graduation of women and minorities. When affirmative action programs were recently dismantled in California and Texas, minority admissions fell drastically (Farley 2000). Similarly, affirmative action in employment has led to reductions in occupational segregation by increasing hiring and promotion into occupations and industries that formerly excluded women and minorities, as well as reductions in race and gender differentials in wages and income (Reskin 1998, 44–59). Affirmative action programs cannot be blamed for not helping the urban underclass. Affirmative action programs are not designed to create jobs. Macroeconomic changes that have led to declining job opportunity for the urban underclass, and the structure of political power that produces macroeconomic policies formulated by the more privileged to serve their class-based interests (taxation, minimum wage, employment, inflation, and the like) are more likely culprits.

Finally, it has been argued by "pragmatists" that affirmative action is "dead in the water"—that affirmative action programs not only have little political support, they are opposed by the large majority of Americans. Again, there is less to this argument than one might imagine. Sociologist Barbara Reskin (1998, 75–79) has shown that U.S. business has supported affirmative action for at least fifteen years. Surveys show that corporate support for affirmative action is based on the recognition that it is "good business," that affirmative action does not lead to reduced productivity, and that given its benefits, the price tag for affirmative action is low. She also reviewed the results of numerous public opinion polls, which show that people's responses in such polls depend largely on how pollsters characterize affirmative action. Specifically, most Americans disapprove of "quotas" or "preferential hiring," but about 70% support affirmative action programs that pollsters describe as not involving "quotas" or "preferences." When pollsters ask about affirmative action in general or about the practices that actual affirmative action programs include, the majority of whites and African Americans are supportive.

Nevertheless, race-based or sex-based affirmative action programs are a "hard sell" to the American public, especially during periods of economic slowdown or decline (Wilson 1987; Conley 1999). The most fervent backlash against such programs comes from "angry white men," who feel especially threatened. Part of this resentment stems from the perception that under the provisions of some of these programs, wealthy people of color and wealthy women stand to gain advantages over economically disadvantaged white men. In this case, the objection is not so much against affirmative action in principle but against specific provisions of some forms of affirmative action that target minorities and women. One potential for reform, then, is to develop affirmative action programs for the economically underprivileged, regardless of race or sex. Such an essentially class-based affirmative action program may be more politically palatable and overcome many of the objections related to charges of "reverse discrimination."

An economically means-tested affirmative action policy using net worth as a criterion of eligibility would promote asset accumulation, which would clearly improve the chances of children for educational and occupational success, as well as for intergenerational wealth transfers, which we have argued provide a nonmerit basis for opportunity. Racial minorities, disproportionately represented among the economically underprivileged, would disproportionately but not exclusively benefit from such arrangements. Along these lines, Dalton Conley (1999) has presented persuasive evidence that the basic and persisting problem for minorities is continuing inability to accumulate wealth. He points out that African Americans may have improving educational and occupational opportunities but have not made much economic progress because at every educational, income, and occupational level they have fewer assets than white Americans. Asset-building policies such as government assistance for home purchases, starting and expanding businesses, and tax incentives targeted to those of modest means to encourage savings and investments could help stimulate wealth creation. To lack capital in a capitalist society is to be at a distinct economic and social disadvantage.

## Noblesse Oblige

Noblesse oblige has its roots in feudal Europe, where it meant the sense of obligation that the nobility had toward the peasantry. The difference between slave societies and estate societies is that slaves had no rights but peasants did. Although the peasantry did not own land in its own name and had to forfeit to the nobility all but a meager portion of their crops to live on, the nobility, in exchange for the loyalty of its subjects, was expected to provide the peasants with land to work, protection from thieves and invaders, and occasional collective celebrations, especially at harvest. These expectations were implicit rather than explicit—a set of moral obligations embedded in the culture of the group. These felt obligations of the rich toward the poor became known as noblesse oblige, a term that has its modern-day equivalent in the view that "to whom much is given, much is expected."

In modern times, noblesse oblige essentially means a combination of philanthropy and a desire to "give something back" through public service or service to humanity. Both philanthropy and progressive taxation are possible ways to reduce levels of inequality and restore more equity to the system, that is, to reduce the nonmerit effects of inheritance across generations. The primary difference between the two is that the former is voluntary and those who benefit are selected by the giver, whereas the latter is nonvoluntary and the objects of beneficence are not chosen by the giver. Through charitable giving, the wealthy can control who receives their largesse, the purposes for which they might receive it, the amounts given, and the pace at which amounts are given.

The political Right tends to favor this type of giving. The control that it affords can be seen as an extension of individual property rights—the right to dispose of one's property as one sees fit. Private donations at the local level are preferred to public taxation at the national level. The political Left, however, is leery of philanthropy as a justification for inequality itself. The Left points out that much of this "charity" is directed toward the rich themselves in the form of support for the arts and "highbrow" culture, exclusive boarding school and ivy-league alma maters, and other upper-class institutions. Such "donations" can also be used for expressly political purposes in support of causes and groups that reflect the interests of the rich, perhaps even extending rather than reducing the degree of inequality.

Despite the apprehensions of the Left, at least some of this largesse eventually makes its way to the truly needy. Robber barons of the Gilded Age, feeling pressure to justify growing accumulations of wealth, extended charitable giving to poor to the national level, often creating charitable foundations in their names dedicated to helping those less fortunate than themselves. However, there appears to have been a historical decline in the ethos of noblesse oblige among those who have amassed new fortunes since the end of World War II (Hall and Marcus 1998).

If philanthropy is directed to the poor in significant amounts, then it does have the effect of both reducing the distance from the top to the bottom and reducing the nonmerit advantages of inheritance. One potential "solution" to the problem of inequality, then, would be to encourage a greater sense of noblesse oblige among the wealthy in ways that level the playing field, increasing the potential for meritocracy while decreasing the intergenerational effects of inheritance.

## Robin Hood Soak the Rich Taxation

Another way to both decrease the nonmerit advantages of inheritance and increase opportunities for those who start out life in the lower segment of the system would be to impose a more heavily progressive system of taxation on income and wealth. Such tax schemes would not mean simple redistribution of wealth from the rich to the poor in the form of cash disbursements. Revenue from more progressive taxation, for instance, could be used to provide greater access to quality education at all levels, health care, public transportation, and other critical services. In this way, the gap in opportunities between the rich and the poor would be reduced and a more level playing field would be established. Such proposals, however, are highly controversial and typically meet with stiff resistance from the rich and powerful. Resistance to wealth taxation has most recently coalesced around the push to eliminate the estate tax, renamed the "death tax" by its opponents because it seems to tax the dead. In fact, the estate is taxed and its inheritors receive the remainder. Exclusions are generous, and only the largest bequests are subject to the tax. Exclusions are also provided for the transfer of the value of family businesses and family farms. Individuals can avoid heavy estate tax through inter vivos giving and careful estate planning. Estate taxes, however, are only one way of taxing wealth. Tax on wealth could also be based on its possession (assets tax), its use (consumption tax), or its exchange (transfer tax) (cf. Wolff 2002).

Those who oppose such taxes often label them "confiscatory" and argue that they discourage work, savings, and investment. "Supply side" advocates argue that taxing wealth in any form discourages investments that would otherwise create more jobs and a "trickle down" effect of wealth creation. "Supply-siders" argue that the sum of individual decisions with regard to the stewardship of resources is collectively more productive, efficient, and efficacious than collective decisions that emerge from the political process. Those who advance this position tend to view inheritance as a natural rather than a civil right, which should not be limited or abridged by the state.

The argument in favor of progressive wealth taxation suggests that unchecked accumulation of wealth increases social inequality to an unacceptable level. According to this view, taxes should be based on an ability to pay principle, with the wealthiest being taxed the most. In this sense, progressive taxation shifts the notion of noblesse oblige from one of "to whom much is given, much is expected" to the philosophy of "to whom much is given, much is *required.*" The case in favor of estate taxation argues that inheritance rights are not natural rights but civil rights granted by the state, which has the power to both regulate and tax wealth in all its forms. According to this view, the state is coheir to claims of private property, the individual accumulation of which was made possible, protected, and promoted by the state.

Tax policy, in the final analysis, is determined by the outcome of political contests. It involves a combination of customs, values, and political clout. Tax policy highlights the tension between freedom of choice at the individual level and equality of opportunity at the societal level. As long as advantages of wealth can be transferred undiminished across generations, true equality of opportunity cannot be realized. And herein lies the great American contradiction. Americans desperately want to believe that the system is fair and that everyone has an equal chance to get ahead. But we also emphatically endorse the right of individuals, with minimal state intervention, to dispose of their property as they personally see fit. We simply can't have it both ways. Inheritance and meritocracy are zero-sum principles of distribution; the more there is of one, the less there is of the other.

## IS A MERITOCRATIC SOCIETY NECESSARILY A FAIR AND JUST SOCIETY?

For all the reasons discussed in this book, true equality of opportunity is highly unlikely. The system, however, could be made much more fair, much more open, and much more meritocratic than it is. Most Americans, sometimes grudgingly, acknowledge that because of discrimination on the bases of sex, race, creed, or other characteristics irrelevant to individual ability, the system has not always been entirely fair or just. The assumption is, however, that these forms of discrimination are rapidly being eliminated, and that their ultimate elimination will finally bring about true equality of opportunity. But as we have demonstrated in this book, even if all such forms of discrimination and their residual effects were somehow miraculously eliminated, we would still not have genuine equality of opportunity or a system entirely based on merit. Other nonmerit factors, including inheritance and patterns of social and economic organization that are external yet constraining to individuals, operate to modify and reduce the effects of individual merit on life chances.

While true equality of opportunity is probably not possible, what is less well acknowledged by both the Left and the Right is that true equality of opportunity may not be entirely desirable. British sociologist Michael Young, in his fictional satire, *The Rise of the Meritocracy* (1961), envisioned what a society truly based on merit would look like. In this futuristic society, individuals are assigned their place in society exclusively based on a system of rigid tests. Those who score highest on the tests fill the most important positions and get the most rewards. A strict hierarchy of merit is created and maintained. What at first seems like an eminently fair and just system in practice degenerates into a ruthless regime. The meritocratic elite feels righteously superior to all those below it and holds those at the bottom of the system in utter contempt. The meritocratic elite, secure in its lofty status, exercises complete and total domination of society. Those at the bottom of the system are incapable of challenging the elite and are permanently deprived of the capacity to rise up against their oppressors.

One possible advantage of a nonmeritocratic society is that at any point in time there are, for whatever combination of reasons, at least some of those at the top of the system who are less capable and competent than at least some of those at the bottom. Such discrepancies should render humility for those at the top and hope and dignity for those at the bottom. But this can only happen if it is widely acknowledged that inheritance, luck, and a variety of other circumstances beyond the merit of individuals are important in affecting where one ends up in the system. This is why the *myth* of meritocracy is harmful: it provides an incomplete explanation for success and failure, mistakenly exalting the rich and unjustly condemning the poor. We may always have the rich and the poor among us, but we need neither exalt the former nor condemn the latter.

# REFERENCES

Conley, Dalton. 1999. *Being Black, Living in the Red: Race, Wealth, and Social Policy in America.* Berkeley: University of California Press.

Farley, John E. 2000. *Majority-Minority Relations.* Upper Saddle River, N.J.: Prentice Hall.

Hall, Peter Dobkin, and George E. Marcus. 1998. "Why Should Men Leave Great Fortunes to Their Children? Dynasty and Inheritance in America." Pp. 139–71 in *Inheritance and Wealth in America,* edited by Robert K. Miller Jr. and Stephen J. McNamee. New York: Plenum.

Mishel, Lawrence, Jared Bernstein, and Heather Boushey. 2003. *The State of Working America: 2002–2003.* Ithaca, N.Y.: Cornell University Press.

Reskin, Barbara F. 1998. *The Realities of Affirmative Action in Employment.* Washington, D.C.: American Sociological Association.

Schor, Juliet. 1998. *The Overspent American: Why We Want What We Don't Need.* New York: Basic Books.

Sullivan, Theresa, Elizabeth Warren, and Jay Lawrence Westbrook. 2000. *The Fragile Middle Class: Americans in Debt*. New Haven, Conn.: Yale University Press.

U.S. Census Bureau. 1953. Table 205 in *1953 Statistical Abstracts of the United States*. Washington, D.C.: U.S. Government Printing Office.

———. 1998. *Measuring 50 Years of Economic Change Using the March Current Population Survey*. Washington, D.C.: U.S. Government Printing Office.

———. 2002. Table 576 in *2002 Statistical Abstract of the United States*. Washington, D.C.: U.S. Government Printing Office.

U.S. Department of Education. 2002. *What Students Pay for College: Changes in Net Price of College Attendance between 1992–93 and 1999–2000*. Washington, D.C.: U.S. Government Printing Office.

Warren, Elizabeth, and Amelia Warren Tyagi. 2003. *The Two-Income Trap: Why Middle-Class Mothers and Fathers Are Going Broke*. New York: Basic Books.

Wilson, William Julius. 1987. *The Truly Disadvantaged*. Chicago: University of Chicago Press.

Wolff, Edward C. 2002. *Top Heavy: Increasing Inequality of Wealth in America and What Can Be Done about It*. New York: New Press.

Young, Michael. 1961. *The Rise of the Meritocracy, 1870–2033: An Essay on Education and Equality*. Baltimore: Penguin Books.

# Index

AARP (American Association of Retired Persons), 187–88

academia, meritocracy in, issues with, 40–43

ADA (Americans with Disabilities Act), 185–86

Adams, James Truslow, 2

affirmative action, 161–63; criticism of, 162, 202–3; definition of, 202; support for, 202–5

AGE (Americans for Generational Equity), 188

age discrimination, 186–88

Age Discrimination in Employment Act, 187

ageism, definition of, 187

agricultural sector, trends in, 117–21, 118f

Aldrich, Nelson W., Jr., 64

Alger, Horatio, 5

Allen, Paul, 148–51

Altair, 149–50

Altria Company, 146–47

American Association of Retired Persons (AARP), 187–88

American Dream, 1–20; downsizing, 9–12; factors in, 1; origins of, individualism and, 4–9; outcomes of,

9; sustainability of, 18–19; tenets of, 2; term, 2

American Revolution, and individualism, 6–7

Americans for Generational Equity (AGE), 188

Americans with Disabilities Act (ADA), 185–86

Andreasen, Marta, 38

Aniston, Jennifer, 26

Anka, Paul, 137

artistic talent, and success, 26–28

asceticism, and capitalism, 4–5

assets tax, 206

athletic ability, and success, 26–28

attitudes: research on, lack of, 31–35; and success, 28–35

attractiveness, discrimination by, 192–94

Auletta, Ken, 30

automobile industry: oligopoly in, 146; trends in, 119–20

baby boomers, and job availability, 125–27

Baker, James, III, 86

Baltzell, E. Digby, 63, 65

beauty industry, 194

Bell, Daniel, 123

Bellow, Adam, 78–79
Bentsen, Lloyd, III, 84
bequests, 61–62
Bernhardt, Annette, 126–27
Bills, David, 139
Biltmore Estate, 66
biology: and inheritance, 51; and
    nepotism, 78
Blau, Peter, 103
Bluestone, Barry, 120
Boardman, Susan, 34
Boesky, Ivan, 39
"boomerang" children, 59
Bourdieu, Pierre, 72, 80, 102
*Bowers v. Hardwick*, 182
Bowles, Samuel, 103
*Brown v. Topeka Kansas Board of
    Education*, 163
Buffett, Warren, 67
bureaucratic job values, 35
Bush, Barbara Pierce, 84–85
Bush, George Herbert Walker, 84
Bush, George Walker ("W"), 84–87, 95
Bush, Laura Welch, 85
Bush, Prescott Sheldon, 84
busing, 164–65
Butler, Robert, 187

Calvinism, and capitalism, 5
capital, socializing of, 145
capitalism, 7–9; moral character and, 38;
    Protestant ethic and, 4–5; and self-
    employment, 138
Carlin, George, 1
Carnegie, Andrew, 97, 137
caste societies, justifying ideology in, 3
Catholics, 5; discrimination against,
    188–89
Chambliss, William, 27
character, and success, 36–39
Cheney, Dick, 86
Cheney, Elizabeth, 87
child care, women and, 173–74
Church of Jesus Christ of Latter-Day
    Saints, discrimination against, 189
cities, inner: and busing, 164–65; jobs
    in, 128

Civil Rights Act, 157, 167, 176
class. *See* social class
Cockerham, William, 60
cognitive ability. *See* intelligence
cohort, and job availability, 125–27
Coleman, James S., 72
college education. *See* higher education
Collins, Randall, 99, 124
comparable worth, 171
competition: corporations and, 120–21;
    costs of, 43–44; discrimination and,
    155
computer occupations, trends in,
    123–25
Conant, James Bryant, 101
Conley, Dalton, 204
Connally, William, III, 84
connections. *See* social capital
Constitution, 6–7
constructive competition, 44
consumption: changing patterns of, 5–6;
    conspicuous, 65–66; tax on, 206
Cooley, Mason, 21, 117
Cooper, Cynthia, 38
coping strategies, 199–201
corporations: and competition, 120–21;
    conglomerations of, 146–47; history
    of, 144–48; mergers of, 146; versus
    self-employment, 138, 148
"correspondence principle," 103
Cose, Ellis, 173
Coutsoukis, Platon, 66
credential inflation, 11, 98–100, 124
credentialism, 98–100
credential underemployment, 123
cultural capital, 71, 79–84, 90, 198; and
    Bush, 84–87; definition of, 14, 71;
    and education, 102–3; inheritance
    and, 57; lack of, 79–80; local versus
    national, 81–82; transmission of,
    81–83
culture of poverty theory, 29–31

Dean, John, 37
debt: education and, 109; trends in,
    200–201
declassing, 88

Defense of Marriage Act, 182
deference, 2
DeLorean, John, 38
democracy, framers and, 6–7
dense networks, 75
destructive competition, 44
Devaney, F. John, 9
diligence, and capitalism, 4–5
disabled, discrimination against, 184–86
discrimination, 17–18, 198–99; definition of, 156; institutionalized, 156, 168, 176; multiple, 177–78; other types of, 181–95; racism and sexism, 155–80; and status attainment, 106
domestic partnerships, 182
Domhoff, G. William, 66–67
downsizing, 120
dual-income households, 199–200
Duncan, Otis Dudley, 103

Edison, Thomas, 137
education, 95–116, 198; and class, 102–3; effects of, 95–96, 96*t*; expansion of, and social mobility, 109–10; history of, 96–98; and intelligence, 24; level of, trends in, 97, 97*t*; and mobility, 100–102; racism in, 163–65; social capital and, 73; and success, 14–15
egotism, versus individualism, Tocqueville on, 7
Ehrenreich, Barbara, 36
Eitzen, Stanley, 26–27
employers, and attitude, 32
entrepreneurial capitalists, 140–41
entrepreneurship, 137–53; Gates and, 149; job values of, 35; personality of, 148; and success, 16–17. *See also* self-employment
equality, Tocqueville on, 7
Equal Pay Act, 171
estate tax, 61–62, 206; abolition of, 67
Etcoff, Nancy, 192–93
ethnic minorities: discrimination against, 157–68, 189; networks and, 75–77; and self-employment, 142
exclusivity, of wealthy, 63–64

family, versus career, women and, 173–74
family background. *See* socioeconomic background
*fear of success syndrome,* 174
female-headed households, 199–200
feudal societies: economic structure of, 8; justifying ideology in, 3
Fitzgerald, F. Scott, 62
Flynn, James, 24
"Flynn Effect," 24
Ford, Henry, 137
foreign policy, and racism, 158
franchisees, 139
free markets, 7–9; and self-employment, 138
free riding, 76
Friedan, Betty, 155
frontier image, 8–9

Galbraith, John Kenneth, 56
gambling, 131–33
Gates, Mary, 149
Gates, William, II, 67, 149
Gates, William (Bill), III, 137, 148–51
gays, discrimination against, 182–83
gender: and multiple discrimination, 177–78; and self-employment, 141–42; and wages, 170–71. *See also* sexism
generational issues, 188; and job availability, 125–27
Gere, Richard, 80
Gilded Age, 65–66
Gini Ratio, 53
Gintis, Herbert, 103
glass ceiling, 172
Gokhale, Jagadeesh, 55
Gould, Mark, 31
Granovetter, Mark, 73–74
Gray Panthers, 188
"the Great U-Turn," 120

habitus, 80
Handcock, Mark, 126–27
Hanks, Tom, 26
hard work: consumption as reward of, 6; and success, 35–36

Harrington, Charles, 34
Harrison, Bennett, 120
Harrison, Rex, 80
Hauser, Robert, 105
health, wealth and, 59–61
health care: costs, trends in, 12; racism and, 158
Hepburn, Audrey, 80
Herrnstein, Richard, 21–25
heterosexism, 182–83
hierarchy of needs, 30
higher education: racism and, 165; socioeconomic background and, 110–13; trends in, 10–11, 98*t*
Hochschild, Arlie, 174–75
Hochschild, Jennifer, 2
Homans, George Casper, 45n3
homophobia, 182–83
housework, women and, 174–75
housing: racism and, 165–68; trends in, 9–10
Huber, Richard, 34, 37
Hugo, Victor, 181
human capital theory, 102; versus innate abilities, 39
hyperagency, 66–67

ideologies of inequality, 2–3; and discrimination, 156
inclusive fitness-maximizing theory of selection, 51
income: definition of, 51; education and, 95–96, 96*t*; inequality in, inheritance and, 51–56; racism and, 160–61; self-employment and, 143; shares of, 51–52, 52*t*
individualism: and education, 96–97; and origins of American Dream, 4–9; and self-employment, 137–38; Tocqueville on, 7
industrial societies, justifying ideology in, 3
industriousness, and success, 32
inequality: coping strategies for, 199–201; free market and, 8; group/aggregate, 77; ideologies justifying, 2–3

information technology occupations, trends in, 123–25
inheritance, 13–14, 49–70, 197–98; cumulative advantages of, 56–61; definition of, 56; effects of, 50*f*
innate talents/abilities, and success, 21–28
innovation, corporations and, 147–48
institutionalized discrimination, 156, 176; interconnectedness of, 168
integrity, and success, 37–38
intelligence: measurement of, issues in, 23; and status attainment, 104; and success, 21–25
Interstate Commerce Commission, 145
inter vivos gifts, 58
irregular economy: income in, 143; self-employment and, 140
Islam, discrimination against, 190
isolation, of wealthy, 64–65

Jefferson, Thomas, 7
Jencks, Christopher, 32, 38
Jews, discrimination against, 189
jobs: age discrimination in, 187; availability of, 121–23; cohort and, 125–27; and disability, 184; and health, 60; with highest projected growth, 122*t*; history of, 117–21, 118*f*; luck and, 117; racism and, 160–61; region and, 127–30; sexism and, 169–76; and success, 15–16
job values, and success, 35

Keating, Charles, 39
Keister, Lisa, 55, 62
King, Martin Luther, Jr., 155
Kroc, Ray, 137

legal system: and corporations, 145; racism in, 158–60
lesbians, discrimination against, 182–83
Levy, Frank, 127–28
Lewis, Ethan, 66
Lewis, Oscar, 29
life expectancy, wealth and, 59–60
lifestyle, of wealthy, 65–66

Lin, Nan, 77
Livingstone, D. W., 122, 124
locus of control, internal versus
    external, 34
lookism, 192–94
lotteries, 131–33
Lucas, George, 26
luck, 117–35, 198; effects of, 130–31;
    and success, 16

Mannon, John, 43
manufacturing sector, trends in, 117–21,
    118*f*
marriage: same-sex, 182; and success, 1;
    wealthy and, 63, 65
Marx, Karl, 140
Maslow, Abraham, 30
McGuffey, William, 5
Mead, George Herbert, 45n3
mental illness, poverty and, 61
mentoring: sexism and, 172–73; social
    capital and, 72
merit, 197–99; case for, 21–48; elements
    of, 13, 21; emphasis on, costs of,
    43–44; versus inheritance, 50*f*;
    selection by, issues in, 40–43; social
    construction of, 107–9
meritocracy, 1–2, 197–99; education
    and, 101–2; fairness of, 207–8;
    Jefferson on, 7; myth of, 208;
    recommendations for, 201–7
*Meritor Savings Bank v. Vinson,*
    175–76
Microsoft, 148–51
Milken, Michael, 39
mind-power ethic, 34
mobility: downward, rarity of, 58–59;
    educational expansion and, 109–10;
    education and, 100–102
moral character, and success, 36–39
Mormons, discrimination against, 189
Morris, Martina, 126–27
Morris, Michael, 30
most qualified candidate, myth of,
    40–43
Murray, Charles, 21–25
Muslims, discrimination against, 190

National Aeronautics and Space
    Administration (NASA), 45n1
National Basketball Association draft, 28
needs, hierarchy of, 30
nepotism, 78–79
net worth, shares of, 51–52, 52*t*
new middle class, 141
new nepotism, 78–79
Nixon, Richard M., 37
noblesse oblige, 205–6

occupations. *See* jobs
office holding: racism and, 158–59;
    women and, 176–77
old boy networks, 172–73
Older Workers Benefit Protection Act,
    187
old middle class, 141
oligopoly, definition of, 145–46
Opel, John, 150
Organization of Petroleum Exporting
    Countries (OPEC), 119, 146
Orwell, George, 197
OWL (Older Women's League), 188
ownership class, 13–14

Packard, Vance, 88
parental rescue, 58–59
Paterson, Tim, 150
pay equity, 171
Peale, Norman Vincent, 34
performance underemployment, 123
persuasion, and justification of
    inequality, 2–3
petty bourgeoisie, 140–41
philanthropy, 205–6
Pierce, Marvin, 84
Pierce, Pauline Robinson, 84
pink-collar ghetto, 169–70
political power: race and, 158–60;
    wealthy and, 66–67; women and,
    176–77
postindustrial society thesis, 123–25
poverty: culture of, theory on, 29–31;
    feminization of, 178; and health, 60;
    multiple discrimination and, 177–78
Powell, Colin, 86

Powell, Michael, 87
privacy, of wealthy, 64–65
property, and wealth, 54
Protestant ethic, 4–5; and mind power, 34; on moral character, 37
Puritans, 4–5

quality of life, and childhood, 57
quotas, 204

race: and athletic success, 27; and intelligence, controversies on, 24–25; and multiple discrimination, 177–78; and self-employment, 142; as social construct, 25
racism, 155, 157–68, 178–79; justifying ideology of, falsehood in, 3
"the random walk hypothesis," 130–31
Rayman, Paula, 121
Reagan administration, 120
Reed, John Shelton, 191
region: discrimination by, 190–92; and job issues, 127–30
Rehabilitation Act, 185
Rehnquist, Janet, 87
relative deprivation, 61
religion: discrimination by, 188–90; and origins of American Dream, 4–6
rentier capitalists, 140
reproductive freedom, 174
Reskin, Barbara, 204
retirement, secure, trends in, 12
reverse inheritance, 51
Riesman, David, 45n3
Roberts, Ed, 150
Roberts, Julia, 80
Roosevelt, Franklin Delano, 117
Rosenau, Pauline Vaillancourt, 44
Rosenfeld, Jeffrey P., 49
Rustbelt, 127–30
Ryan, William, 40

"salvation anxiety," 5
Scalia, Eugene, 86–87
Schervish, Paul, 66

school quality, and educational attainment, 107–9
science occupations, trends in, 123–25
Scott, Mark, 126–27
second shift, 174–75
segregation: de facto, 163; in housing, 166–67
self-actualization, need for, 30
self-employment, 137–53, 198; characteristics of, 141–44; dependent, 139; history of, 137–38; nonvoluntary forms of, 16, 142–43; and success, 16–17; trends in, 11–12, 138–40
service sector, trends in, 117–21, 118*f*
sexism, 155, 169–79; justifying ideology of, falsehood in, 3
sexual harassment, 175–76
Sheridan, Jennifer, 105
Sherman Anti-Trust Act, 145
Sinatra, Frank, 137
slave societies, justifying ideology in, 3
small businesses, 147
Smith, Adam, 7–8
snobbery, 87–89
social capital, 71–78, 90, 198; and Bush, 84–87; definition of, 14, 71; disadvantages of, 75–77; effects of, 73–74; inheritance and, 57–58; and stock market, 132–33; women and, 77, 172
social class: and education, 95; and multiple discrimination, 177–78; self-employment and, 140–41; and value of hard work, 36
social climbing, 71, 87–89; definition of, 14
social reproduction theory, 102–3; cultural capital and, 81–83; education and, 95, 102–3, 112–13
Social Security system, 12, 188
socioeconomic background: and cultural capital, 82–83; and higher education, 110–13; measurement of, issues in, 24; and status attainment,

24, 104, 106; and value of hard work, 36

Southerners, discrimination against, 190–92

Spielberg, Steven, 26

Stanley, Thomas, 33

status attainment research, 103–5; limitations of, 105–7

status declassing, 88

status lending, 88

stock market, 132–33

Stone, Barron, 38

structural hole, 75

structural mobility, 59

subemployment, 123

subjective underemployment, 123

success: factors affecting, 1, 13–19, 197–99; justification of, 37

Sunbelt, 127–30

talent, and success, 21–28

talent-use gap, 122–23

taxation: estate tax, 61–62, 67; progressive, 205–7

teachers, minority, 164

technology occupations, trends in, 123–25

Thurmond, J. Strom, Jr., 86

Thurow, Lester, 53, 130–31

Tocqueville, Alexis de, 7

tracking, 107–8; racism and, 161, 164

transfer tax, 206

transgendered individuals, 183

trusts, 62

truth, versus ideology, 3

Turner, Frederick Jackson, 8–9

underclass, theory of, 30–31

underemployment, 11, 121–22; types of, 122–23

unfairness: approaches to, 201–7; coping strategies for, 199–201; factors in, 197–99

values: Puritan, 4–5; and success, 28–35

Vanderbilt, George, 66

wages: cohort and, 126; gender and, 170–71; and income inequality, 53; recession in, 197–209; region and, 128–30

Wal-Mart, 54, 147

Walton, Sam, 54, 66, 137

Warren, John Robert, 105

Watkins, Sherron, 38

wealth: conservation of, 55–56, 62; definition of, 51–52; inequality in, inheritance and, 51–56; opportunity for, trends in, 11–12

wealthy, 54–55; characteristics of, 62–67; responsibilities of, 205–6

Weber, Max, 4–5

welfare reform, 158

white-collar crime, 38–39

Wiley, Norbert, 28

Wilson, William, 30

Winfrey, Oprah, 26

Wisconsin School, 104

Wolfe, Tom, 45n2

women, and social capital, 77, 172. *See also* sexism

Woods, Tiger, 26

work ethic, 6

work hours, increase in, 200

Wright, Erik Olin, 140–41

Yankee advantage, 190–92

Young, Michael, 208

zoning, 167

# About the Authors

**Stephen J. McNamee** is associate dean of the College of Arts and Sciences and professor of sociology at the University of North Carolina at Wilmington. He is the recipient of the University of North Carolina at Wilmington Distinguished Teaching Professorship Award and the University of North Carolina's Board of Governor's Teaching Award. He is coeditor with Robert K. Miller Jr. of *Inheritance and Wealth in America*. McNamee has published in the areas of inequality, theory, organizations, and the labor force, and he is currently developing a theory on the social construction of life meaning.

**Robert K. Miller Jr.** is professor of sociology and associate chair in the Department of Sociology and Criminal Justice at the University of North Carolina at Wilmington. He has published numerous journal articles and book chapters in several areas of sociology, but his major areas of research interest continue to be in inequality and inheritance. Miller coedited *Inheritance and Wealth in America* with Stephen J. McNamee and is a recent contributor with Jeffrey Rosenfeld and Stephen J. McNamee to the *Handbook of Sociology of Death and Dying*.